National Women's Social & Politi

The Women's M

Words by
E. M. MACAULAY.

Music by
ROUGET DELISLE.

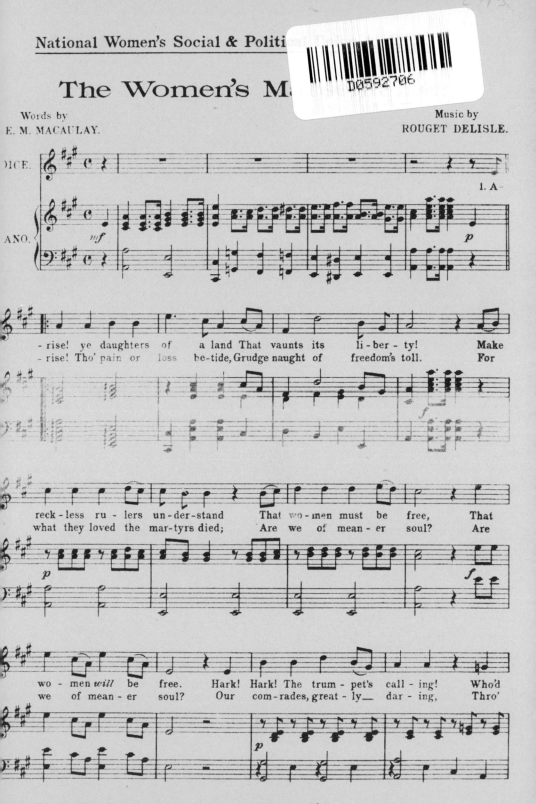

1. A-rise! ye daughters of a land That vaunts its li-ber-ty! Make
-rise! Tho' pain or loss be-tide, Grudge naught of freedom's toll. For

reck-less ru-lers un-der-stand That wo-men must be free, That
what they loved the mar-tyrs died; Are we of mean-er soul? Are

wo-men will be free. Hark! Hark! The trum-pet's call-ing! Who'd
we of mean-er soul? Our com-rades, great-ly_ dar-ing, Thro'

ublished by the Women's Press, 156, Charing Cross Road. Price 1ᵈ

Freedom's Cause

Emmeline Pankhurst being arrested, May 1914.

Freedom's Cause

LIVES OF THE SUFFRAGETTES

FRAN ABRAMS

P

PROFILE BOOKS

First published in Great Britain in 2003 by
PROFILE BOOKS LTD
58A Hatton Garden
London ECIN 8LX
www.profilebooks.co.uk

10 9 8 7 6 5 4 3 2 1

Typeset in Minion by MacGuru
info@macguru.org.uk

Printed and bound in Great Britain by
Clays, Bungay, Suffolk

A CIP catalogue record for this book is available from the British Library.

ISBN 1 86197 425 6

Contents

ACKNOWLEDGEMENTS

Thanks are due to the many staff of libraries and archives where material was gathered for this book, in particular, all the staff of the Women's Library at London Metropolitan University, where the bulk of the research was carried out. I am grateful to them both for their help and advice and for their permission to quote from unpublished materials, and to the following: The West Yorkshire Archive Service, The Wren Library at Trinity College, Cambridge; the International Institute of Social History in Amsterdam; The National Library of Scotland; The Principal and Chapter of Pusey House, Oxford; Manchester Archives and Local Studies department at Manchester Central Libary; The Public Record Office of Northern Ireland; the National Library of Ireland; the curators of the ILP and Fabian collections at the London School of Economics and Policital Science; the curator of the Trades Union Congress Library at London Metropolitan University; the archivist of the Suffragette Fellowship Collection at the Museum of London; The British Library; The British Library Newspaper Library at Colindale; The Public Record Office at Kew, in London; Westminster Local Studies and Archive Department; Camden Local Studies and Archives Centre; Sheffield Local Studies Library; and to Geoffrey Bourne, who donated May Billinghurst's papers to the Women's Library. I would also like to thank Sir Josslyn Gore-Booth for permission to quote from the Lissadell Papers, and both June Purvis and Brian Harrison for advice on oral history materials at The Women's Library.

Thanks are due to all at Profile Books, particularly Andrew Franklin for commissioning this book and John Davey for editing it. I would also like to thank Penny Daniel, Ruth Killick and Bela Cunha for their unfailing good humour, energy and patience.

Thanks, too, to John Farrell for his invaluable help with the Constance Markievicz chapter, Judith Thompson and Angie Ruane for reading and commenting on the manuscript, Jane Lewis for very kindly letting me see one of Emmeline Pankhurst's letters, Kathy and John Emmett for their gifts of copies of *The Suffragette* and *The Workers' Dreadnought*, and last but most definitely not least, my partner Phil Solomon for his unstinting support. All the mistakes are, of course, my own work.

Women's Suffrage: Key Dates

1792	Mary Wollstonecraft tentatively mentions women's suffrage in *A Vindication of the Rights of Woman*.
1832	Parliamentary franchise for men widened by the Great Electoral Reform Act. Henry Hunt MP, presents the first women's petition on the subject, from Mary Smith of Stanmore in Yorkshire.
1865	Society for the promotion of women's suffrage formed in Manchester.
1867	John Stuart Mill presents the second women's suffrage petition in Parliament. London National Society for Women's Suffrage founded. The second Reform Act further widens the franchise for men.
1884	Moves to include votes for women in the third Reform Act are rejected by William Gladstone.
1897	National Union of Women's Suffrage Societies formed with Millicent Garrett Fawcett as president.
1903	Women's Social and Political Union founded in Manchester by Emmeline Pankhurst.
1905	Christabel Pankhurst and Annie Kenney go to prison after causing a disturbance at a Liberal meeting in Manchester.
1906	General election. Liberals returned to power with Sir Henry Campbell-Bannerman as Prime Minister.
1908	Herbert Asquith replaces Campbell-Bannerman as Prime Minister.
1909	First force feeding of suffragette hunger strikers in prison.
1910–11	A battle over Lloyd George's radical budget and over reform of the House of Lords results in two general elections. Conciliation Committee formed to try to find a mutually

acceptable women's suffrage measure.

1911   Conciliation Bill passes its second reading with a large majority but is then blocked.

1912 March   Mass window-smashing raids in the West End of London lead to hundreds of arrests. Christabel flees to Paris.

1912 October Frederick and Emmeline Pethick-Lawrence are expelled from the Women's Social and Political Union.

1913   Militancy increases. Emily Wilding Davison dies after throwing herself under the King's horse at the Derby.

1914   Truce declared after the outbreak of the First World War. Suffragette prisoners released.

1916   Speaker's Conference convened to discuss inclusion of women in a bill to enfranchise soldiers. Lloyd George becomes Prime Minister.

1917   The House of Commons passes Clause 4 of the Representation of the People Bill, which gives the vote to women householders aged thirty and over.

1918   First general election in which women can vote. Constance Markievicz becomes the first woman elected to Parliament.

1928   Women win the right to vote at twenty-one.

1929   Fourteen women MPs elected at the general election.

Emily Davison, a prominent member of the movement, threw herself under the King's horse, Anmer, at the Derby. She died as a result of her injuries.

Introduction

The Queen is most anxious to enlist everyone who can speak or write to join in checking this mad, wicked folly of 'Women's Rights', with all its attendant horrors, on which her poor feeble sex is bent, forgetting every sense of womanly feelings and propriety. Feminists ought to get a good whipping. Were woman to 'unsex' themselves by claiming equality with men, they would become the most hateful, heathen and disgusting of beings and would surely perish without male protection.

Queen Victoria, March 1870[1]

When the queen took up her pen to protest at the criminal lunacy with which some members of her sex were pursuing the notion of equality, the suffragettes were barely a twinkle in Mrs Pankhurst's eye. Even at this early stage, though, suffragist campaigners were provoking outrage – offset by small pockets of joy – in London's comfortable drawing rooms. It was by then two years since the first public meeting calling for a women's parliamentary franchise, and yet the issue was hardly a new one. It had been a low, barely discernible hum beneath the political hubbub since before Victoria ascended the throne. As early as 1831, the *Westminster Review* had published two articles advocating votes for women. The demand was quickly dropped amid suggestions it might delay the full enfranchisement of men, but it had lit a small flame. In the following year, when the great Electoral Reform Act was being debated, a wealthy lady from Yorkshire named Mary Smith caused mirth at Westminster with a petition asking that unmarried women of property should be able to vote in parliamentary elections. In 1838 an early draft of the Chartists' *Charter of Rights and Liberties* included the same idea. In 1866 the notion was again raised in Parliament via a further petition, and public meetings in support of it began to take place around the country.

The story of how women won the vote has been documented many times, and from virtually every angle. The history of the constitutional suffragists has been written, along with many accounts of the militant suffragette movement which gripped the nation's consciousness between 1906 and 1914. There is even a book on the campaigners who opposed the notion of votes for women,[2] and there are full biographies of many of the major players in the game. All these leave a number of questions unanswered. The histories of the movement, of necessity, spell out the progress of the cause itself rather than telling us where its advocates came from and why they got involved. The biographies, while they can shed light on what motivated a particular individual to act in a particular way, cannot tell us what general factors brought together the various participants, with their disparate personalities, views and backgrounds.

This book tells the history of the suffrage movement through the lives of some of those who were caught up in it. It looks at where they came from, how and why they got involved in the movement, and to what effect. Did the women – and men – who devoted their lives to this cause have anything in common? This goes to the heart of one of the great issues concerning people who make history – is greatness inherent, or does it emerge only in exceptional circumstances? Without the women's movement, would these individuals have changed the world in some other way, or would they have led blameless, unexceptional lives? The dozen short biographies in this book consider these questions and give the reader the evidence by which to judge whether or not there might have been something innately extraordinary about these people. Could their future paths have been predicted, it asks, or were they just ordinary individuals who fell by accident or coincidence into the great swell of the franchise cause?

Once embroiled, many of the militants devoted themselves entirely to the cause. Again, this book searches for clues as to why large numbers of middle-class women were willing to give up wealth, leisure, freedom and ultimately even their lives for their beliefs. What was it about the leaders of the suffragette movement that enabled them to incite their followers to such extremes of devotion? What facets of their personalities, their backgrounds or their inbred belief systems led them to build an organisation so fervent, so tightly constructed, so inspirational? Was it them, or was it simply the cause itself, that provoked such extreme reactions? Or was it a combination of the force of personality with the force of history, the culmination of a century of social change?

From the modern perspective many of the events in this book seem so outlandish, so extreme, as to appear virtually inexplicable. How could women who had grown up bound by the social mores personified by Queen Victoria go out and chain themselves to railings? How could they go to prison and starve themselves for political rights, the very thought of which could drive the respectable matrons of the nation to paroxysms of horror? From our twenty-first century viewpoint we tend to see these actions as having been way ahead of their time. Many of these stories reveal a more complex truth, that the women who fought for the vote were often following a pattern rather than breaking a mould. In one sense some of them were not rebelling but following family tradition, picking up the strands of their mothers' and grandmothers' own political activism. Emmeline Pankhurst's grandmother, for example, sent her husband to the great franchise meeting of 1819 on St Peter's Fields in Manchester, now remembered as the Peterloo massacre. Later, in the 1840s, she joined the Anti-Corn Law League to protest against the protectionist measures which kept the price of bread artificially high. These great agitations were characterised by riots, strikes and mass meetings which were frequently put down by the authorities with a great deal of bloodshed. Through the backgrounds of these characters we can see that some women in the nineteenth century were no strangers to political violence.

The Victorian age, these women's lives remind us, was no more homogeneous than any other. If the notion of marching in the streets was anathema to the well-heeled matriarchs of the capital, it was near second nature to some of the working women of Lancashire. Looking at history through the lives of a group of individuals has this further advantage – it lets us see events from a number of different perspectives. While some of the characters in this book were at the centre of the organisations they championed, others were at their margins. The central view is represented here in the chapters on Emmeline Pankhurst, Fred Pethick-Lawrence and to some extent Annie Kenney. The margins are brought to life through personalities such as May Billinghurst, who represents the many women who played their part but never became household names. The extreme fringes of militancy are portrayed through the life of Emily Wilding Davison, and the movement in Scotland and the north through Adela Pankhurst. The constitutional suffragists are seen through the story of Millicent Fawcett, and the 'antis' through Mary Ward. Others represented here were less single-mindedly devoted to the cause: Constance Markievicz, the Irish rebel and first woman MP, and Margaret Bondfield, the first woman cabinet minister, had passing but intriguing relations with it. Others, like Keir Hardie, made key contributions but are chiefly remembered for other aspects of their life's work. Drawing together these lives sheds a new light on the full spectrum of the suffrage cornucopia, on relations between and among the sexes, and on the times more generally.

The characters of the book have many differences but they also have much in common. They are all children of the nineteenth century, which began in the aftermath of the French Revolution and during which, in Britain especially, the Industrial Revolution transformed every aspect of society. During those 100 years, huge new classes of women mingled in fast-growing urban centres. The wretched masses of the industrial North toiled day and night in the cotton and woollen mills of Lancashire and Yorkshire, in the pits and the metal-bashing factories of the Midlands and in the heavy industries of the Scottish lowlands. The Industrial Revolution created other, less downtrodden classes too. It brought together an urban middle class of women who often had great stores of energy and time on their hands. These were the wives of the newly enriched, the scions of merchant families, whose self-confidence was of a new brand, whose wealth came not from the land but from silk-printing, coal trading and beer-brewing. This new stratum of society had its intellectuals, among them the nonconformist preachers whose influence grew daily within the cities' smog. As the century wore on, increasing numbers of schoolteachers reached out tentatively for the knowledge and enlightenment their craft required.

One refrain in this vast chorus was to play a key role in the birth of the women's franchise movement. While some of the women in this book – no strangers to active politics – were beginning to put their mothers' experiences to new uses, their more genteel sisters were reaching the same point by a different route. These underemployed women had often grown up in respectable homes ruled by virtuous Victorian nonconformism, with its careful adherence to duty and its belief in the quiet alleviation of the poor's worst sufferings. Deprived of an outlet for their energies, some of them took to visiting the appalling slums which were the detritus of urbanisation.[3] These seemingly innocuous activities started to act upon them as a radicalising force. Shocked by the conditions they found, they began to talk and think about politics, and from there it was but a small step to a tentative demand for political rights. From such beginnings came the entry into the suffrage movement of workers such as May Billinghurst, as well as of inspirational leaders like Emmeline Pethick-Lawrence.

Many of these individuals were born into families at the centre of successful reforming movements. Their fathers, brothers and mothers had seen off slavery; they had widened the franchise; they had ushered in a host of small measures to help the urban poor. Now they began to think it was time to act on their own behalf. For many, the first real political act was to insist upon an education – for themselves and then for others. Soon, as a result of their agitations, educational establishments for women started opening up. In 1848 a series of lectures for governesses solidified into the new Queen's College for Women. The following year came Bedford College, which even had women on its management board. These institutions, later followed by Newnham Hall in Cambridge and Somerville Hall and Lady Margaret Hall in Oxford, inspired a generation of ambitious young women.

Having gained an education, what many of these newly empowered women wanted was economic freedom. Soon they were forcing their way – sometimes literally – through the doors of the medical establishment, the legal system and a host of other professions and trades. Through the first Women's Employment Bureau, set up in the 1850s, and their own newspaper, the *Englishwoman's Journal*, which dated from around the same time, they sallied forth. Soon there were female house-painters, watchmakers, even hairdressers. New trades became female domains, too: telegraphy, the retail business and nursing, which was by now experiencing a boom thanks to the example of Florence Nightingale.

From here, full citizenship beckoned. John Stuart Mill, elected in 1865 as MP for the City of Westminster, was prepared to put the case in Parliament. Other MPs were behind him, including the up-and-coming Liberal Henry Fawcett. Committees for women's suffrage sprang up, not just in London but also in Manchester, where the campaign was led by a chemical manufacturer's daughter named Lydia Becker. In 1870 came the first Suffrage Bill, introduced by Jacob Bright, and despite some opposition it passed its second reading by 124 votes to 91. For a brief instant it seemed the issue might be resolved almost before it had arisen. Then, while the bill was in committee, Gladstone pronounced himself against the idea and effectively killed it for a generation. When the bill was read a third time there was a majority of 100 against it. Yet it was not in the nature of these women to be downhearted. They embarked on a slow, steady agitation which would continue through five further parliamentary defeats in the next two decades.

Although the vote was not yet won by the end of the nineteenth century, the women involved in the suffrage movement had achieved a number of other important victories. Until 1870, married women in England had been bound by 'couverture', a legal convention which placed them under the protection of their husbands and deprived them of any legal status. This meant they could not independently own property or have any parental rights. Women whose husbands abandoned them, even those who were forced out of their marital homes by extreme violence, could legally be left destitute and unable to contact their children. Elizabeth Wolstenholme Elmy, an early figure in the suffrage movement, played a major role in campaigning for the act which allowed married women to keep some money of their own. Elizabeth also helped to inspire Josephine Butler's campaign against the Contagious Diseases Acts, which led to the repeal of repressive laws through which women could be subjected to repeated arrest and detention under the mere suspicion of prostitution. Such reforms did nothing to ease the pressure for full political rights. Indeed, they served to throw the injustice of women's disenfranchisement into ever starker relief. As the Victorian age drew to a close, middle-class women could justifiably have claimed they had prepared themselves for political freedom. Many were better educated than most voting men; some had professional jobs; some had a rich and detailed knowledge of the nation's legal system and political structures.

The intellectual battle, too, seemed finally to be swinging in the women's favour. At the general election of 1895 more than half the successful candidates were prepared to say on the hustings that they supported votes for women. In 1897, for the first time in twenty-seven years, a suffrage bill passed its second reading in Parliament. It was talked out in its later stages, but the development was encouraging. Now the more radical political classes of the North began to become involved, too, with the Independent Labour Party and the textile unions being lobbied on the subject by women members. But how to translate this into action? It was all very well that MPs now professed to be in favour of women's votes, but how to get them to actually *do* something about it? In some parts of the movement, particularly those parts that with the Pankhursts had become firmly attached to the now-burgeoning labour movement, there was growing frustration. The women's armouries were complete. The battleground was set, and the final struggle for suffrage began.

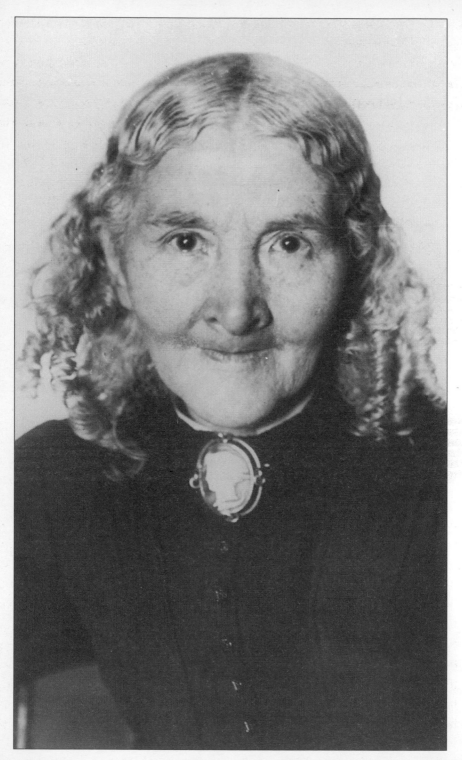

Elizabeth Wolstenholme Elmy

I

Elizabeth Wolstenholme Elmy – A Long Struggle

Sitting by my side is a woman who this month celebrates the 43rd anniversary of her work in this movement. She could tell us that if it had not been for this new militant agitation she would have left this life with a broken heart, because she would have felt that the whole of her life work had been a failure. It is about time that the House of Commons got rushed a bit!

Emmeline Pethick-Lawrence introducing Elizabeth Wolstenholme Elmy to the audience at a suffragette meeting in the Royal Albert Hall, in October 1908. Leaders of the movement were in prison for urging demonstrators to 'Rush the House of Commons!'[1]

Several women might easily have claimed to be the mothers of the suffragette movement, but few with as much justification as Elizabeth Wolstenholme Elmy. Aged seventy when the militant Women's Social and Political Union (WSPU) began breathing its fire on the body politic in 1903, she comfortably jumped the divide between the old and the new. She spent the last decades of the nineteenth century whipping, cajoling and entreating the suffrage movement into being, and the early years of the twentieth gleefully celebrating the birth of its delinquent child. The militants honoured her with a special title: 'Nestor of the Woman Suffrage Movement'. But in her long political life she had experienced far more grind than glory. To say this extraordinary woman worked tirelessly to improve the lot of her sisters would be an almost laughable understatement. Well into her seventies she continued to rise daily at 3 a.m. to put in six or eight hours of political work before starting the washing, cooking and other housework that were her lot as a far from wealthy woman.

Very early on in Elizabeth's long life there were signs she would need to learn self-reliance and determination. The daughter of a Methodist minister from Cheetham Hill, Manchester, she lost her mother while she was still an infant and her father at the age of ten.[2] Her remaining childhood was spent in the care of her stepmother, with trustees overseeing her financial needs. But despite her parents' short-lived presence in her life, it seems they left her both with their nonconformist work ethic and with a strong network of family friends who were committed social reformers. Among these were the Brights, wealthy cotton manufacturers whose sons, John and Jacob, were prominent in many of the great nineteenth-century political movements. John Bright had been a leading campaigner against the protectionist Corn Laws, and years later Elizabeth would recall how she watched 'with deep emotion' the great celebration which took place in Manchester on their repeal in 1846.

Hers was not a background where faint heart or surrender were seen as acceptable. And even at an early age Elizabeth found herself in frequent conflict with the guardians in whose care she was left. She could see quite clearly that her older brother, Joseph, later a Cambridge scholar and a professor of mathematics, was no cleverer than she was. But while he was encouraged in his academic work she was forbidden to read and was told at the age of fourteen that she had 'learnt as much as any woman needed to know'. Elizabeth demurred. Eventually her guardians surrendered and she was sent for two years to the Moravian School at Fulneck, near Leeds, where she was taught in an atmosphere 'of mingled liberty and repression'. Two years later, though, when she expressed a desire to continue her studies at the newly founded Bedford College for Women, she was unable to persuade them. Elizabeth was grounded, but she was not deterred. She could be prevented from going to college, but she could not be prevented from studying at home – a course she followed for two more years before her guardians decided it was time for her to earn a living.

At the age of eighteen Elizabeth began work as a governess, but a year or so later it was suggested that she should sink her small inheritance into what was described as 'a high-class boarding school'. With her stepmother, she moved into a school building in Boothstown Lane, Worsley, and took in half a dozen female pupils. For the next twelve years or so she devoted her life to giving her girls a smoother introduction to the world of learning than she had had herself. Despite her inexperience her school gave its pupils 'a fuller education and a more pleasant and common-sense training than was then dreamt of' for most girls, according to her husband. Instead of 'finishing' her pupils as young ladies, she tried to give them the education she would have liked herself, and indeed, several eventually became headmistresses themselves. One of her later pupils was Frances Rowe, who went on to graduate from Newnham College, Cambridge, and to become a militant suffrage campaigner.

Through her educational work Elizabeth came into contact in the mid-1860s with a group of women who were beginning to agitate for improvements in educational provision for women, and in particular for women's higher education.[3] It could be said that this movement, leading as it did to the foundation of women's 'halls' in Oxford and Cambridge, did as much as any other to propel the women's suffrage campaign into being. Once women had freed themselves from the shackles of drawing-room life, it was but a short step to the realisation that there was no concrete reason why they should not be full citizens of their country. In 1865 Elizabeth founded the Manchester Schoolmistresses' Association and two years later, with Josephine Butler, she formed an organisation which ran lectures for girls and helped to popularise the Oxford and Cambridge Local Examinations, already open to girls. In the spring of 1866 she gave evidence on the subject to the first royal commission on secondary education. By now Elizabeth had moved to a new school at Moody Hall, near Congleton in Cheshire, and had been approached about taking on the headships of more than one larger institution. However, she had rejected the Methodism in which she had been raised and her lack of faith prevented her from being appointed. The educational world's loss was the political world's gain, for she began to turn her attentions to a wider range of causes.

Elizabeth had become one of the first members of the Kensington Society, a London-based debating group set up to discuss women's rights, particularly in education. She was also campaigning for women to be admitted to a range of jobs which had hitherto been closed to them – as bank clerks and as inspectors in factories and schools. In 1866 she took up a new issue – the extension that year of the Contagious Diseases Acts, designed to curb prostitution. Under these acts any woman suspected of prostitution in a specified garrison town could be forced to undergo detention and repeated medical examination. If she denied prostitution she was subjected to a trial, at which the word of a single policeman would be enough to secure her conviction. Many women who were wrongly arrested admitted prostitution to avoid the public humiliation of a court case. Men who spread infection were not subjected to any parallel laws. In a pamphlet on the subject Elizabeth argued the issue touched not merely on 'the personal rights of our sex, but the morality of the nation'.[4] So urgent did the issue seem to her that she sent a telegram to her friend Josephine Butler, already known for her work with prostitutes in Liverpool. (Butler would go on to make the campaign a major part of her life's work.) The fact that Elizabeth was prepared to tread such socially delicate ground while still practising as a teacher gives some indication of her capacity for unconventional thought. Never a firebrand but always a radical, this Victorian schoolmistress on many occasions took a calculated step beyond the boundaries of social acceptability, both in her political thinking and in her private relationships.

While the campaign for the repeal of the Contagious Diseases Acts continued – finally succeeding in 1886 – Elizabeth became involved in another campaign which was far more central to the issue of women's liberation. At the time women were forced to give up all legal rights to own property when they married, and if their husbands then abandoned them they were left penniless. In 1868 Elizabeth became secretary of a newly formed Married Women's Property Committee, whose aim was to change this unjust law. Josephine Butler was also on its executive committee along with Dr Richard Pankhurst, a radical Manchester lawyer, who would be joined in the campaign a decade later by his new wife, Emmeline. The eventual success of this movement, which was achieved in 1882 in a bill partially drafted by Richard Pankhurst, was a major milestone in the movement for women's right to self-determination.[5]

These early campaigns, particularly the struggle for property rights, helped Elizabeth to develop a *modus operandi* which would remain peculiarly hers. Possessed of a fearsomely acute brain she would take a piece of proposed legislation, or the detailed argument of an opponent, and strip it down to its bones before rebuilding it, clothed anew in copious facts and figures designed to back her argument. Her grasp of parliamentary procedure was unparalleled in the women's movement and she remained until her death a major source of advice and information for its members. Take, as just one small example, her dissection of the unwieldy 1880 Criminal Code Bill in a paper to the Dialectical Society.[6] Elizabeth reduced this otherwise little-noted statute, designed to codify existing law, to a handful of devastating facts. This bill would legalise the marriage of girls at twelve, overturn helpful legal rulings on marital rape, criminalise women whose babies died in childbirth for lack of medical care and endanger women who were coerced into crime by their husbands, she pointed out succinctly. The bill collapsed a few weeks later.

The second string to Elizabeth's formidable political bow was her assiduity. She wove around her a vast web of correspondents to whom she wrote almost daily, attaching a stream of useful information, newspaper cuttings, pamphlets, letters from other members of her circle: 'I am sending a full list of how members voted on matters affecting women in the last session' ... 'When I receive the Cheltenham Examiner I will willingly write something if possible' ... 'I return some letters and send on some which may interest you ... ' Often, these sheaves of print would be accompanied by commands or requests: 'Could you please copy the enclosed and return it?' ... 'Dear Friend, a four-page leaflet would I think be most fitting' ... 'In order to secure the actual personal attention of the Queen to Mrs Swiney's leaflet I will ask Mrs Butler to write with it herself to the Empress Frederick ... ' One correspondent, Harriet McIlquham, received several thousand over a thirty-year period, most written hurriedly in a spidery hand and all sharply perceptive.[7]

It would seem to the casual observer that these interlinking political networks were constantly forming and reforming themselves into a bewildering array of committees: the Social Science Association, the North of England Council for Promoting the Education of Women, the Committee for Amending the Law in Points Injurious to Women. It was during this period that Elizabeth gained the nickname, 'The Parliamentary Watchdog'.[8] But it was the cause of women's suffrage to which Elizabeth would devote the greater part of her energies. This was, she believed, the very 'taproot' from which all other freedoms for women should stem. Without the vote, women were powerless and voiceless. With it, they would be able far more effectively to assert political pressure for change. Again, she was among the first to stir herself on the subject, get organised and start a committee. The issue itself was not a new one. Mary Wollstonecraft, one of Elizabeth's great heroines, had raised it thus in her *Vindication of the Rights of Woman*, in 1792:

> I may excite laughter by dropping a hint, which I mean to pursue some future time, for I really think that women ought to have representatives, instead of being arbitrarily governed ... But they need not complain, for they are as well represented as a numerous class of hard-working mechanics, who pay for royalty when they can scarcely stop their children's mouths with bread.

Parliament had received its first demand for votes for women in 1832, during the passage of that year's Great Electoral Reform Act, in the form of a petition from a group of women in Yorkshire. One of Elizabeth's own early political acts was to travel to London in July 1865 to hear the election speech of the radical philosopher and MP John Stuart Mill, which contained an impassioned plea for the enfranchisement of women. Within a few months she had set up a Manchester Committee for the Enfranchisement of Women, of which Josephine Butler was a member. Mill had promised to present a petition on women's suffrage to Parliament if its supporters could raise 100 signatures. In a little less than a fortnight they had 1,499 names, 300 of them personally collected by Elizabeth. By 1867 the group had changed its name to the Manchester National Society for Women's Suffrage and its administration had been taken over by Lydia Becker. In 1872 Elizabeth gave up her school and moved to London, where she worked as a parliamentary lobbyist on women's issues for a salary of £300 a year.

Elizabeth's personal life was about to intrude upon her political activities, to such an extent that she would be all but written out of the histories of the respectable parts of the suffrage movement for many years to come. In 1869 she had met Ben Elmy, who had recently become her neighbour in Congleton. Five years her junior, Ben had been born in Rochdale and had worked as a teacher before setting up in the Cheshire town as a silk-crêpe manufacturer. Elizabeth must have felt she had met a kindred spirit – a 'fair trade' campaigner and former president of the National Secular Society. By 1872, just before she moved to London, the couple were rumoured to be cohabiting. Such 'free unions' were not unknown at the time, especially among those of a radical bent, and Elizabeth's involvement with the married women's property campaign had turned her vehemently against marriage, which would mean the formal loss of her status as an independent woman. In addition, her dislike of organised religion left her opposed to a church wedding. Moreover, Mary Wollstonecraft herself had entered into a similar arrangement rather than submit to the inequitable marriage laws.

None of this impressed Elizabeth's political acquaintances, forward-thinking though they were. The vast majority were horrified by her news, particularly when it became apparent towards the end of 1874 that she was pregnant. As Sylvia Pankhurst put it: 'There was much fluttering in the suffrage dovecotes.'[9] Pitted against one another were Josephine Butler, who expressed some support for the couple's informal union and who may have been a witness at a private ceremony they held, and Ursula Bright, who opposed it vehemently. Butler circulated a card backing the couple's decision but even she stopped short of fully endorsing it. 'They have sinned against no law of purity. They blundered, but their action was grave and pure. The English marriage laws are impure. Marriage under English law is an unholy thing as far as the law is concerned. It is a species of legal prostitution, the woman being the man's property,' the card said. Intense pressure was put on the couple to marry, particularly by Ursula Bright, and they were finally persuaded that the causes they cared for would be harmed by publicity about their unconventional match. They were formally married at Kensington register office in October 1874. The matter did not end there, though. Elizabeth lost her job as a lobbyist and, though she was allowed to remain on the Married Women's Property Committee, Lydia Becker, whose support was already waning, withdrew from it.

Josephine Butler told friends the couple now intended to live very quietly in Congleton and stay out of public life, and so it was for a while. Although Elizabeth continued to campaign on married women's property rights and on the suffrage, her name disappeared from the formal reports of the committees she had founded. Later histories of the movement even recorded that Lydia Becker, and not she, had in fact started the first committee for women's suffrage.

The Wolstenholme Elmys' son Frank was born in January 1875. The birth was not an easy one, and again the couple's unconventional views caused yet more discomfort. They believed that much of the pain suffered by women during childbirth was simply the result of a lack of proper education on the subject. So Elizabeth endured the agonies of a difficult labour largely alone. This unfortunate episode sparked a rumour among already-hostile suffrage supporters that she had begged Ben to go for a doctor and that he had refused to do so, relenting only just before the baby was born. Many of Elizabeth's friends, even some of those who might have been expected to support her, loathed Ben. Word was put about that he gave young Frank gin to torment his wife, and according to Sylvia it was whispered that he was 'violently cruel and unfaithful'. No doubt such things would have been said even if Ben had been a model husband but even Sylvia, who had a child outside marriage herself, described him as 'a stout, sallow man' who 'intensely resented and never forgave' the suffragists' interference in his affairs.

Elizabeth, for her part, always spoke and wrote of Ben with the utmost reverence and never betrayed the slightest resentment during the years of debilitating illness which preceded his death. However, her friend Harriet McIlquham later wrote to a mutual friend that 'I feel sure that her life with Mr Elmy has been one of mixed happiness and sorrow ... In many ways I believe he has been a great intellectual help to her, and in other ways a great tax on her energies – possessing a mixed character akin to our Coleridge, or the American poet, EA Poe.' Frank, according to Sylvia, did not thrive and grew up 'puny and frail and lacking in initiative ... Undoubtedly he was stunted from his birth by solitude and by lack of material things, knowing only the care of that work-driven mother.'[10]

Despite their other commitments the couple found time, under the name 'Ellis Ethelmer', to write a series of pamphlets explaining their views on love and marriage. These included some of the first ever sex education materials. Although these were sometimes distributed by Elizabeth from her Congleton address and were thought by some to have been written by her, she always maintained that they were her husband's work. Either way they must have expressed shared views. These works contained some extraordinary statements – for example, that menstruation was the inherited result of sexual abuse and would gradually disappear if women were better treated – but also provided factual information which would have otherwise been unavailable to parents and young people at the time.[11]

Neither such works nor the best efforts of Elizabeth's former friends in the suffrage movement could keep her from her political work for long. In 1881 she spent several months in London with the six-year-old Frank agitating for a new Married Women's Property Bill. The following year, after the final success of the campaign, she turned her attentions to women's parental rights. Women still had no right to custody of their children, even if their husbands had been guilty of the grossest cruelty. Again her campaign was successful, leading to improved rights for mothers under the 1886 Guardianship of Infants Act. And again, it extracted an almost unimaginable quantity of work and energy from its originator. In three years, petitions bearing more than 90,000 signatures were collected and presented to Parliament. Elizabeth calculated that she personally communicated with 10,000 people and distributed nearly half a million leaflets. After the act was passed she sent out 1,500 copies. How she found the time, while bringing up a small child, is hard to fathom. Nor was she wealthy enough to be relieved of domestic duties. 'Dear Friend, I would have written yesterday but unfortunately it was washing day,' she explained once to Harriet McIlquham after an interval of no more than a few days since her last letter. On another occasion, she admitted: 'I had a huge wash yesterday, having been obliged to put it off by my poor right arm and I was so tired after being at work from 4.30am to 6pm.'

As the 1880s drew to a close the Wolstenholme Elmys' financial situation worsened. Ben's silk business failed because of a flood of cheap imports from Southern Europe and the couple were forced to work long hours for many months while winding up their Congleton factory. In June 1889 Elizabeth told Harriet McIlquham that in addition to political work for the newly formed Women's Franchise League, of which she was secretary, and on campaigns on divorce and contagious diseases, she had been working more than fifty hours a week at the mill.[12] 'We have been finishing all the goods (crêpe finishing work) and Mr Elmy and I do with our own hands, with the help of one man and one woman what … was the work of eight distinct and carefully trained persons,' she explained. But, never one to miss an opportunity for a political campaign, she still found time to write a paper for the Congleton Fair Trade Lodge, explaining how the English worker was 'bidden to starve for want of work at home, that his fellow workers may perish from overwork and misery abroad'. Children in Italy were earning fivepence a day for silk-reeling work, starting at 5 a.m. and working till 10 p.m., a total working week of more than ninety four hours, she said. Ironically, her own week can hardly have been much shorter.

Now, and for the rest of her life, she was forced to accept charity from her friends. In the autumn of 1889 she wrote to Harriet McIlquham thanking her for a gift of home produce: 'Frank has keenly appreciated the apples and pears, and we have all enjoyed the beautiful tomatoes.' Nor was this charity restricted to just the odd food hamper. A little later another letter to Harriet McIlquham revealed her friend was having new clothes made for her, for she could no longer afford to buy them. 'You are quite spoiling me with all your kind attentions, but I won't say any more on this point as I know how you feel,' Elizabeth wrote. Indeed, Elizabeth's friends had difficulty persuading her to accept their gifts at all. Harriet McIlquham wrote to another woman in their circle that she had 'almost offended her' by demanding that she should be paid for the work she did for the cause. Even when she was paid, though, Elizabeth had a tendency to spend the money on more campaigning. One fellow suffrage supporter sent a cheque with the request that 'I wish you for my own peace of mind to accept the enclosed with my one condition that it is spent on *yourself alone.*' Another sent money to Harriet McIlquham for her with the complaint that 'twice last year I sent Mrs Elmy cheques for herself and she put them to the account of the society. This must not go in that way'.

The Wolstenholme Elmys had apparently talked about emigrating to America to start a silk business there. They were not destitute, being left with their home – later mortgaged – furniture, a library and some works of art, but their disposable income was virtually nil. Politically, too, there were frustrations and Elizabeth even considered giving up altogether, albeit briefly. She resigned from the Women's Franchise League after a split on its committee ended her already troubled friendship with Ursula Bright. Afterwards she wrote angrily to Harriet McIlquham: 'I do not intend ever again to take any part whatever in political action on behalf of women. I have done my part and more.' She could not maintain her resolve, though, and within a year she had set up yet another suffrage group, the Women's Emancipation Union. Three years later its work was occupying her for fourteen hours a day, though she was still refusing to take a salary. Instead a group of her friends set up a 'grateful fund' which paid her £1 a week.

The various schisms within the suffrage movement could not fail to affect her. She was too much of a political animal, in every sense, not to get involved. And, on occasion, she was not above turning her sharp wit upon her fellow campaigners. Once, irritated by the attempt of a former member of her Women's Emancipation Union, Mary Cozens, to promote a suffrage bill without consulting her, she wrote to Harriet McIlquham: 'I am inclined to feel with regard to Mrs Bright as well as Miss Cozens that the best thing they could do for the suffrage cause is to go to sleep for a year.' On another occasion she was annoyed by a request for help from Annie Leigh Browne, who was promoting a bill for the election of women councillors: 'I am much more than tired of giving help and information to people who simply insult me in return. I have tried continuously to keep on friendly terms with Miss Browne … in return I have been treated with constant insult.' She concludes that she will help, but 'for the Union, and not as Miss Browne's "slavey"'.

The 1890s were a time of disillusion for suffrage campaigners. Despite the proliferation of different suffrage societies there was a sense that little progress was being made. In 1896 Elizabeth wrote to Harriet McIlquham: 'I have quite decided that unless we succeed in advancing the cause very visibly this session, I shall give up all public work as a simple waste of time. Without the suffrage we win nothing, no matter what painful effort we put

forth.' Her output of letters, newspapers, leaflets and exhortations continued unabated, but two years later she was again telling her friend that she
had no inclination to take up any new causes. 'During the last 10 years I
have spent enough effort in trying to secure amendment of the law on divorce and of the law of inheritance as it affects women to have carried several bills through Parliament had they been for the benefit of male
electors,' she explained caustically.

At home, there was little relief from the constant strain. In 1895 Elizabeth was forced to send out a letter to members of the Women's Emancipation Union apologising for the fact that its annual meeting had had to be
postponed 'owing to the terrible illness, almost unto death, of my husband
and my own tedious and harassing ill-health'. Later, in 1897, she told Harriet McIlquham she was anxious about a planned overnight lobbying trip
to London: 'Mr Elmy is not well and this most variable weather tries him
severely, so that I shall be anxious both for him and Frank all the time I am
away.' It seems Ben suffered from chest complaints, though why the 22-
year-old Frank should have been the cause of such anxiety is not clear.
Sometimes it all seemed too much. By then, of course, Elizabeth was in her
sixties and the strain of between six and eight hours' suffrage work each
day was taking its toll. 'I am old and hope many mornings that the end may
be soon and sudden – and indeed I am so tired (we, my husband and I, are
so tired) in brain, head and body, that we long for rest,' she wrote. Had she
known how much longer the struggle would go on maybe she would really have given up, though this seems unlikely. She was pathologically
incapable of it. And, despite her advancing years, she was about to enter a
phase of her political life which would be almost childlike in its joyfulness.

Hitherto the women's suffrage movement had conducted its business
in a low-key, ladylike manner. When a delegate suggested to a shocked
women's conference in 1892 that if they had a regiment of women who
could shoot, they would have the franchise in a week, no one thought she
was serious. In 1898 the movement's leadership even vetoed a timid suggestion that perhaps an outdoor meeting in Hyde Park would be in order.
The suffragists at that time did not 'do' outdoors – such shenanigans were
left to the hoodlums of the Independent Labour Party and the Marxist Social Democratic Federation. But in Lancashire, not too far from where
Elizabeth Wolstenholme Elmy had her base, Christabel Pankhurst and a
group of her friends started in the early years of the twentieth century to
do just that. By 1903, when Emmeline Pankhurst founded the WSPU as an

offshoot of the Independent Labour Party, they had already begun organising among the textile workers. Elizabeth was soon in close touch with Christabel – she had known her parents for years – and became a firm admirer of her work. Irritated by the inaction of the staid National Union of Women's Suffrage Societies, she wrote that the suffrage campaign gathering force in the textile towns was of more value to their cause than all the work of the National Union put together.

Soon Elizabeth was actively supporting the work of the new WSPU. In May 1905 she helped the new union in her old stamping ground, the central lobby of the House of Commons, trying to win support and time for a suffrage bill which was being introduced by an MP named Bamford Slack. The bill was doomed to failure but Elizabeth's gloom was dispelled by the renewal of the fight, and she was in her element. When news came from the chamber that the bill had been 'talked out', Emmeline Pankhurst suggested an impromptu meeting outside. Elizabeth, although usually more eloquent on paper than on a public platform, rose to address the small crowd that had gathered. Each time she began to speak the police moved her audience on, though, and eventually the Labour leader, Keir Hardie, a key supporter of the suffragettes, persuaded the officers to allow a meeting outside Westminster Abbey. 'And so we were led off,' Sylvia recalled later, 'Keir Hardie hand in hand with old Mrs Elmy, to Broad Sanctuary, by the Abbey gates, where … we passed a resolution of indignation against the Government.'[13] Emmeline Pankhurst described this unauthorised gathering as the first militant suffragette act. Elizabeth was equally delighted by the day's events. Afterwards she wrote to Harriet McIlquham that she was 'desperately tired, but so happy'. Two years later she told Sylvia she had hoped to go to prison that day. She had come to believe women would not win the vote until they suffered imprisonment 'and even death itself, for the sake of our great common cause', she wrote.

For a time, though, even her enthusiasm for the newly revived cause was dampened by the parlous state of Ben's health. In February 1906 she reported that he was now 'too weak to sit up even to have his bed made' and that his breathing was 'painful and difficult'. Her fellow campaigners were anxious about her. Writing to Harriet McIlquham, another WEU member, Louisa Martindale, asked: 'Can she manage all the nursing herself? I know the uprising of women has brightened and revived her, but there is an end of human strength.' Not, it seems, where Elizabeth was concerned. Ben died on 3 March, and Christabel Pankhurst spoke movingly of his work for womanhood at his cremation on 7 March. Five days later his widow was back at work, delighted that the *Manchester Guardian* had decided to print one of her letters in full. This was a sign of the times, she said. The women's cause was finally gaining ground.

However, Elizabeth was not in good shape at this time, and her former pupil Frances Rowe wrote anxiously to Harriet McIlquham: 'Can nothing persuade her to take a rest and nurse up her strength instead of spending it? There is no-one in England with her knowledge of the women's cause. She must not be reckless of herself.' But the old lady was indefatigable. In October 1906 she was back in London, accompanied by Frank this time, to take up a seat on the national executive of the WSPU before attending another suffrage demonstration at Westminster. This time, ten women were arrested. Elizabeth was delighted, for the cause was headline news at last. 'Everything is going on splendidly,' she wrote to Harriet McIlquham, though she was disappointed that the police appeared to have deliberately avoided arresting either her or another elderly demonstrator, Charlotte Despard. 'We both felt aggrieved that we were thought unworthy of the crown they have placed on our dear sisters' heads.' Again, she tried to make a public speech outside Parliament but was moved on by the police. The next day she went to Westminster Police Court to try to have herself listed as a witness, but was instead locked into an anteroom with a number of other demonstrators. In a letter to the *Manchester Guardian* later that week,[14] she accused the police of brutality – though she confided to Harriet McIlquham that 'of course, our friends resisted because they meant to go to prison'.

The next couple of years were delirious ones for Elizabeth. She believed the rise of militancy would bring victory and she became one of a handful of elderly 'constitutional' suffrage campaigners who threw themselves wholeheartedly behind the new tactics. In a letter to the *Manchester Guardian* in February 1907 she pledged her support to a women's tax-evasion campaign: 'I for one am weary of being deceived and betrayed session after session, and therefore I have joined the ranks of the "political strikers",' she wrote.[15] As she barely had any income it is unlikely that this would have caused the Inland Revenue much pain, but the sentiment was a radical one none the less. The excitement may even have done her health some good for in June 1908 she was in top form for a huge suffrage demonstration in London's Hyde Park. The day was a glorious, sunny one, and Elizabeth marched the whole way to the park from Euston station, accompanied by Emmeline Pankhurst and carrying a bouquet of purple and white flowers bordered by green ferns – the three colours of the suf-fragette movement.[16]

During the latter part of that year Elizabeth travelled to a variety of suf-frage demonstrations including one in Heaton Park, Manchester, at which she was presented with a bouquet, having just been named as 'Nestor', or sage, of the suffrage movement.[17] She made speeches, appeared on plat-forms and lapped up the praise which, belatedly, was heaped upon her by her newfound friends. She was having a wonderful time. Sadly, though, age seems to have caught up with her at around this time. She remained active, offering a sort of information centre to the movement from her Congleton home and writing regular letters to the newspapers, but after 1908 she appeared less frequently at suffrage events and did not renew her bid to get arrested. She remained a figure who commanded respect and in 1911 her friend Louisa Martindale published a 'public testimonial' to raise money for her.

Later, though, as militancy reached its height, Elizabeth's attitude to it changed. She had come to believe that the vote was almost won, and that with a careful approach women could achieve their objective very soon. In July 1912 she was particularly incensed when a group of women were caught with petrol, matches, glass-cutters and skeleton keys in the garden of a government minister. A Conciliation Bill on which all hopes had been pinned had just collapsed, yet Elizabeth still felt victory could be just around the corner. 'Now that our cause is on the verge of success,' she wrote to the *Manchester Guardian*,

> I wish to add my protest against the madness which seems to have seized a few persons whose anti-social and criminal actions would seem designed to wreck the whole movement … I appeal to our friends in the ministry and in Parliament not to be deterred from setting right a great wrong by the folly or criminality of a few persons.[18]

But such righteous indignation must have been fired by political consider-ations rather than by personal disgust. A year later she reverted to her for-mer support for the militants. She wrote to the *Manchester Guardian* that the blame for suffragette law-breaking must lie with the government, which had failed to deliver votes for women. 'Upon those who continue to deny to us this right must rest the blame for every violent deed committed by any one of those women who are still denied this right of citizenship. Those who have refused and still refuse us the vote are the real culprits, and need to be exposed as such,' she wrote.[19]

To the end, this indomitable campaigner remained the suffrage movement's greatest repository of knowledge, history and political know-how. Although she maintained some links with the non-militant National Union of Women's Suffrage Societies, at the end her heart was with the militants. Elizabeth Wolstenholme Elmy died, aged eighty-four, in a Manchester nursing home on 12 March 1918 after falling down stairs and hitting her head. Six days earlier royal assent had been given to the Representation of the People Act which granted the vote to women over thirty. In its obituary the *Manchester Guardian* recorded she had lived just long enough to be told the good news.[20]

If a single person can shift the tide of a political movement by sheer force of will and determination, that person was Elizabeth Wolstenholme Elmy. In writing of her another veteran suffrage campaigner, Dora Montefiore, said she put her in mind of Elizabeth Barrett Browning's adage that it takes a soul to move a body and a high-souled man to move the masses. 'I often thought it was the little white hovering soul of Mrs Wolstenholme Elmy which eventually moved a somewhat inert mass of suffrage endeavour and set it on the road of militant activity,' she concluded.[21] Sylvia was even more fulsome: 'When others faltered because the cause was unpopular and the goal seemed far away, Mrs Elmy remained constant and steadfast and accomplished an immensity of work. The women of today and tomorrow will never know how much they owe to her.'[22]

Emmeline Pankhurst.

II

Emmeline Pankhurst – Matriarch

Be militant each in your own way ... those of you who can break windows, break them. Those of you who can still further attack the secret idol of property so as to make the Government realise that property is as greatly endangered by woman suffrage as it was by the Chartists of old – do so. And my last word is to the Government: I incite this meeting to rebellion! I say to the Government: You have not dared to take the leaders of Ulster for their incitement to rebellion. Take me if you dare!

Emmeline Pankhurst in a speech at the Albert Hall, October 1912

When Emmeline Pankhurst gathered a few women at her Manchester home on 10 October 1903 to announce the formation of the new Women's Social and Political Union, what did she think she was doing? Creating a feminist cell which would shake up the city's male politicians, certainly. Starting a suffrage group which would breathe new life into a staid, forty-year-old movement, probably. But even the ambitious, dynamic Emmeline could hardly have imagined the extent to which that day she was branding her name on the future histories of the new century that had just begun.

For many people, Emmeline Pankhurst *was* the suffragette movement. Her name conjures up the movement's purple, white and green colours, women chained to railings, hunger strikes, the glory of victory. It is hard to imagine any summary of the struggle for the vote that does not have Emmeline Pankhurst close to its heart. Alone among the many women who fought, went to prison and even died for the vote she has her own statue, erected just two years after her death, outside the Houses of Parliament. She was one of the greatest orators of the twentieth century, moving her audiences to laughter and to tears, delivering powerful and finely crafted speeches without notes. If one person is ever credited with winning the vote for women, it is usually Mrs Pankhurst.

Yet despite being such an all-pervasive figure in the modern political consciousness she remains, to those who take more than a passing interest in her life, a paradox. Who was the real Emmeline Pankhurst? Was she the tiny, oppressed, birdlike figure once photographed being lifted effortlessly from the ground by a burly policeman? Was she the harridan who amassed an army of women to terrorise London with window-smashing raids; the woman convicted of conspiracy to blow up the home of Lloyd George? Or was she the demure, carefully groomed, middle-aged woman often photographed in embroidered high-necked blouses with a substantial brooch pinned to her bosom? How did this high-minded girl from radical Lancashire stock come first to marry a Socialist, then to campaign against Labour MPs during the women's campaign, and finally to stand as a parliamentary candidate for the Conservative Party? What sort of mother could bury both her sons as well as her husband and then turn her back on two of her three remaining daughters because of political differences? How could a woman who loved the latest couture, the best society parties, the most exquisite food and wine, give up her home, her possessions and finally her health for her politics?

From her earliest days there are clues to the forces that drove this extraordinary woman. Even the date she gave as her birthday, Bastille Day 1858, seems to resonate with her later life, her revolutionary fervour and her love of Paris. Emmeline Goulden was born to be a radical. Her mother, Jane, was a campaigner against slavery, and one of Emmeline's earliest memories was of being taken to a bazaar in Manchester to raise money for newly emancipated slaves. Her father, Robert Goulden, had social upheaval in his blood. His father had been at the Peterloo massacre of 1819, a franchise demonstration broken up by soldiers amid terrible scenes of violence; his mother had been a member in the 1840s of the Anti-Corn Law League.

But the young Emmeline's life was a comfortable one, far removed from the strictures she would later choose to impose on herself. Her father was the self-made owner of a cotton-printing company at Seedley, near Manchester, and by the time Emmeline arrived – one of ten children and the oldest of five girls – the family were relatively well-heeled. They were able to afford a large house, boarding schools for the children and summer holidays with relatives in the Isle of Man. With so many children and numerous visitors – Robert and Jane loved to entertain – the house was always busy. Emmeline, an outgoing child, revelled in this and became something of a star, learning to read and play the piano at an early age; her brothers referred to her as 'the dictionary'. But her young life was not without its frustrations. Her father often set her to read the newspaper to him at breakfast, yet did not believe her education was as important as her brothers'. 'She should have been a lad!' he would often say. The remark was made with pride, but it grated on the girl's nerves.[1]

Even though her parents sent her to boarding school, Emmeline always felt her brothers' education was taken far more seriously by her parents than her own. The main criterion in the choice of her school was that the head was a 'gentlewoman', and her lessons seemed to concentrate mainly on domestic skills. She would say later: 'It used to puzzle me to understand why I was under such a particular obligation to make home attractive to my brothers. We were on excellent terms of friendship, but it was never suggested to them as a duty that they should make home attractive to me. Why not? Nobody seemed to know.'[2]

These feelings were translated into an early propensity for political radicalism. Emmeline Goulden was eight when the Radical MP John Stuart Mill presented his women's suffrage petition to Parliament, aided by Elizabeth Wolstenholme Elmy. The issue was much discussed in the Goulden household, which was well connected with Manchester radical politics, and Emmeline and her younger sister Mary soon decided to do something about it themselves. During the general election of 1868, they dressed themselves in red petticoats which they hid under green skirts, these being the Liberal colours of the day. Then they walked to a polling station about a mile from their home, lifted their skirts to display their petticoats and paraded up and down several times before being tracked down by their nursemaid and dragged home in disgrace. It was not 'done' for young ladies to display their petticoats in public, they were reminded. But Emmeline was not deterred. She was only fourteen when she attended her first suffrage meeting, hosted by the veteran women's suffrage campaigner Lydia Becker.

These activities were curtailed by another development which was to prove deeply formative. At fifteen, Emmeline was sent to Paris to study. There she was to develop both a lifelong love of France and a lifelong friendship with Noemie Rochefort, whose father was a prominent communist, republican and journalist. The two girls met at the Ecole Normale, where they learned chemistry and book-keeping as well as embroidery. So taken with France was Emmeline that she even planned to marry a Frenchman she met through the Rochefort family. She dreamed of a fashionable life in Paris, moving in the same circles as her now married schoolfriend, and was furious when the engagement fell through because her father refused to pay the required dowry. She remained thereafter a great advocate of the French '*dot*' system, believing it gave married women their own independent resources.

It did not take Emmeline Goulden long to forget her heartbroken suitor, though. No sooner had she returned to Manchester, aged twenty, than she had fallen into the midst of its burgeoning peace movement, and into the arms of her future husband, Dr Richard Marsden Pankhurst. Dr Pankhurst, a well-known lawyer and campaigning figure, was twenty years her senior, but was soon smitten by her striking looks. Sylvia Pankhurst describes her mother at this time as a real beauty:

> She returned to Manchester having learnt to wear her hair and her clothes like a Parisian, a graceful, elegant young lady, much more mature in appearance than girls of her age today, with a slender, svelte figure, raven black hair, an olive skin with a slight flush of red in the cheeks, delicately pencilled black eyebrows, beautiful expressive eyes of an unusually deep violet blue, above all a magnificent carriage and a voice of remarkable melody ... She was romantic, believed in constancy, held flirtation degrading, would only give herself to an important man.[3]

Again, the issue of women's property rights reared its head. Emmeline offered, as Elizabeth Wolstenholme Elmy had, to enter into a 'free union' which would dispense with the legal constraints under which married women then had to live. Possibly worried that such a move might embroil them in the sort of controversy experienced by the Elmys four years earlier, Richard Pankhurst refused and the couple were legally married in 1879. Realising the need to keep his energetic young bride occupied, he soon persuaded his Manchester suffrage friends to co-opt her on to some of their committees. He also drew up a programme of study for her, hoping to fill in some of the gaps in her education, but she did not take well to the work, according to Sylvia: 'She was temperamentally unable to devote herself to study; her desire was for action.' She was also temperamentally unsuited to writing: 'She wrote only occasional brief appeals for funds or for militant action. Deprecating even these as "stilted", she declared she felt, with pen in hand, as though "in the dentists chair".'[4] Throughout her life her correspondence tended to be brief, businesslike and to the point.

The marriage was a happy one. Sylvia said her mother 'adored her husband with all that ardent and impassioned loyalty of which she was capable, whilst he remained the most tender and affectionate of lovers'. Emmeline gave birth to four children in five years: Christabel in 1880, Sylvia in 1882, Frank in 1884 and Adela in 1885. Managing a household was not her forte, though, and she soon acquired a maid, Susannah, to take over the task. After the birth of Adela Emmeline was often unwell and would take to her bed complaining of headaches, something she would continue to do in later life when she was depressed. As Sylvia put it, Emmeline's many talents did not stretch to careful husbanding of the family's income, for she liked the finer things in life and was often ignorant of their cost: 'The maid could stretch it farther than her mistress, who was apt to spend too much on the bonbons and to discover she had nothing left for the muttons.'[5]

Emmeline's lack of financial acumen was not the only reason the family was cash-strapped. Her husband's earning power was often impaired by his tendency to put his political beliefs before his need to earn a living, and he lost several valuable legal clients as a result. In 1883 Richard stood in a Manchester by-election as an independent candidate, with Emmeline's father as his election agent. He polled just 6,000 votes to his Tory opponent's 18,000 and lost a great deal of work as a result. Worse, Robert Goulden's business was boycotted by Tory-supporting merchants. Shocked and shamed, the Pankhursts decided to leave Manchester and move south. They took the lease on a house in Hampstead Road, then a deeply unfashionable part of London, and Emmeline, determined to make a fresh start, opened a fancy goods shop which she named Emerson's. It sold items in the arts and crafts style which she would have liked to have had in her own home – and indeed many of them did end up there after they failed to sell. Two of the few successful lines were little milking stools and photograph frames painted in art enamel by Emmeline's sister Mary. Richard immersed himself again in politics. In the 1885 general election he stood as a Liberal and Radical candidate for Rotherhithe, but again the exercise was not a success. After a dirty campaign in which he was accused of radical atheism, he lost. The ensuing legal case, in which he attempted to sue his rival for slander, put a further drain on the family's already slender resources.

Emmeline got involved in politics, too, supporting the match girls in their famous 1886 strike against poor and unhealthy working conditions. The match girls' leader, Annie Besant, continued to visit and attend soirées at the Pankhurst home for some years after the strike ended. In her autobiography Emmeline described the experience in positive terms: 'I threw myself into this strike with enthusiasm, working with the girls and with some women of prominence ... It was a time of tremendous unrest, of labour agitations, of strikes and lockouts.'[6] By this time, Emmeline needed little instruction in the art of political agitation but she must certainly have learned something from the match girls about the power of militancy. At around the same time she attended a political rally in Trafalgar Square which ended in a riot.

Oddly, Emmeline's autobiography does not mention the tragedy which hit her family three years after the move to London: her youngest son, Frank, caught diphtheria while she and her husband were away in Manchester and died soon after their return. Bad drains in the Hampstead Road house were blamed and the family moved again – this time to a rather smarter address in Russell Square, Bloomsbury. Emerson's moved too, to a shop off Oxford Street, and for a time enjoyed quite a success with a range of furniture in the William Morris style. Despite the terrible blow which precipitated it, the move led to some better times for the family. Another son, Harry, was born in 1889 but the birth did not curtail the burgeoning social scene in which Emmeline was becoming involved.

Finally her dream of hosting a fashionable 'salon', shattered many years earlier in Paris, had come to fruition. According to Sylvia[7] the Russell Square house was soon a gathering point for socialists, fabians, anarchists, free-thinkers and radicals of every hue. Among the frequent visitors to the Pankhursts' gatherings were Keir Hardie, founder of the Independent Labour Party and now a close friend, William Morris and Eleanor Marx, daughter of Karl. And where the Pankhursts went, the issue of women's suffrage usually followed. At around this time a group of ladies gathered at their home to form the new Women's Franchise League. The Wolstenholme Elmys were leading lights, along with Josephine Butler and the veteran American women's rights campaigner Elizabeth Cady Stanton. Emmeline was not a great speaker at this stage in her life. Often her longest sentence at these political meetings was : 'I second the motion.' But she clearly set great store by these gatherings at her home and would lay on elaborate teas, music by celebrated artists, speeches by famous politicians. She was at the centre of a vibrant political network and, as always when she found herself in a place full of life and action, she was enjoying herself.

There was just one thing left to make Emmeline's life complete – getting her husband elected to Parliament. Sylvia generously attributes this urge to the appalling social conditions her mother had seen in the back streets of Manchester, and the need to redress them. However, driving personal ambition must also have played a part. From an early age, Emmeline Pankhurst had been determined to 'be someone'. She had hoped to achieve this by marrying a prominent man, but it was fast becoming clear even her beloved and well-connected husband might not be able fully to meet her need for fame. Richard Pankhurst was never to be an MP. In 1895 he stood again for Parliament, this time for Keir Hardie's Independent Labour Party. Again, he failed.

By this time the family had returned to Manchester. Emerson's had closed after a move to Regent Street left it overstretched, and the Pankhursts had left their Russell Square home when its lease ran out. Back on home turf, Emmeline was about to achieve electoral success on her own account. In 1894 she took a seat on the Chorlton Board of Poor Law Guardians, the body which oversaw the area's workhouses. Now she saw real evidence of how the poor had to live and it made a deep impression on her. Fond of the social whirl and of high society she may have been, but Emmeline Pankhurst was always capable of attaching herself to an idea, deeply and without guile. In fact she was never happier than when she had a project to occupy her. She was shocked by the conditions she found in the workhouse, and gratified that she was able to make some improvements to the lives of the inmates: chairs for the elderly, margarine to lubricate the dry-bread diet, cottage homes in the country where children could recover from their chronic bronchitis.

An even more important part of Emmeline's political education came soon after, in May 1896. For some time the Manchester Independent Labour Party had been holding Sunday rallies at a piece of open ground called Boggart Hole Clough. Radicals of all kinds had been using the land for years, but the local authorities were becoming irritated by the popularity of these labour meetings and decided to stop them. When one of the party's speakers was fined, a protest movement began to swell. The weekly crowds grew from a few hundred to 5,000, then to 50,000. At the centre of it all was the striking figure of Emmeline Pankhurst, her pink straw bonnet clearly visible in the crowd, her open umbrella stuck in the ground as a receptacle for donations to the fighting fund. A summons to appear before the bench had little effect on her activities but it caused a stir in the city – after all, she was the wife of a prominent if controversial lawyer. Repeatedly she challenged the court to imprison her but it did not oblige. Keir Hardie came to lend support and was summoned in his turn. The ongoing fracas was the talk of Manchester's political circles. Eventually the council was forced to give in, but not before Emmeline had gained some invaluable lessons in public speaking. Never again would she be diffident on a public platform. If she could face the rowdy and by no means universally sympathetic crowds at Boggart Hole Clough, she was ready for anything.

Another family tragedy was about to interrupt Emmeline's political career, though. In June 1898, while taking Christabel to stay with her friend Noemie in Switzerland, she was recalled by a telegram from her husband: 'Please come home. I am not well.' Knowing Richard would not recall her for any minor ailment, and half fearing his message might be designed to disguise the fact that one of the children was ill, she set off back. After crossing the channel she boarded a train and, glancing over the shoulder of a fellow passenger, read the news of her husband's death in that day's newspaper. Richard, long plagued by stomach problems, had suffered a perforated ulcer and had not recovered. 'Faithful and True My Loving Comrade', a quote from Walt Whitman, were the words she chose for his gravestone.

The next few years were grim ones. Already in some difficulties financially, they were forced to move to a smaller house – 62 Nelson Street, off Manchester's Oxford Road – and Emmeline's brother Herbert moved in to share the expense. Emmeline managed to secure a job as registrar of births and deaths – at the time, women were not allowed to register marriages. Christabel was recalled from Switzerland to manage a new branch of Emerson's – a task she resented deeply and performed to the least of her considerable abilities.

Richard's death proved to be the catalyst for the foundation of the suffragette movement. Labour members in Salford raised money to build a new Pankhurst Memorial Hall and Sylvia, a talented young artist, was engaged to decorate it. While carrying out the work she was astonished to learn that women were barred from the social club which had already opened there. In recent years Emmeline had fought her suffrage battles largely from within the labour movement and had pinned her hopes on the party's support, but on hearing this she decided the time had come to break with mainstream politics. It was becoming increasingly clear Labour was not the answer to the women's prayers. Several members of the party's executive were actively hostile to women's suffrage and when one of them, Philip Snowden, came to lecture at Pankhurst Hall the day after its opening Christabel refused to speak to him.

There were other catalysts, too. Christabel had become friendly with the secretary of the North of England Women's Suffrage Society, Esther Roper, who was scornful of the prospects of Labour ever helping women to win the vote. Esther and her friend Eva Gore-Booth, secretary of the Women's Trade Union Council, were also quietly critical of Emmeline, saying she had abandoned the women's cause since the death of her husband and had given herself over to 'this new Labour Party and personal ambition'. (As well as becoming a registrar, Emmeline had been co-opted on to the school board by the Independent Labour Party.) These comments stung, according to Sylvia, because Emmeline was more than a little jealous of Christabel's new friendships.[8] Christabel was her mother's favourite daughter, the one junior member of the family who could do no wrong. Whether by accident or design, the new movement was destined to bring Emmeline closer to Christabel. It would mould her relationships with all her daughters for the rest of her life.

And so Emmeline flung herself anew into the political fray, this time in pursuit of the cause which would become synonymous with her name. Emmeline's own version of events, given in an autobiography written for the US market, was a slightly different one – that she decided to found the WSPU after a visit to Manchester by the American suffrage campaigner Susan B. Anthony.[9] But whatever the cause, the aim and the methods were clear from the start. This new movement was to win votes for women on the same terms as men, and its permanent motto was to be 'Deeds Not Words'.

A seismic shift was taking place in Emmeline's inner political world. No longer were the aims of Labour, to raise the status of the working class and relieve poverty, at the centre of her thinking. Instead, as Sylvia commented rather bitterly: 'Her impressionable nature was now to be influenced by a narrowly exclusive feminist school ... refusing to admit that the welfare of the working woman ... was in any degree involved in raising the status of the working class as a whole.'[10] Sylvia added perceptively that it was characteristic of her mother to seize the franchise struggle as if it were the only cause in the world at that moment, and furthermore to believe to her very core that the battle must be won *now*, without so much as a moment's delay.

The WSPU was quite a different political beast from the suffrage campaigns that went before. Emmeline describes in her autobiography how the ladies had always sent a deputation to meet friendly MPs after the opening of Parliament. The ceremony was formal, with the MPs profusely thanked for their sympathy and the women assured that their elected friends would vote for their cause whenever they had a chance. More than a little offence was caused, therefore, when the new leader of the WSPU demanded to know what the MPs were going to *do* to win votes for women. Worse was to come. The women turned their attentions to the Liberal government, appearing wherever a minister was due to give a speech and crying out: 'Will the Liberal Party give votes for women?' Invariably, they were thrown out. It was not Emmeline who set this pace, but Christabel and her friends. Although Emmeline was always at the centre of events, lobbying, harrying, campaigning, speech-making, she did not for some time depart so far from the behaviour expected of a respectable widow as to actually get arrested or thrown out of a meeting-hall herself. In 1906 that began to change. In February the women held a huge rally in Caxton Hall, and a deputation went to the House of Commons to demand the vote. In the ardour of that crowd of women, many of them bussed in from the East End for the occasion, Emmeline saw the potential of direct action:

> Those women had followed me to the House of Commons. They had defied the police. They were awake at last. They were prepared to do something that women had never done before – fight for themselves. Women had always fought for men, and for their children. Now they were ready to fight for their own human rights. Our militant movement was established.[11]

Up to this point Emmeline had been dividing her time between her job as registrar, Emerson's and the cause. But Emerson's was sinking, yet again, and she had been rebuked for her frequent absences from the registrarship. Determined as ever to make her mark on the world, she turned her full attention to the women's movement. Her politics would never be the same again, she said in her autobiography: 'We threw away all our conventional notions of what was "ladylike" and "good form", and we applied to our methods the one test question, Will it help?'[12] Not only did she give up her job, her shop and her tenuous hold on respectability, but she also gave up her home – a tremendous sacrifice in one so attached to material goods. Never again, in the two decades and more she had left to live, would she have anything that could be described as a permanent dwelling-place. Her life would be an endless round of suitcases, trains, boats, hotels, platforms and friends' spare rooms. Although she always had a roof over her head, she would never again be truly domesticated. At the time, though, the decision was simple: the cause demanded it, and the cause was all-consuming. Travelling from town to town, raising the rafters with her speeches wherever the political circus led her, she was in her element. Although Emmeline was not invincible, her illnesses and depressions were usually connected with a sense of purposelessness, a feeling that she was getting nowhere. Once, when political travails were all but consuming Emmeline, Sylvia confessed to her mother that she was loath to leave her. Emmeline turned and punched her playfully on the arm, exclaiming: 'Don't look at me like that! Bless you, your old mother likes it. This is what I call life!' Sylvia wrote later that the remark came as a revelation to both of them, though she did not believe it to be entirely true. Her mother was, she said, 'as many-mooded as the sea'. Indeed, even when the struggle was at its height she was sometimes depressed. She felt pushed aside by Christabel and her young, energetic friends, she told Sylvia: 'Despite the public cheers she often felt herself a lonely outsider, and complained of it to me with tears. When the spur of the cause flagged, her life seemed harsh and joyless.'[13]

But more often than not, during these years, there was a speech to be made, a by-election to be fought. The WSPU women made by-elections their speciality, arriving as soon as the poll was announced to urge voters to oppose the Liberals until their government granted the vote. They would fill a vacant shop with suffragette literature and rent a flat-bed lorry on which to make speeches around the town. Even *Tribune*, an antisuffragette newspaper, acknowledged that 'their staying power, judging them by the standards of men, was extraordinary … They rose earlier and retired late. They are better speakers, more logical, better informed.'

Violence was a routine part of political life at the time, and the women had to withstand a great deal of it. At Colne Valley the local Liberals bought pea-shooters for the crowd and when the peas ran out they furnished them with rotten oranges. In Mid-Devon during the Christmas of 1907 Emmeline and her companion Nellie Martel were set upon by furious Liberals after a Unionist gain – a success for the suffragettes was a seat lost to the Liberal government. Emmeline confessed later that when she came to after a blow to the head, lying on the ground with a group of men in a ring around her, she fully believed she was about to be raped or even murdered:

A long time seemed to pass, while the ring of men slowly drew closer. I looked at them, in their drab clothes smeared with yellow pit-clay, and they appeared so underfed, so puny and sodden, that a poignant pity for them swept over me. 'Poor souls,' I thought, then I said suddenly: 'Are none of you *men*?' Then one of the youths darted toward me, and I knew that whatever was going to happen to me was about to begin.[14]

At that moment the police arrived and rescued her, but that night the local Conservative club was attacked and the next morning the body of one of its members was found in the mill-race. Violence and politics, then, were already intertwined in Emmeline's mind. The progress of the suffragettes into ever more serious illegality, when seen in this context, does not seem quite so outlandish.

By the time the movement had been active for five years large numbers of suffragettes had gone to prison, quite deliberately, for the cause. Emmeline had avoided being taken into custody, though, because she feared the WSPU would be rudderless without her. In February 1908, still suffering badly from an ankle injury she sustained in the Mid-Devon fracas, she decided the time was right. Parliament was using a law against 'Tumultous Petitions' enacted by Charles II to prevent the women from presenting their case at Westminster, and a major demonstration was pending. After discusssing the issue with Christabel, Emmeline announced at a supporters' meeting that she planned to lead a deputation of thirteen women to the door of the House of Commons in defiance of the act. What followed was something of a formality. As soon as the small band entered Parliament Square its leader was formally arrested. She was bailed that night but sentenced the following morning to six weeks in the 'second division', a section of the prison where few privileges were on offer.

Emmeline knew what to expect – she had by then heard graphic descriptions of prison life from Sylvia and Adela as well as from Christabel. She was shocked, though, when the wardress asked her to undress in order to put on her prison uniform – stained underwear, rough brown and red striped stockings and a dress with arrows on it. She was given coarse but clean sheets, a towel, a mug of cold cocoa and a thick slice of brown bread, and taken to her cell. Second division prisoners were kept in solitary confinement and were let out of their cells only for an hour's exercise each day. They were not allowed to receive letters for four weeks. Even though she had prepared herself for the experience, the reality hit her harder than she had anticipated. She became depressed, reliving her grief over her husband's death and worrying about her children. 'Her bodily functions, ever acutely responsive to her spiritual, flagged dismally. The old migraine laid her low.

After two days she was removed to hospital,' Sylvia wrote later.[15] The prison sanatorium was hardly more cheerful. There Emmeline lay in bed in her own solitary cell, listening to a woman giving birth alone next door.

This grim episode did not prevent Emmeline from getting arrested again quite soon afterwards. In October of the same year she was issued with a summons after publishing a pre-demonstration handbill urging women to 'Rush the House of Commons!' This was judged so inflammatory that she was sentenced to six weeks in the second division, along with Christabel and another prominent suffragette, Flora Drummond. This time, though, the whole series of events was imbued with a far greater sense of *joie de vivre*. The three women had been ordered to appear at Bow Street police station but instead decided to attend a WSPU 'at home' – meetings usually attended by crowds of several hundred. 'It did not suit our convenience to obey the adjourned summons quite so early, so I wrote a polite note to the police saying that we would be in our headquarters, no. 4 Clement's Inn, the next evening at six o'clock and would then be at his disposal,' Emmeline wrote in her autobiography. She spent the day with Christabel and Flora Drummond on the roof garden of Clement's Inn before proceeding to Bow Street in taxis accompanied by the arresting officers, who had arrived as ordered. When the news broke that the women would be unable to attend their demonstration, a sympathetic Liberal MP called James Murray decided to make them more comfortable. He rushed to the Savoy Hotel, where he ordered a full dinner to be delivered to Bow Street complete with damask tablecloths, silver, flowers, candles and fruit. Three waiters were allowed to serve an elaborate meal and Mrs Pankhurst was reported to be 'hugely entertained'.

Christabel had been studying law at Manchester's Victoria University. Women were not allowed to practise at the time, but her legal skills were put to good use in turning suffragette trials into major spectacles surrounded by massive publicity. On this occasion the trio were able to subpoena Lloyd George, the Chancellor of the Exchequer, who had been present when the handbill was issued at an earlier demonstration, and Herbert Gladstone, son of the former Prime Minister and a member of the Liberal government. On such occasions Emmeline was at her best, both regal and voluble, but with the hint of a twinkle in her eye. She was able to hold forth to the court at length, and to treat both the judge and Fleet Street's finest to a sharp exposition of the suffragettes' aims and methods. 'Our rule has always been to be patient, exercise self-restraint, show our so-called superiors that we are not hysterical, to use no violence, but rather to offer ourselves to the violence of others. We are here, not because we are law-breakers; we are here in our efforts to become law-makers,' she told the court with a flourish.[16] The desired result, of course, was not to achieve a shorter sentence but simply to get the message across.

Emmeline was in fine form. The first thing she did after her arrival at Holloway was to send imperiously for the governor. The women were political prisoners, she told him, and would not agree to undress in front of wardresses or to be searched. Surprisingly, the governor acceded to this though he refused to give Emmeline permission to talk to Christabel during exercise periods.

Although the women emerged from prison to a rapturous reception from their supporters and admirers, all was not well in the Pankhurst world. Harry, who had been apprenticed to a Glasgow builder but had lost his job when the company failed, had fallen ill with 'infantile paralysis', or polio. Since arriving unemployed in London he had been acting as an errand boy for the WSPU. He had also been sent for a time to Essex, to work on a farm run by a millionaire philanthropist, Joseph Fels. It was typical of Emmeline that when Harry became ill she swung erratically between a horrified conviction that he was dying and an equally implacable belief that he was on the mend and would soon be completely well. It was during one of the latter phases that she set sail for America and a fund-raising lecture tour, leaving Sylvia to nurse the sick boy. She returned to find him dying. Sylvia reported that when her mother was told Harry would never walk again she exclaimed: 'He would be better dead!'[17] A few days later he was. However, Emmeline's middle daughter never accused her mother of indifference to her son's fate: 'As we drove the sad way to his burial, she was bowed as I had never seen her,' she wrote.

Emmeline barely paused for breath before she was back at work, for there was a general election pending. Just a few days after the funeral she wrote to the WSPU's Bradford organiser before a meeting there to tell her she was hoping there would be no reference to the tragedy: 'If you can arrange it I would be grateful if Bradford friends would just behave to me as if no great sorrow had come just now. It breaks me down to talk about it although I am very grateful for sympathy. I want to get through my work and know that you will help me to do it.'[18] There was more grief to come.

On Christmas Day 1910 Emmeline's sister Mary Clarke, to whom she had always been close, died from a brain haemorrhage shortly after being released from prison. The extraordinary self-restraint, the sheer focus with which Emmeline appears to have handled these losses suggests she was a more buttoned-up, less openly emotional person than she actually was. Although her younger children might all, at times, justifiably have accused her of neglect they could never have accused her of being a strait-laced Victorian matriarch. In fact, she had an enormous sense of fun, and even an anarchic streak which might seem surprising in the light of some of her more conventional prudities – her horror at being asked to undress in front of a prison wardress, for example. It was only a few months after the loss of Harry that she formed a new attachment in which she was able freely to display some of those qualities.

In the summer of 1910 Emmeline was introduced to Ethel Smyth, an endearingly eccentric bisexual composer who cheerfully confessed to having little or no political background and to caring even less about votes for women – until she met and fell passionately in love with the founder of the WSPU. At first glance Ethel Smyth made a curious companion for a political leader who, despite the violence which attached itself to her movement, remained resolutely feminine. While Emmeline usually had some lace about her person Ethel always dressed in tweeds, deerstalker and tie. Emmeline tended to attack every venture with passion while her new friend regarded the world with a wry, amused cynicism. Ethel, unlike Emmeline, had few sexual or personal inhibitions. But the two women, who at fifty-two were exactly the same age, immediately formed so close an attachment that Ethel decided to give two years of her life to the cause. After that, she said, she would go back to her music. She was as good as her word, though the friendship endured even after she had left the political fray. Ethel's insights into the mind of her friend are incisive and enlightening, untainted by the family tensions which strained the memoirs of the younger generation of Pankhursts. Although it is clear from her writing that her admiration for Emmeline Pankhurst went much further than mere political esteem or platonic affection, it seems unlikely the relationship was a physical one. As Smyth herself noted, her friend had rarely if ever formed close attachments to other women in the past and, if anything, preferred friendships with men. The composer described the Emmeline Pankhurst she knew thus: 'A graceful woman rather under middle height, one would have said a delicate-looking woman, but the well-knit figure, the quick deft movement, the clear complexion, the soft bright eyes that on occasion could emit lambent flame, betokened excellent health.'[19] On census night in 1911, when the suffragettes stayed out all night in an act of 'resistance' to being counted while not recognised as full citizens, the pair watched the dawn break over London together, from the window of Emmeline's hotel room. 'Suddenly it came to us that all was well; for a second we were standing on the spot in a madly spinning world where nothing stirs, where there is eternal stillness … Neither of us ever forgot that dawn,' Ethel wrote later.

But Smyth was also able to describe another aspect of the suffragette leader – a humorous side only she seemed to see. Once, on the way to a meeting together in the WSPU car, they were surrounded by anti-suffrage demonstrators, one of whom fell under the wheels:

> In a twinkling Mrs Pankhurst was on the pavement, her arm round the blowzy victim of Suffragette brutality, while with the innate authority that never failed she ordered a policeman to fetch an ambulance. And so manifest was her distress, so obviously sincere her bitter regret … that in less time than it takes to tell the story it was the crowd that was comforting Mrs Pankhurst … And all this time, Mrs Pankhurst's face, soft with pity, radiant with love, was the face of an angel, and her arm still encircled the lady, who was now quite recovered. But as she settled down somewhat violently in her seat, Mrs Pankhurst might have been heard ejaculating in a furious undertone, 'Drunken old beast! I wish we'd run her over!'

Emmeline did not always share her friend's sense of the ridiculous. In early 1912 she enlisted Ethel's help in preparing for an escalation of suffragette militancy – the women were planning a series of stone-throwing raids in London. Unlike the stouter and more countrified Ethel, Emmeline had never thrown a stone in her life. So the two women went one evening to an isolated part of Hook Heath, near Ethel's Surrey home. 'Near the largest fir tree we could find I dumped down a collection of nice round stones,' Ethel recalled. 'One has heard of people failing to hit a haystack; what followed was rather on those lines. I imagine Mrs Pankhurst had not played ball games in her youth, and the first stone flew backwards out of her hand, narrowly missing my dog.' Emmeline was furious and frustrated, and her expression darkened at each failed attempt. When at last she hit the tree she was suddenly wreathed in smiles, but she was both mystified and annoyed when Ethel collapsed, helpless with laughter.

Ethel noted that despite two attempts, Emmeline failed to hit the

Downing Street window she later singled out for her attentions. Despite this the raids, precipitated by the collapse of the Conciliation Bill on which suffrage hopes had been pinned for two years, were a spectacular success. On two separate days, at a preordained time and with no warning, hundreds of smartly dressed women from Oxford Street to Whitehall, all along Piccadilly and Bond Street, produced hammers from their muffs and laid waste hundreds of square feet of shop frontage. Emmeline was arrested along with a total of 220 other protesters, including Ethel. Ethel described the time the women spent together in Holloway as rather a hoot. The regime had been relaxed. Emmeline was allowed access to WSPU files and had her own food sent in, including a daily half-pint of Château Lafitte. Ethel helped to organise athletic sports in the prison yard, which was even decorated by the women in the suffragette colours. As the women prisoners marched round the exercise yard singing 'March of the Women', an anthem she had composed for them, Ethel looked on from the window of her cell, marking time with a toothbrush.

Emmeline's final prison sentence was to be far less congenial. Suffragettes had set off an explosive device in an empty house owned by Lloyd George and Emmeline, as she always did, had opted to take full public responsibility for the act. 'I have advised, I have incited, I have inspired,' she told a public meeting in Cardiff. The following day, in the Home Secretary's room, the decision was taken to charge her with conspiracy. She was sentenced to three years' penal servitude. It was 1913 and by then suffragette prisoners were regularly hunger-striking. The government had initiated moves to bring in a 'cat and mouse' act which would allow them to be repeatedly released then rearrested when they were judged fit. Emmeline had refused food before, during a short spell in prison the previous year, but on that occasion she had swiftly been freed on medical grounds. This time she knew she faced repeated release and rearrest. Despite the ghastliness of this realisation, her contemporary description of the experience of going without food was down-to-earth, even rather bland, compared to the horrors described by some suffragettes. But certainly she suffered just as much as they did, and for years she had recurring gastric trouble as a result. 'The actual hunger pangs last only about twenty-four hours with most prisoners,' she wrote in her autobiography, published while her sentence continued.

I generally suffer most on the second day. After that there is no very desperate craving for food. Weakness and mental depression take its place.

Great disturbances of digestion divert the desire for food to a longing for relief from pain. Often there is intense headache, with fits of dizziness, or slight delirium. Complete exhaustion and a feeling of isolation from earth mark the final stages of the ordeal. Recovery is often protracted, and entire recovery of normal health is sometimes discouragingly slow.[20]

Emmeline became depressed and ill during her hunger strike and, believing she might die, she wrote to Ethel with her last wishes. The episode led Ethel to make one of her most percipient judgements about her friend's character. The letter, Ethel said, contained instructions not about her family but about the elderly mother of her wardress, Miss Harper. She would like the old lady to be looked after, she wrote. The request demonstrates the shakiness of Emmeline's mental state, but according to Ethel it also highlights one of the key qualities that marked her out. 'The whole incident is typical of this strange woman, who lived less in the past and more wholeheartedly in the present and future than anyone I have ever known,' she wrote.[21] These few words encapsulate the driving force behind Emmeline Pankhurst. When she committed herself to something, as she did to the suffragette movement, she did so to the exclusion of all else. Thus she found herself constantly living in the moment, shutting out the bigger picture of the background to her life. Thus she could expend huge amounts of mental energy, when the moment allowed it, on worrying about her family or dwelling on the loss of her husband. But when the day demanded some other emotion, it was to that immediate feeling she would surrender herself.

There was to be little joy in the next year of Emmeline's life. She spent it, as she had known she would, either in prison and on hunger strike, or recuperating in a suffragette refuge or nursing home. Soon she was not just hunger striking but thirst striking too. This produced far worse effects: 'The muscles waste, the skin becomes shrunken and flabby … the body becomes cold and shivery, there is constant headache and nausea and sometimes there is fever. The mouth and tongue become coated and swollen, the throat thickens and the voice sinks to a thready whisper,' she wrote.[22] By the summer of 1913 Emmeline was in desperate need of a break. During one of her spells of freedom she managed to escape in disguise to Paris, whence Christabel had fled in order to avoid prison. The two spent the summer there and in October Emmeline sailed for America, returning home in December with more than £4,000 for the suffragette coffers. She was arrested on board ship at Plymouth and began anew the grind of hunger strike, release and slow recovery.

Perhaps fortunately for Emmeline's health and for that of the other suffragette hunger strikers, war was about to intervene to bring an end to their self-imposed endurance test. When the declaration came, Emmeline was out of prison and had been smuggled to France to recuperate. She was in St Malo with Ethel, who had been shocked when she saw her friend again after their long separation. She could barely stand and was merely 'the ghost of what had been Mrs Pankhurst'. Within a short time she was swimming in the sea, though, and teaching Ethel to swim too. The war was not unexpected but it threw into stark relief the position in which the suffragette movement then found itself. Over the past two years the atmosphere surrounding the struggle had become so tense, so extreme, that there was no way forward but death for large numbers of women. The war provided an escape route for those campaigners, a means of bowing out gracefully. The government had become as entrenched as had the women – neither side would be seen to give in. If the government granted the vote, it would appear to have bowed to terror tactics. If the women called an end to their activities, their struggle would appear to have been in vain. War changed everything.

Perhaps, given her tendency to go with the moment, it is significant that Emmeline Pankhurst was alone in St Malo with the unapologetically jingoistic Ethel when the declaration of war came. Certainly she wasted no time in winding up the movement and urging her supporters to turn their energies to war work. As Ethel put it, 'Mrs Pankhurst declared that it was now not a question of Votes for Women, but of having any country left to vote in. The Suffrage ship was put out of commission for the duration of the war, and the militants began to tackle the common task.'[23] *The Suffragette*, now the official organ of the movement, hit the streets one last time on 7 August 1914 with an appeal to members to 'protect our Union through everything … for the sake of the human race!' The following week, it did not appear. By then, negotiations for the release of prisoners had taken place and the militant campaign of the WSPU was over.

Emmeline spent much of the war trying to rally support abroad for the allies. She went on another lecture tour in America, where she had always been a popular speaker, and in 1917 spent several months in Russia endeavouring to persuade its politicians to turn their backs on the internal turmoil in their own country and help Britain and France. These activities were not enough to fulfil her restless spirit, though. Now and for the rest of her life she would be frequently depressed, and would suffer bouts of illness supposedly connected to her privations in prison, but probably also linked to her less than serene state of mind. As a means of supporting the war effort she even adopted four orphaned 'war babies'.

There was an increasingly moralistic tone to Emmeline's pronouncements. Although the family had never been religious, Christabel was now dabbling in evangelical Christianity and it seems her newfound cause had some effect on her mother. In America, Emmeline had planned to lecture on 'social hygiene' – the prevention of venereal disease – but wrote to Ethel that 'Somehow when I came to do it I couldn't go in for personal money-making in war time – so I stick to considering the lilies as usual.' Hardly surprisingly given this unworldliness and the demands of the four small children she now had to care for, Emmeline was increasingly beset by money worries.

Seemingly without much effort from the former militants, the government was coming round to their point of view. Herbert Asquith, Prime Minister from 1908 until 1916, had been seen as the devil incarnate during the Cat and Mouse period. But now he was changing – not least because there was still the threat that militancy could resume once the war was over if the vote was not won. There was another reason, though – squaddies and able-seamen returning from the war would expect some reward, too, and many of them still did not have the vote. It would be easy to give votes to some women, at least, as part of the same measure. When Asquith promised that women who had done war work should be included in any postwar extension of the franchise, Emmeline objected. Hang the women, she said. Male soldiers and sailors should have the vote now – the women would not let themselves be used as an impediment to that.

However, Emmeline could not resist the potential prize of a victory in the old fight for the vote. By now Asquith had resigned and the new Prime Minister, David Lloyd George, had offered concessions to the Irish in return for support in the war. Emmeline felt the women should demand the same for themselves. Emmeline Pankhurst met Lloyd George and told him the women would accept whatever wartime measures the government felt it could offer. The WSPU mantra – Votes for Women on the same terms as men – had now been abandoned completely. She told Lloyd George to do whatever he thought was just and practicable in the war circumstances – whatever might pass through the Commons. And so women got the vote but the bedrock on which the WSPU was built – the concept of equal rights with men – was allowed to crumble. It would be another ten years before women would vote on the same terms as men, and for now they made do with a franchise that extended only to property-owning or uni-versity-educated women over thirty.

With the women's war over, what future was there for Emmeline? Sadly, there was little to sustain her fighting spirit and her essential ebullience. In fifteen years she had barely paused to draw breath, let alone to take stock of her life and achievements. Now she found herself to all intents and pur-poses alone: her husband and two sons dead, two of her daughters es-tranged from her because they had clung to their father's socialism while she had drifted away from it. Sylvia never managed to heal her breach. She would meet her mother again many years later but would never be fully forgiven – not least because she compounded her political sins by giving birth to a son out of wedlock. Even Ethel had fallen out with her former idol after she dared to criticise Christabel while writing to Emmeline. Her letter came back with a curt note: 'My dear Ethel, I return your letter. You may wish to destroy it. I would if I were you.' The two women would meet again, several years later in London, and Ethel would describe her former friend as a rather sad character. Her manner, she would say, was 'shy and uncertain': 'I think she would have liked us to be on affectionate terms.'[24] Unmoved, Ethel did not attempt to make contact again.

Emmeline found herself looking west across the Atlantic again, this time to Canada. There, at least, she was still held in high enough esteem to earn a living from lecturing. A testimonial fund for her had not had a large response – less than £3,000, of which more than half was spent on a country cottage which was later sold because she could not afford its up-keep. By the summer of 1920 she was in Victoria, Canada, with her four adopted 'war babies' and Sister Pine, a nurse who had often helped hunger-striking suffragettes and who was now engaged to look after the children. Hard times for Emmeline never extended to changing nappies or getting up in the night with bottles. For a while, the move seemed to have been a good one. She was engaged by the newly formed National Council for Combatting Venereal Disease as a campaigner in a moral crusade against promiscuity. The work suited her – it took her back on the road, on to the series of platforms with which her life had become synonymous. Again she was living out of a suitcase, going from town to town, from hotel to hotel. As one historian later put it: 'Domestication, to her, was a form of idleness, a pretty haven into which one put for refitting. She had to know that there was a series of platforms, a string of audiences, ahead.'[25] In Toronto she made headlines by telling reporters venereal disease was closely related to an infectious mental disease called Bolshevism – both were caused by a mistaken and promiscuous flouting of traditional decencies. Even this moralising always had a feminist streak, though. When she was told by the mayor of Bathurst, New Brunswick, that a prominent new building was 'a home for fallen women', she responded tartly: 'And where, pray, is your home for fallen men?'[26]

But by now Emmeline was sixty-seven, and the rigours of the lifestyle had begun to tell on her. In 1924 severe bronchitis and exhaustion kept her from working for six months, and the harsh Canadian climate did not aid her recovery. She decided to leave, taking her adopted children to Bermuda, where she enjoyed some rare relaxation, sunbathing and teaching the girls to swim in the sea. But the trip diminished her already scarce resources, and she decided to part with two of them, sending them back to England to alternative homes. One of the remaining two, Betty, was adopted by Christabel and the fourth, Mary, remained with Emmeline. Even after lightening her burden in this way, Emmeline decided she could not return to Canada. She put what little was left of her money into an English tea-room on the Riviera which she planned to run with Christabel and another former suffragette, Mabel Tuke. But like Emerson's before it the venture was doomed to failure. Although a few visitors were attracted by the celebrity of the owners, it did not thrive. Christabel hated the whole enterprise and seems to have found her mother's presence irritating. It was not long before Emmeline was packed off to London, and little longer before Christabel closed the tea-room and followed her.

The name of Emmeline Pankhurst was still one to be reckoned with, though. On her return some of the old militants organised a banquet to welcome her, and persuaded her to stand as a Conservative candidate in the unwinnable seat of Whitechapel and St George's. Emmeline decided to settle in the constituency in order to commit herself fully to the task. But the romantic notion of living surrounded by the people she hoped to embrace soon gave way to petulance when she saw the flat she was to live in. 'I hate small rooms!' she wailed. She was never happy in the few months she spent there. She felt exiled, unwanted and unneeded. The damp atmosphere in the flat did not help her bronchial condition and soon she left to stay with friends in Chipping Ongar in Essex, consumed by exhaustion and depression. She wept for hours, saying she did not believe she would ever be able to speak in public again. She became uncharacteristically reminiscent, talking about her husband, her sons and the times she had spent in Paris with Christabel. The news of Sylvia's baby horrified her. When Sylvia phoned to try to talk to her mother, Emmeline put the phone down. It was clear to those few people who remained close to Emmeline Pankhurst that she had not long to live. In May 1928 Christabel had her moved to a nursing home in Hampstead and it was there, on 14 June, a month short of her seventieth birthday, that she died.

The news of the death of such a towering political figure brought a gathering of the militant clans. Former suffragettes kept watch on her coffin at St John's, Smith Square, the night before her funeral and there was a guard of honour as it was carried to its final resting place in Brompton Cemetery. Even Ethel did her bit. Two years later, when Emmeline's statue was unveiled outside Parliament, she conducted her 'March of the Women' at the ceremony. In death, as in much of her life, Emmeline was able to gather people around her and to unite them in a purpose. It was one of her many talents.

She left behind her sadness and bewilderment among those once close to her who had been rejected. But those two qualities – the ability to unify and to cast aside without compunction – surely had some relation to each other. The key quality Emmeline Pankhurst possessed, the one above all that made her the great reformer she was, was her ability to lose herself in the cause. Outside of that, nothing mattered. When there was a prize to be won, she pursued it to the exclusion of all else – family, friends, the principles she had hitherto espoused. For her, the immediate goal was all. When she knew what that goal was, she was consumed by it and was happy; when she was uncertain, or had no clear goal, her vitality quickly drained away.

Sylvia wrote to her mother's former friends for their opinions when she was working on her biography, *Life of Emmeline Pankhurst*. One of the most incisive and generous replies came from Emmeline Pethick-Lawrence, the former treasurer of the WSPU, who had herself been thrown out of the movement after a policy disagreement: 'I believe she conceived her objective in the spirit of generous enthusiasm. In the end it obsessed her like a passion and she completely identified her own career with it in order to obtain it. She threw scruple, affection, honour, legality and her own principles to the winds.'[27]

Annie Kenney dressed as a mill girl.

III

Annie Kenney – Mill to Militancy

Inspector Mather said he was on duty on Friday night, and at 8.50 visited the Free-trade Hall when the Liberal meeting was in progress. Police assistance was called for during the meeting, and he was present when these ladies were ejected. Superintendent Watson asked them to behave as ladies should, and not create further disturbance. They were then at liberty to leave. Miss Pankhurst, however, turned and spat in the Superintendent's face, repeating the same conduct by spitting in the witness's face, and also striking him in the mouth … On the way to the Detective Office, Miss Kenney, in clinging to her friend, trod upon her skirt, and the garment was left behind.

Manchester Guardian, *Monday 16 October 1905*

In October 1905 a young woman rose to her feet during a Liberal Party rally in Manchester's Free Trade Hall. She was thin and rather nervous-looking but the sound she made was loud enough to reverberate both through the hall and the wider political community. 'Will the Liberal government give votes for women?' she yelled, the strength of her lungs belying her frail appearance. When no response came, her audience watched as she climbed on to her seat and repeated her question. This was Annie Kenney, and she had come with her friend Christabel Pankhurst to get arrested. After the pair were dragged outside Christabel completed their night's work. The incident proved a turning point for the Women's Social and Political Union and a milestone in the life of Annie Kenney.

The following day, for the first time, the WSPU made headlines. Annie became the mill girl who went to prison for the vote. As such she was one of the suffragettes' best propaganda tools, useful both in winning workers over to the cause and in convincing supporters that the movement was more than just a group of well-heeled, if well-meaning socialites. It was an image she came to resent deeply, not least because her role within the movement would far outgrow it. For now, though, it had its uses, and long after she had escaped the cotton mill she would be required to wear clogs and shawl for the cause.

There had been few indicators in Annie's early life of what she was to become. Born in September 1879, the fifth of eleven children, she was premature and was lucky to survive her first year. She was always fragile in appearance and those who met her often feared for her health, but in fact she was a sturdy child. Annie was outgoing and often the centre of attention, and she had a tendency to lead her friends into tomboyish scrapes. On occasion she could be spotted at the top of a high wall, encouraging the other children to climb it, or waltzing out on to the centre of a frozen lake, declaring just before the crack came that the ice was quite safe. In Sunday School plays, she loved to play the 'Mary Ann' character, and to 'run wild, wave pots and pans about … and rush around and have a rollicking time'.[1]

In her autobiography Annie described her home life as warm, and she adored her mother. Her father was not often engaged with his children, she recalled, preferring to spend time with friends at the club or with his nose in a book: 'Father never seemed to have any confidence in his children, and he had very little in himself. Had he possessed this essential quality, perhaps the whole course of our lives would have been changed. My mother always said she ought to have been the man and Father the woman.' But while her father, who worked in the mill like her mother, was able to spend his evenings 'educating himself and having a good time', the young Annie noted that her mother did not have the same privileges: 'Never had she an evening in which to read or to cultivate her mind. It was work, work, work: until at midnight she would still be at work darning stockings. It did not seem to me fair, and the sense of the unfairness of it to mother has never ceased to rankle.'

It was from her mother, rather than her father, that Annie gained her intellectual nourishment: 'Mother allowed us great freedom of expression on all subjects, whether it was dancing or the Athanasian Creed, Spiritualism, Haeckel, Walt Whitman, Blatchford, or Paine, I grew up with a smattering of knowledge on many questions.' This was not as unusual as it might seem, for the burgeoning workers' education movements of the late nineteenth century had made a clear mark on the culture of the North-west of England, and many working families were widely read and politically aware. Annie's family was certainly among them. At school she did not shine, though. Her spelling would always remain erratic, perhaps because she never concentrated, choosing instead to chatter to her best friend, Alice Hurst. She hated lessons and the only subject she enjoyed was poetry, though she said she could learn anything that really interested her. She had mixed feelings when her mother told her at the age of ten that she was old enough to go to work in the mill. She took part-time lessons till she was thirteen, but benefited little from the experience.

There was scant time for study, in any case. Once she was a full-time worker at the mill Annie had to get up at five in the morning to start at six, and finished work at 5.30 p.m. After that, unlike her brothers, she was expected to help with washing, cooking and scrubbing floors. She still retained many childlike qualities, though – something which would continue to be remarked on much later in her life. At fourteen, when she had any free time at all, she played with her dolls. When relating details of this phase of her life Annie glossed over certain aspects. Those who knew her related, for example, that she had lost a finger in an accident at the mill, but she left this out of her autobiography. She told Fred Pethick-Lawrence, husband of the suffragette treasurer, that when she was in her mid-teens the factory where she worked closed. For fifteen months she and her co-workers continued to rise at 5 a.m. as usual and tramped from mill to mill looking for work.

Annie's political education began in her late teens when she started paying regular visits to Oldham library to read the *Rational Review* or Robert Blatchford's newspaper, *The Clarion*. Thousands of men and women in the Lancashire factories owed their education to Blatchford, Annie said. Through him, she learned of Walt Whitman, William Morris, Edward Carpenter, Ruskin, Omar Khayyam and the early English poets. She and her siblings would invite their friends home to Sunday tea and the air would hum to the sound of arguments about Darwin or Spencer. One of Annie's brothers, Rowland, went on to edit the *Daily Herald* while three of her sisters joined the suffragettes and two became teachers.

At Christmas 1904, when Annie was twenty-five, her mother became ill and died. The cement that had kept Annie's home life together slipped away with her, she recalled. A few months after her mother's death Annie was invited by a friend from the Clarion Choir, which she had joined to meet other *Clarion* readers, to a meeting of the Oldham Trades Council at which Christabel Pankhurst was due to speak. The name 'Pankhurst' meant nothing to Annie, for in its first eighteen months the WSPU had

had little impact. She returned home so excited she could barely eat for a week. From that day on and for the next fifteen years, Christabel Pankhurst would be Annie Kenney's muse and her idol.

Annie quite simply adored Christabel. Wherever Christabel led, she would follow. Others might see themselves as great leaders; Annie saw herself as a great follower – of Christabel. She described herself as Christabel's 'first-born militant and mascot'.[2] As a fellow suffragette would write of her later, she became

> Christabel's devotee in a sense that was mystical ... she neither gave nor looked to receive any expression of personal tenderness: her devotion took the form of unquestioning faith and absolute obedience ... Just as no ordinary Christian can find that perfect freedom in complete surrender, so no ordinary individual could have given what Annie gave – the surrender of her whole personality to Christabel. That surrender endowed her with fearlessness and power that was not self limited and was therefore incalculable.[3]

The relationship would be mirrored, though never matched in its intensity, by a number of later relationships between Annie and other suffragettes. The extent of their physical nature has never been revealed, but it is certain that in some sense these were romantic attachments. One historian who argues that Annie must have had sexual feelings for other women adds that lesbianism was barely recognised at the time.[4] Such relationships, even when they involved sharing beds, excited little comment. Already, Christabel had formed a close friendship with Esther Roper and Eva Gore-Booth, suffrage campaigners who lived together in Manchester. Her relationship with Eva, in particular, had become intense enough to excite a great deal of comment from her family – according to Sylvia.[5]

Christabel was emphatically not a woman who let her emotions run away with her, and she did not do so in Annie's case. But their first meeting set a pattern that would govern every sphere of Annie's existence for the next fifteen years. In Annie's own account of her life, she explained the power of her emotions in the context of the WSPU, and the manner in which it was run by Christabel: 'For the first few years the militant movement was more like a religious revival than a political movement. It stirred the emotions, it aroused passions, it awakened the human chord which responds to the battle-call of freedom ... the one thing demanded was loyalty to policy and unselfish devotion to the cause.' Annie threw herself into that maelstrom with all the passion of which she was capable, and her deep involvement in it, as well as her relationships with some of its key figures, could only intensify as the suffragettes became increasingly isolated from the rest of society.

Walking to the station with Christabel after that first meeting, Annie impetuously offered to organise a meeting of factory women in Oldham. Christabel expected to hear little more of the enthusiastic young woman, and was impressed when a few days later she received a batch of handbills in the post. Soon Annie was treating the Pankhursts' Nelson Street house as a second home. Annie and Christabel began a tour of the Lancashire Wakes weeks, setting up their stall next to a medicine man or a preacher. Sometimes Sylvia would take the chair, always introducing Annie in the same way: 'I have a young woman here to speak to you who has worked as a half-time hand in the cotton mill.'[6] She described Annie at the time as 'eager and impulsive in manner, with a thin, haggard face, and restless knotted hands. The wild, distraught expression, apt to occasion solicitude, was found on better acquaintance to be less common than a bubbling merriment, in which the crow's feet wrinkled quaintly about a pair of twinkling, bright blue eyes.' Despite Annie's apparently robust attitude to life, those who met her often feared for her health. 'Upon those who saw her only on the platform or in the height of a propaganda discussion, she often made a distressful impression. She seemed to be burning herself up! We thought it impossible that she could live long,' another suffragette, Beatrice Harraden, once said of her. Actually Annie was much sturdier than a superficial observer might judge. Sylvia said she had a vigorous constitution 'and possessed also a substantial dose of what the Scotch call "canny"'. Annie was short and thin-faced, and her most youthful feature was her thick, luxuriant hair, which she piled on top of her head in a loose knot. In those photographs which show her in her own clothes, rather than in her mill girl's outfit, she is usually dressed more plainly than the fashion-conscious Christabel, often in a pinafore dress and blouse.

As a speaker Annie was ideally suited to the rowdy gatherings she would often be forced to confront in the Lancashire mill towns. Though not at all melodious, her voice was strong and she had a colourful turn of phrase. She was not burdened by shyness, and whether dealing with a boisterous factory worker or a prime minister, she was never afraid to speak her mind. Christabel was able to use this ebullient style to good effect, not least on the evening when she left her mother's home for the Free Trade Hall with the words, 'I shall sleep in prison tonight.' Annie, she had decided, would be the perfect companion for such an exercise; and she was right. After that first night in the cells Christabel was sentenced to seven days' imprisonment, Annie to three. The women's aim, of course, had been to get the WSPU noticed, and the stunt was spectacularly successful. Christabel and Annie were delighted to find themselves elevated to the status of social pariahs. As Annie put it: 'The night's catch was rich in the extreme. The very extremity of abuse, criticism, and condemnation hurled at us by the morning Press … was in itself a sign that astute parliamentarians realised we knew what we were about.'[7] On 16 October 1905 the *Daily Mail* commented: 'If any argument were required against giving to ladies political status and power, it has been furnished in Manchester.'

Annie was in prison for only a few days and in her mind the experience would be overlaid by much more vivid impressions of later spells in Holloway:

> Being my first visit to jail, the newness of the life numbed me. I do remember the plank bed, the skilly, the prison clothes. I also remember going to church and sitting next to Christabel, who looked very coy and pretty in her prison cap … I scarcely ate anything all the time I was in prison, and Christabel told me later that she was glad when she saw the back of me, it worried her to see me looking pale and vacant.[8]

Prison was to bring about a major change in Annie's life – one which had perhaps already become inevitable. Emmeline Pankhurst told her she need not go back to the mill. She could live in Nelson Street and become a full member of the Pankhurst household. Annie emerged from prison to a whole new world: 'Had I found on my return that I had taken on a new body, I should not have been in the least surprised. I felt absolutely changed. The past seemed blotted out.'[9]

Something else had changed, too. In the past the meetings Annie had organised with Christabel had attracted 'a dog, a man, a child and a few stragglers', but now all the world wanted to catch a glimpse of the jailbirds. Displaying an impudence which would set the scene for many future stunts, the women booked Manchester's Free Trade Hall to protest at their imprisonment – and were amazed when they had to turn away hundreds of people. Suddenly the suffragettes were big news, at least in the North of

England. But the North, as Annie put it, was the home of so many other revolutions, 'both bloodless and otherwise'. It was not difficult, at the time, to arouse passions in the political hotbed of the industrial North, where trade unionism and the growing labour movement had created a heightened atmosphere. London was a different story. And London, then as now, was where the nation's political heart was situated. The WSPU began to turn its face to the south.

Annie's first visit to London came a few weeks later, in December 1905. With a new Liberal Prime Minister, Henry Campbell-Bannerman, installed in Downing Street, the Liberal Party had decided to capitalise on its success by holding a rally at the Royal Albert Hall. With the help of political friends Annie obtained two tickets to the private box of John Burns, who had just been made a minister. Disguised in a fur coat and a veil, she managed to enter the hall undetected, and as soon as Campbell-Bannerman rose to his feet she got up and shouted her question: 'Will the Liberal government give votes to women?' The audience started to get up, angrily. Annie opened her coat to reveal a banner round her waist: 'Give Votes to Women'. Everyone laughed, because it was upside down. Soon she was thrown out on to the street, but her mission was accomplished. Annie and other suffragettes would repeat the performance so often that it became purely a ritual. Sylvia, accompanying Annie, sometimes feared the audience would simply think her a madwoman: 'She held the seat of her chair firmly in both hands and started off in a sort of wail which sounded more like a mechanical siren than the human voice, repeating over and over again without a pause the familiar words: "Will the Liberal government give women the vote?"'[10] It was the act of turning up, putting the question and being thrown out that mattered – it kept the women's cause in the public eye.

Annie told Christabel and Emmeline with characteristic impetuosity that if she had two pounds in her pocket she could 'rouse London'. They took her up on the offer. After paying her fare from Manchester she had just a pound and a few shillings left. She enjoyed the experience, and never seemed to entertain a moment of self-doubt. With the warm wind of Christabel's will in her sails, she could do anything. A city had no terrors for her, she claimed. She believed opposition in London meant no more than opposition in a little Lancashire town and she was full of hope and of unquestioning faith that success would be theirs. With the help of Sylvia and of another suffrage campaigner, Dora Montefiore, she began holding meetings in the East End on similar lines to those she had hosted in Lancashire.

If she had an hour or so to spare Annie liked to buy a bag of chestnuts, get on a bus and tour London from terminus to terminus. She also loved to take the bus to Uxbridge, where there was countryside in which she could walk for miles. But she could not always afford to go on pleasure trips such as these. Sometimes she would simply walk on the Embankment and 'make friends with some woman derelict' – Mrs Pankhurst had warned her not to speak to any man in the street except a policeman. Annie was desperately short of money and Sylvia, whose student scholarship had run out, was not much better off. At her rooms in Park Walk, Chelsea, almost every meal included Egyptian lentils, which were a staple of the urban poor at the time because they were one of the cheapest foods available, Annie recalled later.

> One day it would be lentils with an egg perched on top; the following day tomatoes with an egg perched on the top; the day after that, as a change, lentils and tomatoes with an egg perched on top; and the following day again, to make our meals varied, an egg with fried tomatoes perched upon it and cocoa or a glass of milk.[11]

For a treat she would go to a restaurant called Lockhart's in the Strand, but she never chose anything with lentils. 'I used to read the menu at Lockhart's as though it were a new novel,' she said. It was not long before she had told the waitress her life story and given her some suffragette literature.

People were Annie's great strength. A lesser woman would have been intimidated by the grand, highly educated types with whom the suffrage movement brought her into contact. Not Annie. Matters of etiquette never worried her, she said. 'Thoroughbred' people would not mind if she used the wrong knife or said the wrong thing. If people cared about social graces that was probably because they were trying to be something they were not. Emmeline Pankhurst arrived in London that year and sent Annie off to lobby the journalist W. T. Stead for his support. Perhaps Emmeline knew of Stead's fondness for young girls, which Sylvia experienced too. On one occasion Annie had to appeal to Emmeline to ask him not to kiss her when she went to his office. But Annie liked Stead, and he quickly became a father figure. Before their first meeting was over she was sitting on the arm of his chair, telling him all about her life. He responded by telling her she must come to him if she was ever lonely or in trouble. Later he even let her use a room in his house in Smith Square to rest during Westminster lobbies and demonstrations, and he lent her £25 to help her organise her first big London meeting. With Emmeline's permission he invited her to spend time at his house on Hayling Island in Hampshire. He signed his letters to her, 'your affectionate Granddad'. Stead was so bowled over by Annie that later that year he wrote a eulogy to her in his *Review of Reviews*. Annie Kenney was the new Josephine Butler, he gushed. He even compared her to Joan of Arc. Nor was Stead the only person of note to be taken with Annie. The elderly Lady Rosalind Carlisle, wife of a Liberal Unionist MP and a strong supporter of the suffrage, 'made quite a pet of her', according to Sylvia. Lady Carlisle's son Geoffrey, the heir to Castle Howard, would throw his glass eye across the room to amuse her. Presumably Annie's working-class image, though irksome to her later, did her no harm in this context. As she put it herself, she was a mascot for the cause.

But while the well-heeled Pankhursts and their friends empathised with the poor and wanted to help them, Annie saw her connection with them from quite a different angle. She wanted to be part of London society, and they were her route into it. Not least among these wealthy acquaintances was Emmeline Pethick-Lawrence, at whose door Annie arrived one day early in 1906. The wealthy Emmeline had been asked to become WSPU treasurer but had refused, saying she had too many other commitments. Mrs Pankhurst sent Annie. 'She burst in upon me one day in her rather breathless way and threw all my barriers down,' Emmeline recalled later. 'There was something about Annie that touched my heart. She was very simple and seemed to have a whole-hearted faith in the goodness of everybody that she met.'[12] It was the beginning of another intense relationship for Annie. While her devotion to Christabel never dimmed, her attachment to Emmeline Pethick-Lawrence was so strong as to alarm some of those around her. Teresa Billington-Greig wrote later to Annie's sister Jessie:

> It is true that there was an immediate and strong emotional attraction between Emmeline Pethick-Lawrence and Annie Kenney … indeed so emotional and so openly paraded that it frightened me. I saw it as something unbalanced and primitive and possibly dangerous to the movement … but the emotional obsession died out and the partnership … persisted for many years.[13]

Before that first meeting was over Emmeline Pethick-Lawrence had agreed to be WSPU treasurer, a post to which she would bring her flair for both finance and publicity. From then on the union would be put on a far more professional footing, and its annual income would rise from a few pounds to many thousands. She became one of the movement's four pillars, alongside Annie, Christabel and Emmeline Pankhurst. It was not long before Annie was adopted by Emmeline and her husband, Fred, like the Pankhursts before her, as a full family member. During the week she would stay with them at their London home in Clement's Inn; at weekends she would go with them to Holmwood, their country house in Surrey. Annie no longer had to worry about money: 'I was more like an adopted daughter than a friend, and many comforts and a few luxuries were very soon mine that had not been mine before.'[14] Christabel and Emmeline Pankhurst often spent weekends at Holmwood, too, and the group would sit up late in front of a log fire talking over ideas. 'If the beautiful woods there could have spoken, Scotland Yard would have forestalled many a militant attack,' Annie wrote later.[15]

Whatever its nature, the relationship followed a pattern that was to be repeated by Annie and by other suffrage agitators. The political atmosphere in which the suffragettes lived was an intense one, and was bound to lead to equally intense friendships. As time went on and the leaders of the WSPU became increasingly isolated from the rest of society so they became increasingly emotionally dependent on one another. As Annie herself said, they placed themselves outside the conventional mores of the day – there was no one to tell them what to do:

> The changed life into which most of us entered was a revolution in itself. No home life, no one to say what we should do or what we should not do, no family ties, we were free and alone in a great brilliant city, scores of young women scarcely out of their teens met together in a revolutionary movement, outlaws or breakers of laws, independent of everything and everybody, fearless and self-confident.[16]

Annie described the life of the WSPU as highly disciplined, almost monastic: 'It was an unwritten rule that there should be no concerts, no theatres, no smoking; work, and sleep to prepare us for more work, was the unwritten order of the day.'[17] This discipline included being available, at any time the union demanded it, to go to prison. In the popular conception the women went out to demonstrate or cause a disturbance and were arrested as a result. In reality, they usually made up their minds to get arrested – or rather were called to offer themselves for imprisonment by the union's leadership. Some suffragettes described the arrival of a letter from Clement's Inn, requesting that they present themselves on a certain day for arrest. Thus the judicial system became not the punisher of the suffragettes' unruly behaviour, but one of their best publicity tools. This was an idea planted by Annie and Christabel after their debut at the Free Trade Hall in Manchester. In the middle of 1906, eight months after her first imprisonment, Annie's turn came round again. During a deputation to the Prime Minister, Henry Campbell-Bannerman, at which Annie had presented herself in mill girl's attire, he had hinted that the biggest obstacle to giving women the vote was the opposition of the Chancellor of the Exchequer, Herbert Asquith. The WSPU requested a meeting with Asquith. He refused. Annie then turned up with a group of women at the Chancellor's house in Cavendish Square and rang the bell incessantly. She was arrested with two others and sentenced to two months.

Annie did not mind prison. She made friends with the wardresses and ended up feeling sorry for them. She would rather go back to working in a cotton mill than work in a prison, she reflected – the pay was better and you were on your feet less. She gleaned tips from other prisoners on how best to polish the floor of her cell. 'You had your pint of tea in your own tin mug   it was always a relief to hear that it was tea – I should never have guessed it by the taste,' she mused later.[18] Characteristically, she was sent to her cell for breaking the 'no speaking' rule during exercise. But by the end of her time in prison even she felt depressed. On the day of her release she was so excited she could not eat the celebratory breakfast that was waiting for her – the first decent meal she had seen in two months.

Over the following year Annie was usually to be found with the Pethick-Lawrences. In 1907 they took her on the first of a number of holidays, with Christabel and another suffragette, Mary Gawthorpe. The experience was topped by the appearance of Campbell-Bannerman in the restaurant car of the train that was taking them to the Riviera. The women convened a meeting and decided Annie should approach him. She spent a happy hour having a 'nice, homely chat' with him, during which she confided that she had never been abroad before. When he got off, a few stops before her, the Prime Minister stood on the platform waving his hat. Thereafter he always referred to her as 'my little friend Annie Kenney'.

Back in England Annie's life took a new turn. She was made organiser first for Bristol, then for the whole of the West of England. The work

consisted mainly of drumming up support, finding new members and trying to generate enthusiasm for the cause in the area. It was the kind of project Annie enjoyed most – she liked to sow seeds, she said, but once they
were growing strongly she preferred to move on and leave the day-to-day
running to others. Now she was able to leave her Lancashire image behind
and to win recognition for her skills. To the people she met in and around
Bristol she was a figure of authority within the union, trusted by the
Pankhursts and the Pethick-Lawrences. Instead of seeing her as a mascot,
her new acquaintances were more inclined to look up to her.

   None more so, it seems, than Mary Blathwayt, who became to Annie
what Annie had been to Christabel – a dogged, adoring admirer who
would follow her anywhere, do anything for her. Mary, in her late twenties
at the time, had a comfortable but probably rather dull life before Annie
arrived. Soon she was doing Annie's washing, driving her around, washing
her hair, even giving her French lessons. Soon – as she had been at Nelson
Street and at Holmwood – Annie was a member of the family, with her
own room at the Blathwayts' Batheaston home. In December 1908 she gave
Mary a brooch depicting Boudicca. On the back was a message to 'Bay' –
Mary's family pet name – 'From Annie with Love'. On another occasion
Annie gave Mary a rose. Mary recorded in her diary the dates on which she
shared a bed with Annie, and those on which Annie shared with someone
else. In July 1908 Mary wrote in her diary that she had been with Annie
while resting in the afternoon.[19] A month later she was concerned enough
by the arrival of another suffragette to note: 'Miss Browne is sleeping in
Annie's room now.' Adela Pankhurst, too, shared Annie's room when she
came to stay that summer. In September Clara Codd arrived: 'She is sleeping with Annie,' Mary recorded. Clara, a WSPU worker recruited by Annie,
stated in her memoirs that while working in Bristol she always shared a bed
with Annie.[20] Presumably such attachments were regarded as the sort of
romantic friendships often formed by young girls, but to suggest that they
never involved feelings that were more than simply platonic stretches
credulity too far. For Annie, this period was a liberating one, a metamor-
phosis from follower to leader, and she enjoyed both the personal and the
professional benefits immensely.

   Annie spent every weekend at Batheaston, but often she would arrive so
exhausted that she would simply take to her bed for a few days. As an organiser, even with Mary's willing help, she was always overworked. She had
to raise money, book halls, write and distribute handbills, make the tea for

'at homes' and pray that a few people would be sent to eat what she had bought. In the early days she was happy if she got a few shillings and two new members.

Nor was the experience of campaigning in the West of England always a genteel affair, as Emmeline Pankhurst found to her cost when she was attacked at the Mid-Devon by-election. At Poole in the summer of 1909, Mary Blathwayt's mother Emily recorded in her diary, Annie was surrounded by a mob who tore her cloak to pieces and threw a stone which hit her on the head. In Bristol a large crowd of children threw potatoes, stones, turf and dust. At a fête in Canford Park, Dorset, Annie's clothing was slit from neck to hem. But while some might have despaired, Annie entered into the spirit and thoroughly enjoyed herself. 'The election I enjoyed most, and had the greatest fun over, was at Bristol. In one of the centres there was a splendid place for open air meetings. We went there night after night, only to be shouted down by the irate party men and a group of boys. I never got a word in edgeways,' she wrote in her autobiography.[21] One night she and a companion, speaking on a trolley, were hauled by the crowd and left at the gates of the local lunatic asylum. In Somerset she was pelted with rotten eggs, the smell of which lingered for weeks, and in Wales, with fish. 'We took it all in good part. Fish, flesh, fowl or eggs, it made no difference,' she wrote.[22]

Annie was happiest when she was busy, and she frankly admitted that life became a little dull during 1910 when the suffragettes called a truce because it seemed the government was going to allow a suffrage bill to pass through Parliament. There would be no opportunities for boredom in the coming years, though. Annie, recalled to London in the autumn of 1911 as the union teetered on the verge of a fresh outbreak of militancy, was about to find herself with more to do than she could possibly have wished for. In March 1912, in Manchester on a quest to buy the union a printing press for use in the event that its *Votes for Women* were closed down, Annie saw a newspaper placard: 'All Suffragette Leaders Arrested!' She rushed back to London to find a note in her flat: 'All leaders in prison, except Christabel who has escaped, no one knows how, where or why. Do not come to the office until dark. Detectives everywhere.' Annie's main concern was for Christabel. It was three days before an intermediary brought a letter from her and revealed she was in Paris: 'Your keen intuition has always appealed to me ... I trust you implicitly and I give you complete control over the whole movement ... come to me at the first possible moment.' Annie set off immediately. She arrived in Paris to find Christabel had gone out to visit the Princesse de Polignac, having wasted no time in connecting herself with Parisian high society. Waiting for Christabel at the princess's residence, where it transpired she had gone out for a walk, Annie picked up a volume of Sappho's poetry, bound in cherry leather, and began reading it before falling fast asleep.

It was the start of a cloak-and-dagger existence that lasted for more than two years. Each Friday, heavily disguised, Annie would take the boat-train via Le Havre. Sundays were devoted to work but on Saturdays the two would walk along the Seine or visit the Bois de Boulogne. Annie took instructions from Christabel on every little point – which organiser should be placed where, circular letters, fund-raising, lobbying MPs. When she arrived back in London a bulky letter would already be on its way to her with yet more instructions. There was such resentment within the union about Annie's new position that she earned herself the nickname 'Christabel's Blotting Paper'. Annie found this amusing, and took to signing her letters to Christabel, 'The Blotter'.

During the week Annie worked all day at the union's Clement's Inn headquarters, then met militants at her flat at midnight to discuss illegal actions. Christabel had ordered an escalation of militancy, including the burning of empty houses, and it fell to Annie to organise these raids. She did not enjoy this work, nor did she agree with it. She did it because Christabel asked her to, she said later. None the less, it fell to her to ensure that each arsonist left home with the proper equipment – cotton wool, a small bottle of paraffin, wood shavings and matches. 'Combustibles' were stored by Annie in hiding places from where they could be retrieved when needed, and a sympathetic analytical chemist, Edwy Clayton, was engaged to advise on suitable places for attack. In addition to supplying a list of government offices, cotton mills and other buildings, he carried out experiments for the women on chemicals suitable for making explosives. Annie was very upset when he was later arrested and convicted of conspiracy on the basis of papers he had sent to her sister Jessie.

The fun was going out of the movement for Annie. Christabel had left a gap in her life, and the departure of the Pethick-Lawrences soon afterwards in a dispute over the direction of the union was a further blow. Annie was forced to choose between two people she loved more than any others – Christabel and Emmeline Pethick-Lawrence. She followed Christabel, as she always had. 'If all the world were on one side, and Christabel Pankhurst on the other, I would walk straight over to Christabel Pankhurst!' she declared.[23] Emmeline Pethick-Lawrence noted down later that at the final meeting with the Pankhursts, Annie had refused to speak to her. The friendship did not survive. The Pethick-Lawrences' financial acumen was sorely missed, and though there was still £15,000 in the bank in the spring of 1913 it became increasingly hard to raise funds.

It was inevitable that Annie would be arrested at some point, and in April 1913 it happened. She was charged with incitement to riot in connection with a series of speeches she had made. Ironically these speeches were actually copies of orations by the Ulster Unionist leader, Sir Edward Carson. Pressed for time and no great speechwriter, Annie had simply adapted Carson's words to suit her purposes. They had caused such disquiet among the authorities that a detective had even been sent to the Pennine village where Annie had grown up to try to dig up dirt about her private life and her family. The material that was gathered had little effect, for the result was inevitable – a lengthy prison sentence. Annie conducted her own defence. The object was not to keep the sentence down but merely to ensure that long articles and speeches were read out, mainly to annoy the prosecution and gain publicity. Annie's closing speech had to last for hours. 'We never, never took these trials seriously. They were just part of our propaganda,' she wrote.[24]

Annie was in good spirits when she left the Old Bailey in a prison van. In fact, she was looking forward to the rest. She expected to be taken to Holloway, but instead found herself on the way to Maidstone. However, she enjoyed the journey and when the prison van broke down she insisted on buying her wardresses a meal, telling them they should humour her as she would soon be on hunger strike. They should imagine she was a great lady escaping some castle, and that they were her companions, she told them. Annie soon became good friends with the matron and the doctor who were charged with caring for her while she was on hunger strike: 'The doctor was ever so kind and did his best to persuade me to have fruit.'[25] She was released after three days, the first prisoner to be officially released under the Cat and Mouse Act – the government measure allowing for the release of hunger-striking prisoners on licence and their subsequent rearrest when they were fit again.

The cycle of imprisonment, hunger strike, release, recovery and rearrest continued for more than a year. Once out, the 'mouse' had just a few days before her licence expired, when an elaborate game would ensue, with the police in pursuit. There were various safe houses, notably the home of the Brackenbury family at 2 Campden Hill Square, Notting Hill, which was renamed 'Mouse Castle'. With detectives watching the doors, on one occasion Annie escaped in disguise over a side wall into a neighbouring garden and then swapped clothes with a fake 'delivery man' to get away. Once she arrived safely to give a speech by having herself delivered to the London Pavilion in a laundry hamper labelled: 'Marie Lloyd, luggage in advance'.

In the summer of 1913 Annie escaped for a respite to France, where she met up with Christabel in Deauville. Uncharacteristically, though, she became bored with her mentor's company. She found Deauville pretentious and restricting – she could never see the need for white gloves – and moved on to Brittany with her sister Jessie and three other women. 'We laughed all day and all night. The people at the hotel called me "the laughing one" … There is nothing like hard conscientious work to make one enjoy a real holiday – I mean a holiday where you can run wild, not a parade holiday,' Annie wrote in her autobiography.[26]

Back in England she was soon rearrested after trying the actress's baggage trick again, and this time went on thirst as well as hunger strike. This was far worse, she found. When she was released she had to be carried out of the prison. She could not speak, and even though she had herself taken to a meeting in Knightsbridge by ambulance, she was too weak to make a speech. And so it went on. At around this time, Christabel ordered Annie to seek refuge with the Archbishop of Canterbury. To her amazement she gained entry to Lambeth Palace, where she demanded sanctuary as an outlaw under an ancient statute that had never been repealed – it seems that Christabel had been putting her legal training to some use. Annie was soon telling the archbishop about her old vicar, Mr Grundy, and about her confirmation. But when she asked if she could stay he became 'hot and irritated'. Eventually detectives arrived to take her back to Holloway.

Annie was in Scotland when she read of the outbreak of war. There was nothing to do but await orders from Paris. They stated simply that all militants must 'fight for their country as they have fought for the vote'. Annie, now becoming increasingly uncomfortable with Christabel's autocratic style, must have shown some hint of her true feelings because she was soon asked to leave the country. One of the leaders of the movement should be safe in case of invasion, Christabel said. Annie was to board a boat for America. She did not enjoy the experience. Although her fare had been paid, she had little money and few contacts. Determined to make the best of things she got in touch with a suffragette sympathiser who sent her to Alice Paul, an American suffragist who had been with the militants in Britain. Annie did not take to her, and decided to set off on a little tour of her own, visiting states where referenda were due to be held on women's suffrage. She was in California when she heard that Christabel was in America: 'Christabel in America? What was wrong at home? I must go to New York to see if I was needed.'[27] But the train journey was long and by the time Annie arrived in New York, tired and homesick, she had developed tonsillitis. She must have cut a pathetic figure when she presented herself to Christabel, who was preparing to make a speech at the Carnegie Hall urging Americans to enter the war on the side of the Allies. 'Christabel, I feel lonely. I want to go home,' Annie said. She sailed back to England soon afterwards.

Annie was not allowed to remain idle, nor would it have been in her nature to do so. Christabel charged her with organising a campaign to explain the situation in the Balkans to people in England. With her self-confessed loathing for learning, and the near-impossibility of the subject, it was an ambitious task. She enjoyed it, though, and after just a couple of weeks' study she made her first wartime speech in Huddersfield. Annie tended often to play on her own lack of ability – 'I, who could not have reasoned the point of why a cat drank milk!' she remarked, wide-eyed, of her appointment as head of the WSPU – but when she put her mind to learning something, she did not usually have much trouble. Often, she had the force of Christabel's convictions to drive her on.

To be suddenly on the side of the establishment after years of political pariahdom was a strange experience. Emmeline Pankhurst received an invitation to meet Lloyd George, now Minister for Munitions, and she asked Annie to go with her. Lloyd George asked them to help find female recruits for the munitions factories, and Emmeline agreed to organise a procession. At around the same time Annie was even invited to meet Lord Northcliffe, whose newspapers – which included the *Daily Mail* – had been unswervingly hostile to the suffragettes. 'We seemed to be friendly with every one, and every one was friendly with us,' Annie wrote in her autobiography. She immediately struck up a friendship with Lord Northcliffe, who was even prepared to see her when he had given strict orders that he was 'not at home'.

In 1915 Christabel sent Annie abroad again, this time to help Australia's Prime Minister, Billy Hughes, in a referendum campaign on conscription. Hughes had visited London earlier that year and had more than once taken Annie out on long motor drives during which they had talked about Labour politics. Christabel also hoped, it seems, that Annie would be able to persuade Hughes to return to Britain to help the war effort.[28] On her arrival in Sydney Annie sought out Hughes. 'We want you back,' she told him.

'We?' he responded. 'Who are *we*?' Annie thought for a moment before re-plying: '*We* is Christabel. And I feel sure the country would rejoice at news of your return.' Although Hughes was clearly much amused, even Annie's charm could not persuade him to set off for Europe once more. By the time Annie returned, several weeks later, Christabel had again retreated to Paris.

Even the end of the war did not bring the termination of Annie's servi-tude to Christabel. Having returned to England once more Christabel had decided to stand for election in Smethwick, and she kept Annie busy dur-ing her campaign.

> Poor Mr Lloyd George, poor Lord Northcliffe! I was never off their doorsteps. By the time they had answered one question, Christabel thought of another … Strange to say I was never turned away once. Christabel said that was the reason why she sent me! Mr Lloyd George used to be very cross, then he would relax when he saw that I was really sorry to have disturbed him.[29]

Christabel stood as an independent, and her friends persuaded the Conser-vative candidate to withdraw so she could have a straight fight with Labour. Annie's main task, apart from cajoling politicians and newspaper propri-etors, was to raise funds. But she was tired, and she decided this was to be her last job for Christabel. Once the election was over Annie told Christa-bel – who had not been successful – of her decision. At last, she was released from the bond which had held her for so long. 'We had a long talk, and I was free … and so my Suffragette pilgrimage was ended,' Annie wrote.

Annie's involvement in politics ended there. After the war she went to live in St Leonard's with Grace Roe, who had acted as her WSPU understudy while Christabel was in Paris. There the two women devoted themselves to a shared interest in Theosophy, a quasi-religious movement founded by Madame Blavatsky in 1875, and based on Hindu ideas of karma and rein-carnation with nirvana as the eventual aim. Annie had become involved briefly with it in 1912, but had dropped it at the time because Christabel dis-approved. Among several other suffrage campaigners attracted to Theoso-phy was Annie Besant, who had led the Bryant and May match workers in their famous strike of 1888, and who eventually went to live in India.

Annie did not remain in St Leonard's for long. In 1918, while staying on the Isle of Arran with her sister Jessie, she had met James Taylor, and in April 1920 at Lytham parish church she married him. The wedding was noted by Mary Blathwayt, who slipped a copy of the wedding photograph between the pages of her diary, and was attended by Jessie, Grace Roe and another former suffragette, Frances Bartlett. Annie was given away by her brother Rowland. Soon afterwards Emily Blathwayt recorded in her diary: 'Answered Miss Grace Roe's letter. She likes Annie's husband very much and hears they are very happy together.' Annie and James had a honeymoon on the Isle of Arran, and in the following February Annie gave birth to a son, Warwick Kenney Taylor. The family, with whom Grace Roe lived until Warwick's birth, settled in Letchworth in Hertfordshire.

Annie attended Mrs Pankhurst's funeral in 1928, but subsequently slipped from public view, though she continued to write to Christabel, who settled in America. Annie died in the Lister Hospital in Hitchen, Hertfordshire, in 1953, and her ashes were scattered near her birthplace in Lancashire. Unlike some other former militants, Annie had been able to move on and to start another life. She never became simply a well-known ex- suffragette, as Christabel did, or even a rather lost, sad figure, as Emmeline did.

Even if she had never set eyes on Christabel Pankhurst, Annie Kenney would have found a route out of her Lancashire mill town. Before she became a suffragette she was already well on the way to doing so through education and through the trade union or labour movement. Despite that, she had much to thank the WSPU for. It offered her opportunities she could barely have dreamed of as a ten-year-old part-timer in the mill. In return, she gave what Christabel demanded of all those around her – total, unquestioning loyalty. While others parted company with the union in bitterness and disillusion, Annie stayed faithful. Even when her instinct was to question its rigid discipline and its demand for total focus on the one cause, she bit her lip. In this, Annie was the archetypal suffragette, if such a thing existed. But she brought more to the militant movement than that. As one of its earliest members and a leading figure throughout, she was also able to imprint some of her remarkable personality on its soul. She gave it a sense of humour, imbued it with a close comradeship that drew many to the cause and used her winsome, disarming manner to floor even some of its most fervent political enemies. The strength of Annie's devotion to Christabel irked some of their comrades, but it also helped to set the tone for the whole militant movement. Annie herself said, several years after the end of the struggle and after her marriage, that this bond would always persist: 'There is a cord between Christabel and me that nothing can break – the cord of love … We started militancy side by side and we stood together until victory was won.'[30]

Fred and Emmeline Pethick-Lawrence

IV

Fred Pethick-Lawrence – Godfather

Dear Sir,

May I respectfully ask if it is not possible to break up the Suffragette movement by taking action against Mr and Mrs Pethick Lawrence for conspiring
and inciting to serious breaches of the peace. It can very easily be proved
that Mr Pethick Lawrence went to East Ham on one occasion and hired a
number of women at two shillings per day plus their expenses. These
women were drilled into their work by Mr Lawrence and his assistants and
took part in very disorderly scenes ... These women (and many of the
women agitators who are paid £2–£5 per week) know nothing of politics or
Votes for Women questions and are paid for creating disturbance at command of the leaders.

Letter from Miss A. Meechan to the Public Prosecutor, March 1907.
The police found no truth in her allegations.[1]

Fred Pethick-Lawrence did few of the things that nowadays seem to
define in the public mind the activities of a suffragette. Unlike others
among the militants' small but ardent group of male supporters he never
threw a stone, rarely spoke at a demonstration and never disrupted a government minister's meeting. Yet one of the proudest moments in the long
and full life of this unobtrusive man came when he went to prison for the
cause to which he had devoted himself. This imprisonment was perhaps
the most public, the most celebrated episode during the six-year association of Fred and his wife Emmeline with the Women's Social and Political
Union. But it was not their greatest contribution to the fight for women's
enfranchisement. Without them, it is hard to see where the movement
would have gone after the initial excitement of its first acts of militancy,
after the furore surrounding the imprisonment of Christabel and Annie
Kenney. Fred and Emmeline Pethick-Lawrence gave the suffragettes a

backbone. The combination of Emmeline's fund-raising skills and Fred's financial and organisational ability – and his wealth – turned a small band of fiery but disorganised revolutionaries into a national movement with a headquarters, staff and infrastructure that would have been the envy of any mainstream political party.

Fred Lawrence, as he was until his marriage, was born to a life of privilege. The fifth child of wealthy Unitarians, his first home was a comfortable house in Gloucester Gardens, West London. His grandfather was a sheriff of the City of London and had he lived for two more years would have become Lord Mayor. There was, though, a strong reforming streak in the Lawrence family, and Fred was never destined for a life of leisure or a place among the landed classes. His family were 'new money', borne to affluence on the great tide of trade and technological advance which characterised the early years of the nineteenth century. William Lawrence, Fred's grandfather, was a carpenter from Cornwall who travelled to London and set up shop in Hoxton Square on the fringes of the city. As new residential districts sprang up around the centre of trade, Lawrence & Co. mined a rich seam of business. Although the City was then, as now, a Tory bastion, the Lawrences were reformers. William had been involved in the franchise agitation which preceded the Great Reform Act of 1832, and two of Fred's uncles were Liberal MPs.

One of these, Edwin Lawrence, was to be the major influence in Fred's childhood after the death of his father in 1875 when Fred was just three. 'Uncle Edwin' took over the task of educating 'little Freddy', the youngest of five children. Still young himself and full of energy, Edwin played boisterous games with the boy and devised complex betting games in which Fred had to predict the results of his school tests correctly in order to win. He was, Fred said later, a man of almost encyclopaedic knowledge who loved to pass this on to his nephew.[2] By all accounts Fred, who was also doted on by his mother and three elder sisters, was not a child who wanted for attention.

Throughout his life Fred would be a polymath. He loved outdoor games yet as a boy amused himself after 'lights out' by working out the nineteen times table in his head. At school he managed to be both studious and popular. One of his teachers wrote of him: 'He is certainly a real good sterling lad full of every manly quality. Wherever he goes he will do honour to himself and to all who are for him among whom I reckon myself one of the first. I am very glad he came to me and I don't mean to lose sight of him.'[3] There was never any question of Fred following his father and grandfather into a trade apprenticeship. After prep school he was sent to Eton, where he would become captain of the Oppidians – head of the boys who boarded in town rather than in the college. He recorded later that he enjoyed his time there, and would go again if he had the choice, but said he always felt like an outsider: 'I was sometimes told that I was "pi" (short for pious) but I was never a "scug" – the most opprobrious of Eton epithets. Rather they regarded me as an oddity and called me a "sap" (short for sapiens) because I worked hard; and my principal nickname was "The Comet" given me, so they said, because I was a "guiding and a shining light".'[4] Fred's overriding impression of Eton was of its pupils' firm conviction that they were in a class apart, that they had 'a destiny different in kind from that awaiting those of more ordinary clay'.

Fred's career of understated brilliance continued unabated during six years at Trinity College, Cambridge: after three years studying maths, he stayed on for a further three to read natural sciences. As president of the Union Debating Society he once promoted the idea that women should be able to take degrees – with Hillaire Belloc speaking against him. He played billiards for the university as well as excelling at football, tennis and racquets. In 1897 he was made a fellow of his college and seemed set for an academic career. But other influences were already at work. Fred's political consciousness was being honed through the contacts he was making at Cambridge. In his fifth year there he had begun attending lectures by Alfred Marshall, an economist who encouraged Fred to write a prize-winning essay on wage differentials across England.[5] Having thus travelled the country and begun to discover the appalling conditions in which some of his fellow citizens were living, he then accepted an invitation to visit a 'university settlement' in Canning Town, East London, run by a man called Percy Alden. He was deeply impressed. Alden asked him to come to Canning Town and to write a book about conditions there, but there was something else Fred wanted to do first: travel. Throughout his life he would be an inveterate traveller – he had already contemplated visiting Russia but in the event the trip had not materialised. Now he took himself off on a 'grand tour', through India, Ceylon, Australia, New Zealand, China, Japan and the United States.

Fred was not the most effusive of young men. During one of his long sea journeys his companions, seized by the spirit of irony, wrote the following limerick about him:

There was a young fellow called Lawrence,
Whose spirits ran over in torrents.
When they said,
'Pray don't shout,'
He would only yell out,
'All restraints I hold in abhorrence.'

Later in life he would put his reticence down to shyness, to the fear of indifference or ridicule – but he would also admit that as a rather clinical, mathematically minded young man he experienced a 'sheer lack of interest' in those around him: 'Much of what they said or did left me cold or critical, while many things which moved me greatly drew from them no response.'[6] He would always fight shy of talking or writing about his emotional life except to those closest to him. His secretary told an interviewer after his death: 'I just felt he was always afraid of revealing *himself*.'[7]

On his return to England Fred flung himself into a maelstrom of work. Settling in rooms in the Barking Road in London's East End he began researching the book Percy Alden had asked him to write. But he was drawn increasingly into the day-to-day running of the Canning Town settlement, and soon became its treasurer. At the same time he was studying for his bar exams, which he passed in 1899. Although he never practised full time as a barrister he put his legal skills to good use as a 'poor man's lawyer', giving legal advice and support to anyone who needed it.

Although he was becoming increasingly sensitive to the injustice dealt to London's poor – it was in Canning Town that he first met Keir Hardie – Fred was still a long way from being a socialist. His uncles, who were right-wing Liberal Unionist MPs, made an introduction for him to the selection committee at Lambeth North, which adopted him as its prospective candidate. Then, quite suddenly, his life and everything in it changed when he met the woman who would become his wife – Emmeline Pethick.

Fred was smitten. He had never come across a woman like Emmeline. She smoked cigarettes, jumped off London buses while they were moving and went out walking without gloves. Her family background was strikingly similar to his own. Her grandfather, like his, was Cornish and like his had moved east – to Bristol – to go into business. Emmeline grew up among numerous brothers and sisters in a comfortable home

in Weston-Super-Mare and was taken to a range of different nonconformist churches. As a young woman, tired of the strictures of small-
town, middle-class life and dreading the prospect of waiting for a
suitable husband to appear, she took herself off to London and became
a 'sister' to the poor in the West London Mission. She had now left the
mission with her friend Mary Neal to run Maison Esperance, a co-
operative dressmaking business in the Euston Road and a seaside hostel
at Littlehampton for the children of the London poor. When Emmeline
and Mary brought a group of girls for an evening's entertainment at the
Canning Town settlement in 1899, both Emmeline's fate and Fred's were
sealed.

Fred, determined to engineer a means of seeing Emmeline again, offered to buy shares in her business – having reached the age of majority, he had inherited the family fortune. That gave him the excuse to
appear at shareholders' meetings. The pair had met only two or three
times when he proposed. But Emmeline did not at this stage return
Fred's ardent feelings – or if she did, his method of expressing them was
so stilted that she was unsure of their sincerity. She wrote a long, earnest
letter explaining that she could not marry him because he did not share
her socialist beliefs. What about the Boer War? She was against it; he
had barely considered it. And how could she become the wife of a
prospective Liberal Unionist MP?[8] Fred made a decision: if the Boer
War stood between him and marriage to the woman of his dreams, he
must investigate it. He booked a passage to South Africa. Emmeline was
impressed, if still unsure.

Fred returned from South Africa convinced that Emmeline was right.
He told the selection committee at Lambeth North that he no longer
wished to stand for election as their candidate. But another long, agonising
year would pass before Emmeline would agree to marry him. It seems that
at last she managed to break down his emotional reserve: 'My dear Frederick, I am very pleased with you,' she wrote to him the day after their engagement. 'For the first time since I have known you, you have done
something adequate ... As a wooer you have been an utter failure.'[9]
Emmeline had correctly diagnosed one of Fred's key qualities – a tendency
to over-analyse. She, on the other hand, was always in touch with her emotions – as a suffragette her speeches were full of fire and romance; in later
life she would sometimes give herself over to mysticism.

The wedding was not the grand affair that two more ordinary people with their backgrounds might have had. It was held in Canning Town, and the guests included fifty inmates of the St Marylebone workhouse – friends of Emmeline's – and Lloyd George, who was at the time known as a notorious pro-Boer firebrand. Indeed, some of Emmeline's relatives declined to travel with him in the special coach hired to bring guests to the ceremony, and Fred's beloved uncle Edwin stayed away altogether in protest at his nephew's stance on the war. The marriage continued on similarly unconventional lines. One of the newlyweds' first decisions was to take on a double-barrelled surname – partly as a symbol of Fred's desire for Emmeline to keep her own identity but also, as he told her family, so that he might become part of her 'clan' as she had of his. The couple decided to live during the week in a flat in Clement's Inn, in central London, and at the weekends in a large cottage at Holmwood in Surrey. The Mascot had been built by Sir Edwin Lutyens for a family who then found it did not suit them. It suited the Pethick-Lawrences perfectly, and Emmeline set about decorating it in a suitably austere, simple style. In the weeks before their marriage she sent Fred a diagram of the dining room: 'White enamel dresser. Deal table – white enamel legs, covered with green linen tablecloth. Chairs – white enamel with material colour (green) rush. My instincts are all this way as I know yours are – we love simplicity … Only we don't want to do anything feeble, lieber … I know I can talk to Liberty's man and explain our socialism and love of simplicity and we will make him help us.'[10]

And thus began one of the happiest marriages of the twentieth century, as the *Daily Herald* would describe it later. Emmeline drew Fred out and he, for his part, was often happy to organise quietly in the background while she fought battles and won hearts. Fred and Emmeline Pethick-Lawrence were astonishingly ardent and enduring lovers. After more than fifty years of marriage Fred would sometimes pen a note to Emmeline while in the train from their Surrey house to their London flat to tell her how much he loved and missed her. In Clement's Inn, the suffragette headquarters, their third-floor flat was next to the office – but there was no connecting door. Throughout the day their secretaries would clamber down one flight of stairs and up the other, bringing notes from one to the other. Emmeline said of Fred that 'his outstanding qualities of intellect, balanced judgment and practical administration in business and finance became the rock upon which I have built, since then, the structure of my life'.[11]

On their first anniversary Fred gave Emmeline a present which expanded their property portfolio still further – her own flat. She explained later that the rooms in their shared home faced east and she missed the sun. The garden flat at the top of the same building was flooded with light, and Fred had it furnished in oriental fashion with deep couches and a moss-green carpet. It gave her a refuge, particularly later when the WSPU headquarters took over much of the building.

Both Fred and Emmeline loved children. She continued after her marriage to spend an annual holiday with her former charges at the Green Lady Hostel in Littlehampton, and also converted a pair of cottages near their Surrey home into holiday accommodation for city children. Acquaintances talked of how Fred always enjoyed the company of children too – his niece later remembered how he spent a day on the beach building a huge sand maze with walls so high they seemed 'like Hampton Court'.[12] But they never had any children of their own. One letter from Fred to Emmeline, written in the spring of 1903, suggests they may have hoped she was pregnant. He writes that he had been worried because he did not know what was wrong, but now he knows something is 'on the way and will make us both extra happy'. He adds: 'Isn't it splendid dear. My heart is just singing and singing and won't keep quiet.' But in December that year another letter adds: 'I am to you a splendid husband and you to me a splendid wife and it is enough! Du und ich.'

The differences between them must have sometimes created tension – Emmeline untidy, sometimes moody, sometimes inclined to take to her bed when confronted with an unwelcome task; Fred organised to the point of being pernickety. But their home was certainly a harmonious one and they were easy people to be around – their two secretaries, Gladys Groom-Smith and Esther Knowles, both worked for them throughout their adult lives and became part of their family, and even the gardener at Holmwood, Rapley, passed the job to his son after he retired. Fred's compulsive desire for order was mitigated by Emmeline's more emotional approach to life, but his mathematical, clinical mind remained a driving force. His filing system was formidable. Everyone with whom he ever corresponded had their own code number. Letters were cross-referenced and copied into other files where they might later become relevant. Each file contained a card with personal details, and a copy of every reply was placed on the file. Decades after the suffrage struggle, participants would approach Fred to check historical details, knowing he could call them to hand within minutes. He was a man of habit. He never drank tea or coffee and though not teetotal he rarely took alcohol. His breakfast was always one and a half pints of sweetened barley water, half a pint of milk, three pieces of toast and half a pound of jam. Each year he enjoyed counting how many Christmas cards he received, and updating his numerous different card lists so that everyone would receive an appropriate greeting the following year.

Not long before his marriage Fred had inherited a substantial sum of money on the death of his brother and had decided to invest it in a radical newspaper, *The Echo*. During the early years of his marriage he ran the paper while Emmeline continued her work with the Maison Esperance. Its editor was his old friend Percy Alden, who ran the Canning Town settlement. Ramsay MacDonald wrote the 'Labour Notes' and another well-known Labour figure, Henry Brailsford, wrote the leaders. But although the circulation was considered healthy the paper was not a financial success. Reluctantly, he decided to close it. Freed from the daily workload involved in bringing out a newspaper, he and Emmeline decided to take their first foreign trip. Naturally, it had to be to South Africa.

While they were there two news items from England caught their attention. The first was the confirmation that there was going to be a general election in January 1906 – an event that made them decide to hurry home. The second was the imprisonment of Christabel and Annie Kenney for protesting at a Liberal meeting in Manchester. Some of the women the Pethick-Lawrences had met in South Africa had been campaigning for the vote and were disturbed by the news. Surely such bad behaviour would set the cause back years, the women argued?[13] Emmeline thought not. She decided she would like to meet these suffragettes and discover more about them. It would not be long before she would have her chance. Keir Hardie, who had become a good friend after his first meeting with Fred in Canning Town and who had spent weekends with the couple in Surrey, had spotted an opportunity to help the nascent suffragette movement. Soon afterwards Annie Kenney arrived at Emmeline's door, ardent and breathless.

While Emmeline was forming new attachments, both political and personal, in the early months of 1906, Fred stayed in the background. However close his wife's relationship with Annie might have been, he must have known it could never threaten their marriage. If he felt any resentment of these all-consuming activities, he never showed it. Six months later he followed Emmeline's lead and devoted his own life to the women's cause. Up until that point socialism had come first for both of them. 'I failed to see what the average "sheltered" woman of the middle classes had to complain about,' he explained later. ' I do not suppose I should ever have become entangled with the suffragettes if it had not been for my wife.'[14] Fred's call to arms came in the form of a telegram from Emmeline: could he come to London to defend Annie Kenney and two other women who had been arrested for ringing Herbert Asquith's doorbell? He was happy to oblige. But at that stage he still did not see himself becoming as deeply involved as his wife, not least because membership of the union was barred to men (male supporters later set up their own Men's Political Union).

In the autumn of 1906 Emmeline was arrested at the opening of Parliament. Although this was prearranged – each woman taking part was allotted a place to attempt to make a speech in the lobby of the House of Commons – she had not warned Fred of what she planned to do. Fred immediately set to work to capitalise on the incident. A protest meeting was hastily arranged, and an appeal made for funds. 'It is not a question of how much do you feel, but how much are you going to *do*? I am going to give £10 to the WSPU for every day of my wife's sentence, and I should like to know who will follow my example,' Fred demanded.[15] The press had a field day – this poor chap was so henpecked by his harridan of a suffragette wife that he would pay to keep her in prison! The story went around the world. A woman dressed as Emmeline won a prize at a fancy dress ball in Covent Garden, with a placard reading:

Ten pounds a day
He said he'd pay
To keep this face
In Holloway.

Emmeline was delighted – she described it later as 'an inspiration', for any publicity was good publicity. Unfortunately there were no such high jinks in Holloway. She suffered from claustrophobia and the experience of being taken to prison in a Black Maria, with its cramped individual compartments for each prisoner, drove her to the verge of a breakdown. In prison she lay on her plank bed in a sleepless state of nervous exhaustion, and after a few days Fred secured her release and took her to Italy to stay with friends. On his return, he took over her role at the WSPU headquarters. Emmeline, who might have been forgiven for being annoyed at her husband's interference, was pleased and grateful.

Fred turned his analytical brain to the situation. He felt that, while the public were beginning to be aware of the union, there was a danger that it would grow too fast and become a shambles. The union's organisation could be divided into three, he decided. First, there was the headquarters – Fred and Emmeline's flat – which was desperately overstretched and short staffed. He took on more paid workers and rented dedicated office space in another part of the Clement's Inn building. There was a network of fifty or so regional branches, whose relations with headquarters needed to be put on a tighter and more professional footing. Lastly there was the literature published by the union in support of its cause, which was now hived off into a separate company, The Woman's Press. A financial secretary was engaged to do the books. In the following four years the staff of the union continued to increase until eventually it had sixty paid clerical workers and more than twenty rooms in Clement's Inn. By 1910–11 it had an income of £29,000 and a network of fifty paid organisers across the country. By contrast the older, non-militant National Union of Women's Suffrage did not have a dedicated national headquarters until 1911.

Fred also suggested more professional stewarding arrangements for meetings, dividing up helpers according to their functions and to parts of the hall – with Flora Drummond, a leading WSPU figure, in charge of keeping order. What Fred had done was to harness the enthusiasm, the drive and the *joie de vivre* of the early movement. But although he devoted himself full time to the union from 1906, it was not until 1909 that he took on an official position as joint treasurer with Emmeline.

The role Fred took was an unobtrusive one, for he was self-assured enough not to feel the need to ride in at a gallop and take over. Most casual supporters of the movement knew him as a quiet figure who ran the literature stall at the weekly 'at home', which quickly outgrew the union's headquarters and later took over the Queen's Hall or the Portman Rooms. He and Emmeline made a good administrative team: she charismatic, inspiring, driving and cajoling wealthy supporters to make ever larger donations; he careful, organised, with an eye to detail. Emmeline was the public figure, Fred the support system both for her and for the union. At one major fund-raising meeting Emmeline worked the crowd like an evangelical preacher, drawing in thousands of pounds in donations and pledges, while Fred stood at the side of the stage turning the cogs of a machine which recorded the total raised. The Pethick-Lawrences had pledged £1,000 a year of their considerable fortune to the WSPU; others made even bigger donations. The union was able to stage ever larger events, the organising of which fell largely to Fred.[16] Its Hyde Park rally in 1908 was attended by 250,000 people and cost £4,813, including the rent of an extra suite of offices and dedicated staff. A quarter of a mile of park railings were dug up to create more space for the speakers, and thirty special trains ran from around the country.

Fred took on the day-to-day work of ensuring that the *Votes for Women* newspaper, of which he was joint editor with Emmeline, got to the press on time. Her popularity as a speaker at public meetings often took her away from the office but he was usually to be found there, ensuring the machine was running smoothly. Some of the leader columns in the paper were his work and he wrote a number of long articles on policy, but many of his contributions went unsigned. Between 1908 and 1909 the revenue from subscriptions for *Votes for Women* trebled from £6,000 to more than £18,000, and its circulation grew to 30,000. The Woman's Press brought in a further £2,000.

The job of bailing out suffragettes was one of the few things that would draw Fred away from Clement's Inn on a weekday. Because Cannon Row police station, to which women were usually taken if they were arrested in Westminster, did not have overnight accommodation for prisoners at the time it was necessary for them to be given bail. The women came to know Fred affectionately as 'Godfather', and he calculated that over the years he must have stood surety for more than a thousand of them, not one of whom ever broke her bail. In the autumn of 1908 he took on the additional role of defence counsel. At a public meeting in Leeds a WSPU organiser named Jennie Baines had thrown herself at Herbert Asquith crying 'Votes for women and down with tyranny!' She was the first suffragette to be tried by jury. On her behalf Fred tried – without success – to subpoena both Asquith and Herbert Gladstone. Jennie Baines was convicted of unlawful assembly and spent six weeks in Armley jail.

Fred admired Christabel particularly. Vera Brittain, who knew him towards the end of his life, said he was 'captivated' by her and might quite possibly have been in love with her.[17] But he did not share the sexual sectarianism to which she increasingly adhered as time went on. If asked, he would say he joined the movement specifically in order to prevent a 'sex war' which he feared would break out if women did not soon win the vote. Because they had no constitutional outlet for their political grievances, they were bound to continue to use unconstitutional methods, he believed. It would be a disaster if it were to appear that men and women were taking up arms against one another.

Increasingly, though, arms were being taken up, if not against men then against property. Fred was not a natural firebrand but he never publicly criticised the union's militant policy. Indeed, he actively supported it though his support was tested as the suffragettes' demonstrations became more and more controversial. Sylvia Pankhurst described his discomfort when a supporter named Helen Ogston took a dogwhip to a Liberal meeting in the Albert Hall and used it against the stewards when they handled her roughly.[18] In 1911 he published a short book, *Women's Fight for the Vote*, in which he extolled the virtues of making a fuss: 'Nothing has done more to retard the progress of the human race than the exaltation of submission into a high and noble virtue. It may often be expedient to submit; it may even sometimes be morally right to do so in order to avoid a greater evil; but submission is not inherently beautiful – it is generally cowardly and frequently morally wrong.' When Marion Wallace Dunlop began the first suffragette hunger strike in 1909 he wrote to her: 'Nothing has moved me so much – stirred me to the depths of my being – as your heroic action. The power of the human spirit is to me the most sublime thing in life – that compared with which all ordinary things sink into insignificance.'[19]

As WSPU militancy grew, the finger of suspicion began to be pointed at Fred. The suffragette window-smashing raids of March 1912 sent shock waves through the capital, and they had equally far-reaching effects for the Pethick-Lawrences. Four days after the raids, the couple were in their flat at Clement's Inn when the police arrived to arrest them for conspiracy. Fred was taken to Brixton prison and Emmeline to Holloway. He was filled with exultation – at last he had the chance to experience what the suffragettes had been going through for so long – perhaps even to take the limelight.

Fred was not at all unhappy in prison. He said afterwards it reminded him of prep school. He started learning Italian, enjoyed singing hymns in the prison chapel and even wrote to Emmeline that while exercising in the yard he had heard a lark singing in the sky above him.[20] He decided to defend himself, as did Emmeline Pankhurst, who was also charged, while his wife hired a barrister. The Pethick-Lawrences were held on remand for three weeks and were then bailed until the trial, which took place in May. On the eve of the case Fred wrote to Emmeline in almost Churchillian mood:

> Beloved, We are very near to a great day, the greatest that we have seen in our lives … We are to stand where the great and noble have stood before us all down the ages. We are to be linked with those who have won the everlasting homage of the whole human race. If next week you and I were to be crowned King and Queen in the presence of an adulating people, how paltry would be the honour in comparison![21]

At around the same time *Votes for Women* ran a rather odd eulogy setting out 'the secret' of what Fred had done for women and for the wider world. His academic honours, his skill at billiards and his positions in student debating societies were all brought into play. Even his racial origins – 'solid, fair, unemotional' Cornish stock – were held up for examination. The piece rather cryptically suggested his brusqueness could sometimes be offensive: 'He will never know the sweets of personal popularity and would not appreciate them if he did.'

In his speech to the jury Fred tried to emphasise the difference between militancy and violence – he abhorred window-smashing but could not bring himself to criticise women who did it, he said. He read out the statement of a window-smasher who had been badly injured in a demonstration outside Parliament and who said she felt there was little else she could do to make her views known. All three defendants were found guilty and sentenced to nine months' imprisonment. Fred was taken first to Wormwood Scrubs then back to Brixton. After a few days he heard the other WSPU leaders had gone on hunger strike in Holloway, and decided to follow their example. At first his low-key protest attracted little attention, indeed it was three days before the authorities realised what he was up to and removed him to the prison hospital.[22] By then what he described as 'the food habit' had passed off.

He was force fed twice a day for more than ten days – some of the most brutal treatment meted out to any suffrage prisoner. In her memoirs

Emmeline Pankhurst said he was in a state of collapse by the time he was released. He had lost one and a half stone, and his weight-loss was accelerating.[23] He did not complain. Typically he wrote to Emmeline that while exercising by walking up and down his cell, he had worked out that he could make his fingers add up to thirty-five by counting each finger on the left hand not as one but as six. If his thumbs were allowed to count differently from his fingers it would be possible to count on his hands from one to ninety-nine, he said.

If prison was surprisingly easy, what came after was much more trying. The relationship between the Pethick-Lawrences and the Pankhursts, which had been such a strong one throughout the previous six years, was about to come under immense strain. There were two issues on the horizon which needed discussion and resolution, and both were likely to cause friction. The first, and most important, was the future direction of the union's militant policy. Christabel, in exile in Paris, was preparing to push her acolytes to ever more radical, daring and dangerous acts. Fred and Emmeline both had their doubts about this. They feared much of the membership, let alone the public, was not ready to accept an even greater degree of lawlessness, and they wanted to push forward the boundaries by degrees. The second, subsidiary issue, concerned the couple's money. Although the wealth of the Pethick-Lawrences had transformed and sustained the union, it was about to become a problem. The government was preparing to hold Fred responsible for the cost of the March window-smashing raids. He could afford to pay, but Emmeline Pankhurst feared every future act of militancy could be met with a similar claim.

On their release Fred and Emmeline travelled to Boulogne to meet Christabel and her mother for a serious discussion about the way forward. What followed seemed to the Pethick-Lawrences a heated but friendly disagreement. Fred suggested Christabel, who had fled the country to avoid arrest, should return to England and challenge the authorities to imprison her. Christabel thought differently. The talk also turned to militancy and when no consensus could be reached the four agreed to talk further in the autumn after taking a holiday. Surprisingly, given the closeness of their relationship with Emmeline and Christabel, Fred and Emmeline had completely misunderstood their *modus operandi*. They should have realised that no one in the union, not even people as central to its being as themselves, could challenge Christabel and survive. Before leaving, heading first for Switzerland and then for Canada, Fred wrote to Christabel without hint of a breach, addressing her as 'God-daughter' and confirming he was happy to bear the financial cost of militancy. 'Let them do their worst … we ought to give publicity to every step they take,' he wrote. 'No decision as to refunding me from WSPU funds must be taken in our absence.'[24] The letter was not received in the spirit in which it was sent. Christabel and her mother had a further discussion, and reached a decision. Fred and Emmeline must be forced out of the movement, they decreed.

The news, when it reached the Pethick-Lawrences in the form of a letter written by Mrs Pankhurst, came as a total shock.[25] The couple should not return to the UK, she suggested, but should stay in Canada and build up WSPU support there. The letter claimed the real problem was money. The government had seen in Fred's wealth 'a potent weapon' against the movement, she argued, and the movement could be reduced to 'a farce' if every act of militancy were met with a corresponding damages claim. Emmeline Pethick-Lawrence wrote back rejecting the suggestion and acknowledging that they already expected the authorities to target their bank account. 'With regard to militancy we have never for a single instant allowed our individual interests to stand in the way of any necessary action or policy to be pursued by the union and we never shall,' she wrote.[26]

Fred and Emmeline returned to England to the grim realisation that not only had bailiffs taken up residence at their home, The Mascot, but that they had also been thrown out of the union. They felt as if they had been the victims of a sudden bereavement. After six years, they could not take it in. Unable to believe that Christabel would do this to them they demanded to see her. She made the trip from Paris, where she was now living openly, and confirmed what they had already been told. At a meeting in the Albert Hall which had been planned as a welcome for all the leaders, Mrs Pankhurst appeared alone and read a statement saying that after a disagreement about the future direction of militancy, the Pethick-Lawrences had agreed to leave. They would retain control of *Votes for Women* which would no longer be the official organ of the union; the WSPU had already moved to new offices in Kingsway. In her autobiography Emmeline Pethick-Lawrence confirmed this public version of events. There had always been a 'fundamental difference' between the desire of herself and Fred to push militancy forward by degrees and that of Mrs Pankhurst and Christabel which now tended towards 'civil war', she said.[27] Emmeline was inclined to put up a fight against expulsion; Fred persuaded her that to do so would be to split the union. It was better to go quietly and hold their tongues: 'We refused to pull down in this way, stone by stone, the edifice which we had with such care and at such cost assisted to build up,' Fred explained later.[28] There were no public recriminations but it was many years before any of the main protagonists spoke to one another again.

Even the split with the WSPU did not end of this agony – the Pethick-Lawrences were still facing bankruptcy proceedings. An auction of their belongings was held at The Mascot, but raised only £300 towards their £1,100 court costs even though many friends arrived to buy personal possessions and give them back to the couple. Even the auctioneer returned to them a trinket he had bought as a keepsake. The rest of the costs were later taken from Fred's estate, plus a further £5,000 for repairs to shop windows damaged in the raids. Fortunately he had deep pockets and did not have to sell his home. Emmeline wrote to a supporter: 'We are not troubled by the loss of material possessions, knowing how little such things are compared with those things that really matter … Some day I shall have a tablet fixed in our little hall at The Mascot with Milton's words, 'Oh Liberty! Thou choicest treasure!'[29]

The severing of the Pethick-Lawrences' association with Christabel and Emmeline Pankhurst did not end their involvement with the militant suffrage movement. They continued to edit and run *Votes for Women*, and in 1913 Emmeline again went to prison, after a protest against the Cat and Mouse Act. In 1914 she and Fred joined the United Suffragists, a new organisation open to both militants and non-militants, and they handed the paper over to its control.[30] They also kept in touch with Sylvia Pankhurst, who had herself been ejected from the WSPU and now defied her mother and sister in opposing the First World War – a view she shared with the Pethick-Lawrences. In the years that followed Fred drifted, looking for a new outlet for his energies. He found it difficult to cope emotionally with the split. The writer Henry Nevinson said Fred was bitter and angry about what had happened. He was 'very violent' on the subject and in the two years before the outbreak of the First World War it had become 'almost an obsession' with him. In particular, he had been hurt at the way in which the Pankhursts made all the arrangements in secret before springing the separation on himself and Emmeline.[31]

There were further disappointments in store. Emmeline remained busy, making a long trip to the US just after war broke out to help set up the Women's International League which would campaign for peace. Also in 1914 she took in children of strikers in Dublin. Fred was less well occupied. Relieved of the need to support Emmeline in her suffrage work and freed – to an extent – from the stigma of militancy, he set about looking for a parliamentary seat. In Aberdeen South, where he stood in a 1917 by-election as a 'peace by negotiation' candidate, he came bottom of the poll with just 333 votes. He was then adopted as Labour candidate for Hastings but again his opposition to the war got in the way. In 1918, at the age of forty-six, he was conscripted. Although not a pacifist – he was against *this* war, not all wars – he became a conscientious objector. He escaped prison, working on a farm instead, but the Hastings Labour Party dropped him. In 1918 it was Emmeline, not Fred, who was a candidate – in Rusholme, Manchester, where she failed to get elected. Fred tried again, in Islington in 1921, and again failed. Finally, in November 1923, he was elected as Labour MP for Leicester West. It was a particularly triumphant victory, for after his selection Fred learned that Winston Churchill – an old suffragette adversary – would be his opponent. He won with 13,634 votes to Churchill's 9,236.

It is ironic that Fred Pethick-Lawrence, a man, was the only member of the WSPU leadership to become an MP. Women had the vote, but they still had a long way to go in winning political equality. For Fred, with his political uncles, it seemed a natural step – delayed rather than facilitated by the women's suffrage struggle. He was not the only ex-prisoner to sit in Parliament that session, though – a special dinner was held for this elite group, of whom there were eighteen in all. Several had been imprisoned as conscientious objectors during the war, others were former Poplar councillors who had flouted the law over poor relief for the unemployed. George Lansbury had been to prison first for the suffragettes and later as leader of the Poplar revolt.

At first it looked as if Fred's parliamentary career might not be a distinguished one. The press gallery nicknamed him 'Pathetic Lawrence' because his speeches were dull. Fred was hurt by this and asked the actor Wilfred Walter to train him in public speaking. This helped, but oratory was never his strong point. He also found constituency surgeries dull at first, though later he learned to derive satisfaction from seeking solutions to his constituents' problems.

At around this time Fred and Emmeline made a change in their personal lives. A major road was to run past The Mascot, and they decided to give it up. They built a new house at Peaslake in Surrey, designed to be labour-saving so that for the first time they could live without a full-time domestic staff. They kept only the gardener, Rapley, and two full-time secretaries. Fred found domesticity a welcome relief from politics. He enjoyed cooking, digging vegetables and making jam: 'I have found it a pleasant relief from political life to take charge of part of the cooking, which I regard as an extension of the chemistry experiments of my boyhood,'[32] he wrote.

Parliament had its relaxing side, too. There were frequent trips abroad with other MPs, and in the autumn of 1925 he spent several weeks in America. Fred was even challenged to a tennis doubles match by Churchill's wife Clementine in revenge for the loss of her husband's seat. Fred and his partner lost. But in 1929, after Fred had retained his seat at Leicester West, such high jinks came to an end with his elevation to the job of Financial Secretary to the Treasury in Ramsay MacDonald's Labour government. It was the perfect job for him, with his mathematical mind and eye for detail. Although a quiet man he was ambitious and after so many years in his wife's shadow he was determined to move on. He had long harboured a desire for promotion, and had berated himself for losing his temper with the Chancellor, Philip Snowden, during a debate. But as it turned out, Snowden had enjoyed the rough-and-tumble of the altercation and now he brought Fred into his department. When the phone call came, Fred was in Peaslake cooking salmon for Sunday lunch.[33] In his excitement he forgot all about it and found it still boiling away two hours later.

Fred was proud that during his time in this post he was able to introduce a week's paid holiday for all government employees, a measure which affected about 100,000 people including some postal workers, tradesmen in the air force and staff in arsenals and naval dockyards. His spell at the Treasury was short-lived, though. In 1931, after days of financial crisis during which Ramsay MacDonald's cabinet had sat almost continuously, Fred was called to Downing Street with other junior ministers to hear that MacDonald was to form a National Government with the Conservatives. As they all filed out, the Prime Minister stopped Fred and asked if he might stay on. Fred declined. In the ensuing general election only fifty-two of the 263 Labour MPs who had taken this stance were re-elected, and Fred was not among them.

Fred and Emmeline, as they often did when they had little else to do, went travelling, spending long spells over the next few years in Russia, the Middle East and Spain. Emmeline, though still involved with the women's movement as president of the Women's Freedom League, had scaled down her activities, and, at the age of sixty, it seemed Fred's parliamentary career was over. But as it turned out, the most distinguished part of Fred's life at Westminster was yet to come. In 1935 he was again elected, this time as MP for Edinburgh East. During the Second World War he steadily climbed the ladder of promotion within his party, becoming first unofficial deputy to the Labour leader, Bertie Lees-Smith, and then – after Lees-Smith's death from the after-effects of 'flu – chairman of the Parliamentary Labour Party and effectively leader of the opposition, though normal hostilities had been suspended. Although Fred was re-elected in Edinburgh East in 1945, Clement Attlee asked him to become both a peer and a cabinet minister – as Secretary of State for India and Burma. Fred had had a long association with India. He had gone there on his first major visit abroad, in 1897, and in 1931 he had taken part in a round table conference on the country's future. Gandhi, who knew Keir Hardie, had visited the Clement's Inn flat for a frugal meal of raisins and milk and a talk about his work in South Africa.[34] Fred and Sir Stafford Cripps had been among the very few Labour candidates to mention India in their 1945 election addresses, advocating independence at the earliest possible date. The appointment was welcomed by Indian nationalists, and yet it was surprising. Fred was by then seventy-four and it was clear the negotiations to come would tax the strength of a much younger man. The situation between Nehru's Congress Party, which wanted a united India, and Jinnah's Muslim League, which wanted a separate Pakistan, was quickly reaching deadlock. Attlee announced a cabinet mission to India to try to frame a new constitution. It would be led by Fred, with Stafford Cripps, the President of the Board of Trade, and Sir Albert Alexander, the First Lord of the Admiralty.

When the party left England in March they hoped to be home in time for Easter, but this was not to be. Though they spent weeks ensconced in a private house in Delhi from which Cripps was sent out as an emissary to the various parties, the talks seemed barely to have progressed. The tension and uncertainty were hard to bear. Fred wrote to Emmeline: 'Our political weather is subject to the same rapid changes as the physical weather in the English climate. Sun and storm follow one another at short intervals. Yesterday morning it looked as if the conference could not fail to break down, by evening it had come out full sunshine, by this morning there are dark clouds again.'[35] By 16 May he was forced to admit that his mission had failed to agree a constitution for an independent India, and to issue a statement saying an interim government would carry on until progress was made. Gandhi welcomed the statement but a further three weeks went by before Jinnah could persuade the Muslim League to accept it even as a basis for discussion. Fred found the waiting interminable. 'These people talk and deliberate with a sense of all eternity in front of them,' he told Emmeline. On 8 June he wrote to her that, greeted afresh with the immediate prospect of failure, he had experienced a momentary sense of relief that he might soon be going home. 'And then came the reaction as I thought of the terrible time ahead if the calamity in fact materialised. And so I stifled back my desire for personal escape and thanked God that while there was life there was still hope.' The strain was becoming too much. Gandhi, Fred reported irascibly, was being 'very awkward'. 'He suffers from high blood pressure and when he gets an idea he can't let go of it even if it goes contrary to what he has been urging up to the day before. He prefers theoretical perfection as he sees it and is not really interested in the practical consultations of Government which involve mutual accommodation.'

At last, on 25 June, Congress accepted a long-term plan to draft a constitution, though it rejected the proposed interim government, which was then dropped. Jinnah, who had been prepared to enter an interim government if Congress had accepted it, accused the British of bad faith. The mission finally left India with a sense that although they had not succeeded, they had at least convinced Indian politicians of all hues that they were sincere in their desire to give India independence. But at the end of July the Muslim League withdrew its acceptance of the mission's proposals. In August nearly 5,000 people were killed and 15,000 injured in riots. To make matters worse, the Viceroy had heard rumours that Fred was about to retire and to be replaced by Cripps, who was unpopular with the Muslims. Fred was forced to write to Attlee denying the rumours. But the truth was he was tired. He felt he no longer had the mental agility required for such a task. He told Attlee that if he wanted to replace him with a younger man, he would not object. Attlee declined to do so. But the following spring, after an ultimatum by the British government that it intended to transfer power no later than June 1948, Fred wrote again to the Prime Minister: 'My Dear C, I have come to the end of my tether.' This time, Attlee agreed to let him retire. Fred wrote sadly to his secretary, Esther Knowles, that he felt he had left the job unfinished. 'I have had lots of very friendly and much too complimentary letters from all sorts of people about my retirement. I should have liked to have seen the Indian problem solved or on the way to solution during my term of office but it has eluded me and I have had to lay my burden down with no solution in sight.'

Retirement from the cabinet did not mean an end to an active life, or even to a public life. Ten years later, at the age of eighty-six, Fred wrote to a correspondent: 'My principal present activities are the House of Lords, Governor and member of the Executive Committee of Bridewell Hospital, Governor of Stratford-Upon-Avon Memorial Theatre, Trustee of the National Library of Scotland and member of the Political Honours Scrutiny Committee. I am a regular reader of the Economist newspaper.'[36] Fred's entry into the world of Westminster politics had been delayed, but it was certainly not curtailed. Although Emmeline was generally regarded as the more charming, the more outgoing of the two, Fred had an enormous circle of friends with whom he corresponded to the end of his life. Relieved of his daily duties, he found time to write philosophical musings. His secretary, Esther Knowles, received the benefit of his views on the creation along with a eulogy to the month of October. Once, after a dinner at his old Cambridge college, he wrote a long letter to the master, G. M. Trevelyan, in defence of suffragette militancy.

For Emmeline, though, there would be no such energetic battling on to the end. In 1950, a year before she and Fred celebrated their golden wedding with a series of parties for friends and family, she fell in the garden at Peaslake and broke her hip. Fred wrote to Esther Knowles that Emmeline was 'very down'. But, he said, he was bearing in mind that thirty years earlier he had been frustrated and she serene. Emmeline had also become very deaf and suffered from heart trouble, and in her last years she did not stray often from Surrey. On their fiftieth anniversary she wrote to Fred: 'I have not the words to tell you what you are and have ever been to me, and will be to the end. I shall go out like a soap bubble but you will be *there*. PS That's how I feel at the moment. But not always, old darling, for sometimes I am your old rascal.'[37] Three years later Emmeline suffered a series of heart attacks and in March 1954 she died. Fred wrote to a well-wisher in Australia: 'I feel a bit dazed. It is as though I was at a violin concerto with the violinist absent.'[38] Fred gave up the Surrey house, moved to London and kept himself busy at weekends visiting friends around the country.

Fred was not suited to the life of a single man, and craved companion-ship. In February 1957, at the age of eighty-five, he married Helen Mc-Crombie who, as Helen Craggs, had been one of the many suffragettes for whom he had stood bail. They were married in the registry office at Cax-ton Hall, which had been the scene of many a suffrage rally. Fred wrote to another former comrade, Daisy Solomon, that Emmeline had always told him the greatest compliment a man could pay to his dead wife was to marry again. 'So I feel I have her blessing in advance,' he explained.[39] Later that year Fred and Helen visited Pakistan and India, where they stayed with Indira Gandhi and were treated with deep reverence. Their itinerary read like a state visit. 'Sunday Nov 17. 9.30am Arrival at Karachi Airport. Stay at State Guest House. 11.30am Call on the Acting President. 1pm Lunch by UK Community. 4.30pm Call on Minister of Finance.'[40] Afterwards, Fred ac-knowledged in a thank-you note to Indira Gandhi that he was glad to get home for a rest.

Fred made his last speech in the House of Lords on 27 July 1961, five months before his ninetieth birthday. After delivering a closely argued crit-icism of the government's economic strategy, he left for a weekend in Gloucestershire with Helen but 'simply folded up', according to Esther Knowles, who had herself retired two years earlier. He took to his bed and never got out of it again. Helen was so snowed under with letters of con-dolence from Fred's wide circle of acquaintance that it took her many weeks to answer them. The organisations which wrote to express their gratitude for his efforts on their behalf included the Asian Film Society, the Association for Moral and Social Hygiene, the National Marriage Guid-ance Council and the Universities Federation for Animal Welfare. Barbara Castle praised 'a breadth of vision and a generosity of spirit ahead of his time', and Shirley Williams his speeches, which were 'always perfect mod-els of lucidity and cogency'. At his memorial service Clement Attlee read the lesson and Viscount Alexander of Hillsborough, his colleague on the cabinet mission to India, gave the address.

What would the WSPU have been without the Pethick-Lawrences? It is impossible to judge, for the union would certainly have found another benefactor. Their main contribution was neither money nor militant zeal. Fred would have done far less to advance the status of the union if he had gone out and set fire to some pillar-boxes or interrupted a meeting. What he did was to give the union an organisational backbone, a foundation upon which the many and inventive talents of its leadership could be built.

It is hard to say whether Fred Pethick-Lawrence was a right-winger or a left-winger, a radical or a natural member of the establishment. If he had his time again, he wrote once towards the end of his life, he would do it all again in much the same way – he was a socialist yet saw no major contradiction in the idea that he should have been schooled at Eton. Yet no one ever accused him of lacking constancy either in his views or in his personal life, nor of stupidity or thoughtlessness. His was a soul which sought constantly after truth without ever suffering the agony of self-doubt. Fred Pethick-Lawrence entitled his autobiography *Fate Has Been Kind*, and he did so advisedly.

Adela Pankhurst in the suffragette garden at Batheaston, Somerset

V

Adela Pankhurst – Forgotten Sister

There had been much rain the day before – the ground was muddy and very slippery. A gang of young men, some of them students, got behind the crowd and began to push people down the slippery slope … for some reason a specially vicious attack was made upon Adela Pankhurst. My husband realised her danger and rushed to her assistance. It was all that he could do to hold up the tiny figure while the men closed in on her, with faces so expressive of mob hatred that he feared for her life …. from henceforward we took the precaution to speak from lorries … I never met anyone so fearless as were these young girls. I never saw a suffragette, under menace of violence, otherwise than cool and collected.

Emmeline Pethick-Lawrence describing a suffragette meeting in June 1906 attended by 30,000 people at Boggart Hole Clough, Manchester.[1]

It was with little sense of elation that Emmeline Pankhurst gave birth to her fourth child, Adela Constantia Mary, in June 1885. There was no great novelty to the addition of a third girl to the existing brood, and in any case this child was a sickly creature. She had weak legs and bad lungs, and for a time was not expected to live. Emmeline entrusted her care to the family nurse, Susannah Jones, and within a couple of months had gone away to London to support her husband's fruitless efforts to get elected to Parliament in Rotherhithe.

Adela was not born at a happy time for the Pankhurst family. In the months before her birth they had left Emmeline's parental home after a series of rows about politics and money. There the older children had enjoyed an idyllic life surrounded by adoring relatives. Christmas pantomimes had been produced by four aunts and five uncles, with Sylvia allowed to play Cinderella and Christabel her prince. There had been a bustling kitchen where the children's Manx grandmother produced butter, bread, pickles, jams and cakes. The much smaller rented house in Green-heys, south of Manchester city centre, seemed quiet and dull by compari-son.

Adela was forced to wear splints on her legs and did not learn to walk until she was three. She later blamed neglect by her mother for her weak physical constitution. In Emmeline's memoirs Adela and her younger brother Harry would be dismissed, nameless, as 'two other children'. Adela was three when her brother Frank died of diphtheria, old enough to un-derstand her grief-stricken mother when she stormed that 'he had much finer eyes than any of these children'.[2] She was four when her youngest sib-ling, Harry, was born and from then on she was 'a child apart' according to Sylvia. She was left to play on her own or to sit in the kitchen with the ser-vants, who alone among the adults in the household seemed to have time for her. Once, while the family was living in London, she returned from a solitary afternoon in the garden at the centre of Russell Square to report that some big boys had asked her strange questions. Sylvia and Christabel were rebuked for allowing her to play there alone, and after that the chil-dren were confined to the back yard of their own home.

Adela was a bright little thing, though, and never shy in front of strangers. She passed her hours of solitude in making up stories she de-scribed as 'prince tales', and waylayed visitors to the house to ask: 'Shall I tell you a tale?' Often she was rewarded by their undivided attention as she wove her fantasies. The fact that she was small for her age helped by mak-ing her seem more advanced for her years than she really was. Adela would make up plays which she acted out enthusiastically by herself, playing all the characters in turn and appropriating household objects as stage props. Throughout her life she loved to perform. Christabel remembered how both she and Sylvia once 'dried' while delivering a laboriously prepared lecture on cats to an audience of family friends. Adela, aged about five, stepped eagerly into the breach: 'The cat has a nose and a mouth joined to-gether like a monkey or such-like,' she began precociously. Her elder sis-ters, seeing the fruit of their labours crumbling into dust, were furious.

Life in the Pankhurst household was rather earnest at the best of times, with Richard bringing home a different book each day for his children to study – history, botany, astronomy, chemistry, engineering, novels or even fairy tales, for his tastes were eclectic. 'Drudge and drill! Drudge and drill!' he would exhort, in between telling the girls that if they did not grow up to help others they would not have been worth the upbringing. It was a heavy burden, not least because it was assumed they would inherit all their parents' beliefs and attitudes. Years later Adela recalled how her father had attempted to hammer his heartfelt atheism into her: 'I think I was only about six when my father – a most revered person in my existence – assured me there was no God – and I knew inside me that he was wrong.'[3]

Emmeline believed formal education stifled children's individuality, but Adela had more of it than her older sisters. She loved her first school, a small intimate establishment in Southport to which she went briefly at the age of seven. Even at that age she soon won over a band of admirers: 'I established myself then and there as personality,' she recalled.[4] She was less happy at the Manchester Girls' High School. She felt lost among its 500-plus pupils, and did not thrive. She hated the school, hated the dancing classes she had to endure there and missed the carefree summer rambles she took with her mother and Harry during the holidays. Once, feeling fat and unloved, she tried to run away. A gardener discovered her after school in the act of changing out of her uniform, but with her school hat still on her head. When Adela arrived home in a cab, her parents finally took notice for long enough to realise how low she had sunk. She appeared to have had a breakdown, and was refusing to speak. She spent a lonely winter recovering at home before being sent to convalesce with an aunt who lived in Aberdeen. Despite her occasional frailty, though, most people knew Adela as a sunny, vigorous and hard-working girl. She was an attractive and usually cheerful character to whom others warmed, and she did well academically.

Like all the Pankhurst children Adela was a political animal. Harry cajoled her into canvassing for his teacher, who was standing for election to the Board of Guardians, for at the age of ten Harry had found he was not being taken seriously on the doorstep. When the Boer War broke out the whole family joined in a pacifist campaign against it, and at school Adela was hit in the face by a book thrown by a fellow pupil who did not share her anti-war views.

When Adela's teachers suggested she should apply for an Oxford scholarship, Emmeline would not hear of it. Adela later claimed her educational needs had come second to those of her older sisters – Christabel studied law at Manchester's Victoria University and Sylvia went to the Royal College of Art in London.[5] But in the end it was ill-health that put an end to Adela's schooling, for at the age of sixteen she caught scarlet fever which left her with permanent lung damage. Once she was well enough to travel Emmeline sent her to stay with her old schoolfriend Noemie DuFaux in Switzerland.

Adela came back refreshed, revitalised and determined to become a teacher. Emmeline was horrified. Although Richard had frequently urged his children to 'get something to earn your living by that you like and can do',[6] this was not what Emmeline had in mind. Art or law were one thing, but teaching was an occupation for the bright working-class pupil, or for the genteel but impoverished. Although Adela fitted this second category, it was not what her mother had planned. As always, though, Adela knew her own mind. By the winter of 1903, aged eighteen, she was working as a pupil-teacher at an elementary school in Urmston, on the other side of Manchester from the family home. She would catch the 7 a.m. train from the city centre, and return home to a full evening of study. Adela loved her charges, barefoot and ragged as they were, and the sense that she was descending into the underworld appealed to the romantic side of her nature: 'I was at last one of the working masses who were to redeem mankind,' she wrote later.[7]

Adela was at the inaugural meeting of the WSPU in October 1903, though she said she got involved only 'to get my mother and Christabel out of a hole ... I wanted to write books and go in for music.'[8] But whatever her reservations she threw herself into the cause, as she did with most things, enthusiastically. With her penchant for performance she was a natural candidate for the union's first speakers' list, which also included the three other Pankhurst women and Teresa Billington. During the early months the union's main activity was speaking at Independent Labour Party or trade union meetings as well as at any event where people were gathered – wakes weeks, fairs – and in public spaces such as Manchester's Boggart Hole Clough.

Adela was a confident speaker, never cowed by hecklers and always quick to recall a pertinent fact or statistic. During school holidays she spoke all over the North of England and the Midlands, taking a tour of the Potteries then later speaking from a portable platform in Stockton, Leicester, Grimsby, Hartlepool, Leeds, Bradford and Sheffield. The long hours and the damp and windy conditions took their toll on her health. In February 1905 in a letter to a colleague about policy Emmeline mentioned that she had 'got home last night very tired to find my younger girl in bed with a slight attack of pleurisy'. She added: 'Fortunately she is getting better.'[9]

Alongside the rough-and-tumble of the public platform ran the union's fund-raising effort, which was always a more genteel affair. Molly Morris, who joined the union in 1905, aged fifteen, recalled being sent to fetch

Adela from the station in Manchester and going with her to the home of a wealthy sympathiser who talked of the sacrifices women could make for the cause – including cutting out the fish course at breakfast.[10] On one occasion Molly was arrested while chalking the pavement outside Manchester's Free Trade Hall, where Adela and Emmeline Pethick-Lawrence were due to speak. She said the city's chief of police, a Mr Peacock, was sympathetic and suggested she keep an eye out for the law in future when indulging in such activities. 'I can't always get you out of these scrapes, you know,' he told her as he let her go.

The police were not to remain so protective for long. From October 1905, when Annie Kenney and Christabel staged their protest at Sir Edward Grey's meeting and were arrested, the struggle became increasingly rowdy. It was clear Arthur Balfour's Conservative government would not last long, and in December that year the Prime Minister resigned. The Liberal leader, Henry Campbell-Bannerman, was invited to form an administration. While celebrating what they believed would be the end of a reactionary era in which the women's cause had made little progress, the suffragettes now stepped up their campaign against the Liberals. Adela became Winston Churchill's *bête noire* during the ensuing general election, turning up whenever he spoke in the city. Hannah Mitchell, an early WSPU recruit, said that on one such occasion Churchill's henchmen locked Adela in a classroom for several hours to keep her quiet.[11]

Despite all this activity it was another six months before Adela finally managed to get arrested. Dressed up in her mother's best silk coat and hat to look like a respectable Liberal lady, she arrived at a Liberal meeting in Manchester's Belle Vue pleasure park with a tall, scholarly-looking man. Hannah Mitchell, who was also there, had borrowed a smart green costume from a friend. Adela's hat was trimmed with roses and did not suit her, Hannah said, but it had a wide brim which hid her face, almost meeting the high collar of her coat. Adela was the first to rise to put her question – 'Will the government give votes to women?' – and was immediately ejected, followed shortly afterwards by Hannah. As they sat on a wall with two others waiting for their friends to appear, the police arrived. Hannah recalled later: 'I followed Adela who was in the grip of a big burly officer who kept telling her she ought to be smacked and set to work at the wash tubs. She grew so angry that she slapped his hand, which was as big as a ham.'[12]

At Minshull Street police court on the following Monday, Adela and her three friends were all charged with obstruction and Adela faced an additional charge of assaulting a policeman. She was defended by the Independent Labour Party's solicitor and fined ten shillings, though the magistrate's quizzical glance from the slight, girlish figure to the huge, burly policeman spoke volumes. She refused to pay and was sent to Strangeways prison for seven days.

Although Adela wrote a long article in the *Labour Record* shortly afterwards, entitled 'Thoughts in Prison', she said little about how she coped with the experience. It seems incarceration made her sentimental, for she spent the time musing about the lot of the poor. 'As a teacher I had been trying for years in the case of the children with whom I had to deal to stave off the inevitable answer … I had felt the hopeless futility of my work. Now, in prison … it seemed to me that for the first time in my life I was doing something which would help,' she wrote.[13]

A week after her release Adela was to have her most frightening experience yet. At a meeting at Boggart Hole Clough, she was at the centre of a frenzied attack by a gang of youths. When she was offered shelter in a nearby house with Hannah Mitchell the crowd massed outside, yelling. The householder threatened them with a chair. Eventually the two women ran out and jumped on a tram, speeded by a fusillade of cabbages and other missiles grabbed from nearby gardens. Now that the suffragettes' militancy had become famous, large crowds would turn out for all their meetings. Some came to listen, some to sign up to the cause and some simply to heckle. The WSPU was not slow to realise the value of its notoriety. Adela and a group of other former prisoners were sent on a tour around the country to talk about their experiences and promote the cause.

Adela's imprisonment had marked the end of her short-lived career as a teacher, and now she was appointed as a paid regional organiser for the WSPU in West Yorkshire. But even at this early stage, some of her activities must have caused disquiet at the new suffragette headquarters in London. For while the union drifted gradually away from its roots in the Labour movement, Adela stuck doggedly to hers. One of her earliest activities in Yorkshire was to organise local members to support striking textile workers in Daubhill and Hebden Bridge, and two local WSPU members were actually summonsed as strike pickets. Christabel, who had moved to London to become the union's chief organiser, wished nothing to distract her members' attention from the fight for the vote, and could hardly have been pleased. Throughout 1907 the Huddersfield branch of the union made repeated and vain efforts to persuade Christabel to speak there,[14] though Annie Kenney did come to recruit marchers for a demonstration in London.

Adela's daily life took on a pattern that would change little in the following five years, though she herself would move several times. The life of a WSPU organiser was nothing if not full of contrast. One day she might be speaking to a noisy crowd of thousands at an outdoor rally on some windswept moorside; the next helping at a fund-raising 'sewing bee' or toffee-making session. The minutes of the Huddersfield WSPU give a flavour.[15] Early in 1908 Adela presided over a social evening with a whist drive at 7.45 p.m., speeches at 9 p.m., refreshments at 9.15 and a dance at 9.30. The first prize in the whist drive was a framed picture of Mrs Pankhurst. At one meeting Mary Gawthorpe reported Hull was having a jumble sale while Leeds was doing 'a roaring trade' in peppermint creams. A piano organ tour initiated by Mrs Baines was also proving a success. As well as paying Adela's £2 a week salary, each branch was expected to make donations to the national union from its funds.

There was frequent tension over money. After a by-election in Colne Valley the West Yorkshire members were forced to raise extra cash to pay expenses, money that Mrs Pankhurst had promised but failed to deliver. On another occasion a deputation of women demanded assurances from Adela that the union would bear the cost of a planned Town Hall meeting if it made a financial loss. And there was also continuing frustration at the women's inability to get their message across. After a minister's meeting in Bradford Adela reported in *Votes for Women*: 'Dr MacNamara's whole manner whilst speaking on the subject was most offensive, causing a laugh amongst the most ignorant men in the hall. The papers here omit the main point of his reply.'[16]

Adela enjoyed the work, though, and derived a sense of fun from the brash atmosphere of public meetings. After one gathering addressed by Herbert Gladstone she reported she had stood on her chair to ask a question and then handed it forward on a piece of paper when she could not make herself heard. 'Then for some reason or other the men began to fight one another and Mr Gladstone left the platform,' she added.[17] In Sheffield the Secretary of State for War, Richard Burdon Haldane, emerged after a meeting from which Adela had been excluded to find his car plastered with 'Votes for Women' posters. In Pudsey Adela reported she and her fellow speakers had been pelted with rotten oranges: 'None touched us, however, and as the people did not like being hit themselves they soon put a stop to it.'[18] At a dinner in Sheffield addressed by the First Lord of the Admiralty Reginald McKenna, Adela disguised herself as a kitchen maid to gain entrance. Rebuffed, she gathered a crowd of more than 800 to hear her speak on the Town Hall steps before leading them in a pitched battle with police lasting an hour and a half.[19]

Adela was frequently out of step with union policy, but she felt things were going well. In June 1908 she was put in charge of a platform at a huge suffragette rally in Hyde Park – *Votes for Women* described her as the 'Stormy Petrel' of Winston Churchill's election meetings – and in Yorkshire her meetings were attracting ever larger crowds. The Co-op Hall at Cleckheaton was now too small to be used as a venue, she reported, while the new 1,000-seat Town Hall at Ilkley was often full to the doors. A rally on Woodhouse Moor, near Leeds, in the summer of 1908, attracted 100,000 people – twice as many as had been there for a male suffrage meeting in 1884. There were ten platforms, brass bands and fluttering banners, and the *Yorkshire Post* reported that Adela held the attention of a large section of the audience for an hour and a quarter.

Wherever Adela went, she won friends and admirers. Archie Key, the son of the Huddersfield branch secretary Edith Key, confessed later that as a teenage boy he had been 'desperately in love with Adela although she was fully nine years older than I'.[20] While Emmeline and Christabel were 'statuesque tragediennes born to bear the roles of martyrs', Adela and Sylvia were of different stock, he said. Both 'turned out to be rebels within a rebellious family'. When Adela visited Annie Kenney's West Country hideaway, Batheaston, Emily Blathwayt described her as 'a dear little thing of 23 and except when she speaks looks like a timid child'.[21] Although hardworking, she occasionally found time for some fun. She was among a group who went to see Ellen Terry in *Captain Brassbound* at Bradford, all dressed in full Suffragette regalia. They even received a round of applause from the rest of the audience during the interval.

Adela's health often let her down. In February 1909 she was sent to Scotland to help with a rush of by-election campaigns in Forfar, Hawick and Glasgow. When she arrived the local organiser, Helen Fraser, was shocked by her appearance:

> As I met her at the train I could hear her breathing. Horrified, I said, 'Did your mother see you when you left last night?' I thought she said 'Yes.'

Anyhow I took her to the room I had booked and sent for a very well-known woman doctor whose comments on her travelling like that were acid, but she secured a nurse and Adela successfully got rid of her pneumonia.[22]

It was an inauspicious start to a turbulent spell north of the border that was to last for more than a year.

With the by-elections and her illness behind her Adela stayed on in Scotland to help develop the movement there. Basing herself in Aberdeen she embarked on the usual round of 'at homes' and drawing-room meetings interspersed with trips north to Inverness or west to the Isles to recruit new members. She still had opportunities to indulge in her favourite sport of Liberal-baiting. In July 1909 she was arrested at a rowdy protest outside one of Churchill's meetings in Edinburgh. In August she was arrested again at the St Andrew's Hall in Glasgow and charged with malicious damage, for breaking a window in the hall and another in the court. An arrest warrant was issued, but never pursued.

Women were by now being force fed in English prisons, and the struggle was becoming more bitter. In October 1909 Churchill was again in Scotland and Adela was among a group of women who appeared at a garden party he was attending in Abernethy. It was a violent occasion. No sooner had Adela opened the car door than she was dragged out by Liberal stewards, who then tried to overturn the vehicle. One woman was almost strangled with her own scarf and the group were bombarded with turf. Afterwards the *Dundee Courier* demanded an inquiry into why the police had stood by and watched such an unprovoked attack without intervening, and Churchill was forced to dissociate himself from the behaviour of his party workers.

A few days later at a meeting in Dundee the suffragettes took their revenge. As Churchill prepared to speak, they assembled in the garret of a house adjoining the hall. Adela crouched by a window with a two-pound weight on a string, flinging it repeatedly downwards on to the glass roof of the meeting room in an attempt to smash it. In the mêlée, a slate thrown by a man outside missed her head by a couple of inches. Soon the police broke in and arrested Adela with four others. In the past mere imprisonment had been considered a sufficient act of martyrdom for a suffragette, but now the stakes were rising. Adela and her comrades immediately began hunger-striking, and Adela set to work scratching suffragette slogans on the wall of her cell.

In the light of events in England the women must have feared they would be force fed, but the Scottish authorities took a more humane view. A doctor was brought to examine Adela and described her as 'a slender under-sized girl five feet in height and (in health) seven stones in weight'. He added: 'Dr Sturrock, the superintendent of the Perth Criminal Lunatic Department, was impressed by her extraordinary appearance and bearing and did not hesitate to say that she was of a "degenerate type"'. She was deemed unfit for force feeding and released along with her four companions.[23] The group capitalised on the episode by having their photograph taken by a studio in Dundee, holding a window frame with a broken pane. It is one of the most cheerful pictures of Adela from this period.[24] Adela spoke of her prison experiences to an outdoor audience of 10,000 before leaving to recuperate at Batheaston. In an article for *Votes for Women* in November 1909, she related: 'The cold was intense. I suffered from hunger nearly the whole time and from great pain for two days, especially at night. I am filled with admiration and wonder at the courage and endurance of those who in English prisons have gone through under conditions which make ours seem almost nothing.'

Adela did not return to Scotland but her friendship with Helen Fraser, the Scottish organiser of the WSPU, was to last for life. Once she had got over her initial misgivings Helen became a close friend and a great admirer of Adela. She found her very much in the thrall of her mother and older sisters, yet still an individual. 'I am of the opinion that Adela was far from being the last of the four. She was, when I first knew her, fanatically devoted to her mother and Christabel, but she had a mind of her own – an original and often unexpected mind,' she said in her memoirs.[25]

In early 1910, recovered from her prison experience, Adela returned to Yorkshire to organise a by-election campaign in Scarborough. Soon she was again working as Yorkshire organiser, based in Sheffield but covering the whole of the region, speaking to 'a large crowd of sympathetic fishermen' on the coast one day, chalking slogans on the pavements of villages in the Dales the next. A suffrage shop was opened in Sheffield, and funds were raised for a poster site at Sheffield Midland station. Adela was deeply amused to report that a Churchill meeting in Sheffield had been surrounded by barricades and 100 police while she quietly attended a drawing-room meeting at the other end of town.[26] The round of fund-raisers and 'at homes' continued but now Adela branched out into a new activity – 'lantern lectures' on the prevalence of sweated labour. She even wrote an article on the subject for *Votes for Women*, something that cannot have been received with unbridled joy at union headquarters, though her recent hunger strike had won her some goodwill.

The fun was going out of the movement for Adela, though. She was shocked by the violence she had experienced in Scotland, and according to her friend Helen Fraser she had expressed doubts to union headquarters in late 1909 about the turn militancy was taking. Although militancy was largely suspended from the beginning of 1910, when hopes of a suffrage bill began to rise, until late in 1911, when they faded again, Adela was now viewed with suspicion at WSPU headquarters. Her work was placed under new and unwelcome scrutiny, and on one occasion she was called to London to explain why she had organised a public meeting without permission. She even considered resigning but was persuaded by Emmeline Pethick-Lawrence to stay on.

Adela had other problems, too – she was constitutionally unsuited to the lifestyle. The round of open-air meetings and demonstrations, combined with the stress of constantly wondering when the next rebuke from headquarters would come, took its toll. She completely lost her voice. In the middle of 1911 *Votes for Women* announced that she had been obliged to cancel all meetings till the autumn. With Helen Archdale, a friend and fellow suffragette based in Sheffield at the time, she retreated to Wemyss Bay in Scotland, where there was a health 'hydro' popular with left-wing figures including the Pankhursts' old family friend Keir Hardie. Adela returned to Sheffield, but not for long. In October 1911 she moved with Helen Archdale to London, and her involvement as a full-time suffrage campaigner came to an end.

Although Adela's memories of this last spell in Yorkshire were of a 'miserable' time, her successor's experience suggests it may not have been all drudgery. Molly Morris, who became the next organiser in Sheffield, gave a far rosier picture.[27] Her main job was to run the shop, she said. This was not an arduous task, for it seemed the young men of the left in the area had taken to calling in regularly for a chat – Adela had this effect wherever she went. The visits were so frequent that Molly had to discourage them because some of the city's older suffragettes thought their attentions improper. She also aroused the suspicions of her landlady during all-night pavement-chalking trips around South Yorkshire, from which she would return on the tram with the foundry workers on the early shift. Molly recalled having plenty of time, too, for rambles in the Peak District with groups of sympathisers.

Although Adela's health was certainly a factor in her leaving the WSPU, it was probably not the main one. Her refusal to give up her affection for socialism was certainly one, though Sylvia suffered from this complaint too and she managed to hang on in the union for a further two years. But Adela's real problem was Christabel. Somehow, she had managed to enrage her easily riled older sister to the point of apoplexy. 'I would not care if you were multiplied by a hundred, but one of Adela is too many!' she told Sylvia.[28] At the bottom of Christabel's paranoia was an unfounded belief that Adela wanted to leave the union and found a rival organisation – something she flatly denied.

Many years later Adela wrote to her friend Helen Fraser that she believed far too much emphasis had been placed on militancy:

> I never regarded them myself as more than the drum that attracts attention and brings up the crowd to hear the message. The truth about my attitude, though I kept it to myself, was that I had come to realise that militancy was out of control … I knew all too well that after 1910 we were rapidly losing ground. I even tried to tell Christabel this was the case, but unfortunately she took it amiss.[29]

Adela told Helen with some bitterness that from the day she left the movement she was written out of its earlier history by followers of her mother and Christabel:

> [They] will never admit me or mention me as having played any part at all … As soon as I was not employed in politics I discovered that I was absolutely friendless. After all I had put into the movement no-one at headquarters ever enquired about my health or my fortunes. I was like the old soldiers who return from the wars and are turned out to beg in the streets. I knew if I said a single word to any of our members I would be starting a 'Party' so I held my tongue.[30]

In fact Adela was never completely estranged from her colleagues in the suffragette movement. After leaving Sheffield she lived for several months in London with Helen Archdale, who had been appointed as a prisoners' co-ordinator for the national union and who went to prison herself in March 1912 after the suffragettes' stone-throwing raids in central London. Throughout her life Adela would maintain contact with other suffragettes, many of whom had ended up feeling disillusioned with or bruised by the attitudes of the WSPU leadership. For Adela, though, the problem was particularly acute and particularly personal. Not only had she lost the respect of most of her family, she had also been left with no money and no job. Desperate at the prospect of becoming both idle and dependent, she decided to become a gardener – according to Sylvia, about the worst career she could possibly have chosen. 'The desire was a reaction from the knowledge that though a brilliant speaker and one of the hardest workers in the movement, she was often regarded with more disapproval than approbation by Mrs Pankhurst and Christabel, and was the subject of a sharper criticism than the other organisers had to face,' Sylvia recorded in her memoirs.[31]

Adela's first idea was to take up horticultural research but her resources were too slim. Her mother gave her £200 from the proceeds of an American lecture tour – just enough for a basic training course – and made her promise never to speak on a public platform in Britain again. In 1912 Adela embarked on a diploma course at Studley Horticultural College in Worcestershire, and the following year she found a job as head gardener with a family near Bath – though she claimed no one connected with the WSPU would employ her, the Batten-Pooll family were in fact sympathisers. The episode was a disaster. If Adela was unfit for outdoor speaking she was even less fit for gardening, and within months she was again in a state of collapse. She wrote to ask her mother if she would pay her fare to Canada. Emmeline refused. The 28-year-old Adela was a 'naughty child', she wrote to Helen Archdale in the summer of 1913, by which time Adela had left her job and was looking after Helen's children in Switzerland. 'The best thing for A just now is that she must be made to feel a sense of responsibility ... She must stick to her bargain like a good girl.'[32] A few months later, in early 1914, Emmeline had a change of heart. Adela should go to Australia, she decided. She gave her youngest daughter enough money for a one-way ticket, and an address in Melbourne for Vida Goldstein, an Australian suffrage campaigner with whom Adela had sometimes spoken in the UK. After Adela's departure Emmeline wrote rather sadly to Helen Archdale: 'After she had really gone I felt very sad and yet I know it is the only way for her to realise she is really grown up. We have all treated her like a little girl.'[33]

Although Adela had sailed from England in February 1914 with a heavy heart, emigration turned out to be the making of her. She loved looking after the children on the ship, the *Geelong*, and arrived in Australia with a greater sense of optimism than she had felt for years. She soon had a paid post with the Women's Political Association, and within months her opposition to the war in Europe had given her a new campaign to fling herself into – something she did with her usual gusto. Now that she had finally broken free of the straitjacket imposed on her by her mother and eldest sister, there was little they could do to hurt her. Emmeline wrote to Sylvia, who was also campaigning against the war: 'I am ashamed to know where you and Adela stand.'[34] Even this had little or no effect. In Australia Adela became the celebrity she had never been in Britain, and the role suited her. Soon she was a household name. Antipodean visitors to London told Sylvia her sister was 'the most popular woman in Australia'.[35]

It was Adela's finest hour. And to cap things off, in 1917 she met and married Tom Walsh, an organiser for the seamen's union and a widower with three children. Adela, who loved children, was in her element. Later that year she wrote to Sylvia: 'This is the life, isn't it, and I am happy – more than happy – to carry on our father's work.'[36] An acquaintance at the time, Edgar Ross, said Adela even adopted the suffragette methods such as window-smashing in her anti-conscription struggle: 'What I remember most about her was her courage. She would stand, unfearing, in front of jingo-mad soldiers heckling her when speaking on the platform.'[37] Ross also recalled that many of the young men in the socialist movement in Melbourne at the time had their eyes on Adela, 'but she was sort of "above" them, too remote to contemplate for a lover'. Her married life had a rocky start, for six days after her wedding she was sentenced to four months' imprisonment for a series of public order offences including window-smashing and a torchlit procession against conscription.

The following year Adela and Tom resigned from the Victorian Socialist Party, of which Adela had become organiser. Arguably, they had now reached their most left-wing point and would spend the rest of their lives drifting to the right. In 1921 they joined the executive committee of the newly formed Australian Communist Party, but within a couple of years the Walshes views were changing.[38] Adela took part in a public debate with a communist speaker in which she made 'splenetic, hostile remarks on the party and the Communist movement generally'. In 1929 she founded the Australian Women's Guild of Empire, a branch of an organisation set up in London after the 1926 general strike by Adela's former suffragette colleague Flora Drummond.

Adela always made a rather unconvincing right-winger. She saw herself as a champion of the poor, even though her new organisation condemned working mothers, abortion, contraception, communism and trade unions. When she made a tour of the Australian coalfields to attack the unions during a lock-out, she talked mostly about how the children of the miners were suffering. She used her guild to start a welfare agency for families struggling in industrial areas. And she still lived by the suffragette slogan, 'Deeds not Words'. Arriving at the scene of a strike by unemployed workers on government work programmes, she was taunted by a communist leader who shouted: 'You wouldn't do this sort of work yourself.' Adela and her secretary, Enid Metcalfe, put on rubber boots, took up spades and started digging. On another occasion a group of striking seamen threw a bucket of water over her. Adela, unmoved, simply joked that as a sailor's wife she could hardly be expected to be afraid of water.

It was a rumbustious, active and full life. In addition to her three step-daughters Adela had five children of her own – named Richard after her father, Sylvia after her sister, Christian, Ursula, and finally Faith Hope, who died soon after birth. Ursula remembered her mother as a small, fair woman with a brisk common-sense manner that belied a legendary absent-mindedness. One of her chief recollections was of Adela, dressed in a suit ready for some political meeting, giving a last poke to a copper full of washing: 'While discoursing strongly on some issue she would often be seen trying to take her apron off over a large brimmed hat. She cared little about food, her favourite fare being a slice of bread and butter and a cup of tea. We children never felt neglected and felt nothing for her but love, respect and a strange desire to protect her.'[39]

While her political life remained fiery to the end, Adela made her peace with many of her fellow campaigners in the suffragette struggle, chief among these being her mother. A few weeks before her death in 1928, Emmeline wrote to her daughter expressing her regret for the long rift between them. Adela had already re-established contact with Flora Drummond but now she found herself at the centre of a network of ex-militants. Dora Montefiore and Nellie Martel visited her in Australia, and both Helen Archdale and Helen Fraser (later Helen Moyes), looked her up after following her example and emigrating. Her personal life was largely happy and fulfilled, but as the years went by her ideas left her increasingly isolated in the wider world. In the 1920s Adela and Tom had made enemies of their former communist colleagues as they grew increasingly critical of the Soviet Union. In the 1930s they began to develop new sympathies which would separate them even from their most conservative associates.

During the First World War Adela had always refused to believe the outlandish stories that circulated about German atrocities, and some echo of this stance stayed with her. She could never really accept that Fascism was as bad as people said it was. If Hitler hated communism he could not be all bad, she reasoned. And neither could his allies closer to her adopted home – the Japanese, to whose representatives in Australia she became increasingly close. Her friends in the Guild of Empire disliked this new affiliation, and soon after the Second World War broke out she was asked to resign from her paid post with the organisation. The following month Adela and Tom set off on a goodwill mission to Japan. They returned with the message that Australia had no future if it did not ally itself with such a major Asian market. This was not well received.

The Second World War was a wretched time for the Walshes. Tom became ill with cancer and the family lived mainly on the barely adequate secretarial wages of their daughters Sylvia and Christian, and on a military allotment from their son Dick. For a brief spell Adela was a paid organiser with a new Australian national party, Australia First, but conflicts with colleagues forced her to resign after a couple of months. In March 1942 she was interned for her pro-Japanese views after a series of police raids on her home. True to her suffragette credentials she went on hunger strike. The doctors, like their forebears in Scotland thirty years earlier, refused to force feed her and she was released after more than a year in custody, just before Tom's death in April 1943.

Although Adela lived until 1961 she took little part in active politics after the war. In 1949 she wrote to Helen Fraser Moyes that she believed she had paid for seeing the perils of communism too early: 'So long did I warn my supporters that co-operation with Russia and all those who supported the Bolsheviks was the way to disaster and I was ruined and interned for my pains. I do not get much satisfaction in saying "I told you so."'[40] She clung, too, to her belief that Hitler was not as bad as he had been painted. 'Communism has not brought home the bacon ... Taken on achievement, Fascism did very much better while it lasted. Officially we don't admit this but actually I believe most people who are interested know it perfectly well,' she told her friend in a later letter.[41]

As she grew older Adela viewed the suffragette campaign with a sort of incredulity, and gave credit to the constitutional suffragists headed by Millicent Fawcett for the winning of the vote. Christabel and Emmeline had thrown their backs into the war effort in 1914 without first demanding assurances that they would be rewarded later, she pointed out.[42] The postwar government needed to give votes to women because the fighting had left men disillusioned with politics and it needed at least one group of enthusiastic citizens, she believed. But Adela's strongest feeling about the suffrage movement, according to her daughter Ursula, was a surprising one coming from someone who had been involved in militant insurrection so many times in the course of struggles so many and diverse. It might almost have served as an epitaph on her gravestone: 'Looking back over the years she could hardly credit that such a violent struggle should have been necessary.'[43]

Whatever her political foibles Adela remained a big-hearted character, in some ways more like her mother than any of her siblings. Sylvia stuck with her emotional attachment to socialism, Christabel was sphinx-like and calculating, but Adela had the fire and passion with which Emmeline had been able to fling herself at life. Adela rated as her own greatest gift the ability to 'talk to the crowd and keep it up until the cows came home', but she underrated herself. To the suffrage movement she also brought enthusiasm and hard work. To her later campaigns she brought qualities of leadership that, though sometimes misused, were indisputable. Adela Pankhurst was sucked into politics through the predilections of her family. In other circumstances, she might easily have made a success of her life in quite a different field.

James Keir Hardie.

VI

Keir Hardie – Westminster Friend

> I thought the days of my pioneering were over but of late I have felt, with increasing intensity, the injustice inflicted on women by our present laws. The Party is largely my own child and I cannot part from it lightly, or without pain; but at the same time I cannot sever myself from the principles I hold. If it is necessary for me to separate myself from what has been my life's work, I do so in order to remove the stigma resting upon our wives, mothers and sisters of being accounted unfit for citizenship.
>
> *Keir Hardie threatens to resign from the Labour Party over women's suffrage*
> *at its 1907 conference*

The name of Keir Hardie has long been one to be conjured with. Even in the twenty-first century the myth of the Labour Party's founder is still writ large in the collective imagination. In the five years after the party's 1997 return to power, Hardie's image was summoned up in the House of Commons chamber no fewer than 100 times. The phrase, 'if Keir Hardie were alive today', once the anguished howl of traditionalists opposing some change in policy, later became a mantra for modernisers. At the Labour Party's centenary celebration in February 2000 Tony Blair mentioned Hardie's name four times in his speech.

Even in life Hardie was a huge figure. His friend, lover and greatest fan, Sylvia Pankhurst, said that in his darkest hour he 'seemed to loom over us like some great, tragic ruin'.[1] And indeed, his life genuinely encompassed many of the elements necessary for the making of a socialist folk hero. Born in 1856, the illegitimate son of a farm labourer and a miner, in his early days Hardie experienced all the hunger, abuse and ill-treatment at the hands of the bosses that any hagiographer could wish for.

But what of women? What was it in his background, his nature, that made him a champion not just of votes for women but of the rather narrow line peddled by the Women's Social and Political Union? For although the suffrage issue remained just one of a clutch of policies close to Hardie's heart, it was one to which he clung with particular ferocity. One, indeed, for which he was even prepared to compromise his socialist ideals. Throughout the years of the suffragette campaign, Hardie was one of a very few key figures in the Labour movement who stuck by the militants. He did so even when he was vilified by the WSPU for his connection with a party less than committed to the women's cause. There must have been more in this than pure ideological zeal. What were the personal, the psychological reasons for Hardie's attachment to this cause?

James Keir Hardie was a man who liked strong women. He was the first son of an impoverished but ambitious mother, Mary Kerr or Keir, who believed she was born to better things. Her mother's family had been minor landowners fallen on hard times, and despite her often desperate circumstances she worked hard to ensure her son got at least a basic education. In his early childhood Hardie, who never knew his father, was looked after by his grandmother while his mother worked, and enjoyed the unmitigated adoration of both women. As one biographer put it, 'if Freud be correct that the man who is his mother's favourite conquers the world, Hardie started with a stunning lead in the great oedipal drama'.[2]

When little Jamie – as he was called – was three years old, things seemed to look up. His mother met and married a ship's carpenter named David Hardie and soon afterwards the family moved a short distance to Glasgow where he found work in the shipyards. A year or so after the wedding a brother, named David after his father, was born. But times were hard and there was often not enough money to feed the growing family. At the age of eight, Hardie was sent out to work as a messenger boy. From then on he had a variety of different jobs: heating rivets in a shipyard, helping out in a printer's office and later working as a delivery boy for a baker. It was then that things went from bad to worse. David Hardie was out of work and his son's meagre wages were all that kept the family from starvation. Then Hardie was sacked one New Year's Eve for arriving at work late. His youngest brother, Duncan, was dying and his mother was about to give birth to a fourth child. David Hardie was forced to go to sea to earn a living and Mary returned with her sons to a mining village near her former home.

And so, aged ten, James Keir Hardie went to work in the pit, his home life again dominated by his mother and grandmother. At home and during breaks in his twelve-hour underground day he continued his education. And through both home and work, he was drawn inexorably into politics – through his mother into the temperance movement, and through his work into the miners' union, which appointed him a full-time official at the age of twenty-three. By then he had been sacked from the pit for his political activities, and he never again held a working-class job.

At about this time Hardie met and married Lillie Wilson, a fellow temperance campaigner and also the daughter of a publican. He enjoyed the company of women, and Lillie was not the first girl to catch his eye. The marriage was not always a source of joy to either party, though. For Hardie, politics always came first. The day after his wedding he attended a political rally and set the pattern for the rest of his married life. While he travelled the globe in pursuit of his causes, Lillie was left at home, struggling to bring up a growing family. Although his home in Cumnock in Ayrshire, built with a gift from a wealthy philanthropist, would continue to be important to him, it would also be associated in his mind with duty and worry, particularly financial worry. Lillie did not play an active part in his political life; apart from an annual trip to the Labour conference and the odd run-out at election times, she remained largely hidden from public view. Increasingly, Hardie turned elsewhere for relaxation and respite.

It was through his union activities that Hardie first came into contact with the Pankhursts, a family who were to feature large in his political and personal existence. In 1888 he travelled to London to attend a week-long International Workers Congress, and it was there that he met Richard and Emmeline. The couple's radical views attracted Hardie, but there may also have been a more immediate personal bond. A year earlier the Hardies had lost a daughter, Sarah, to scarlet fever, and even more recently the Pankhursts' young son Frank had died of diphtheria. But it was politics that was to forge a lasting friendship between them, and in particular Richard's passion for women's suffrage. The Pankhursts and their associates opened Hardie's eyes to the possibility that women might not just vote, but might become as deeply involved in politics as men. Up until that time Hardie's political landscape had been almost entirely populated by men, but now he met a host of political women: Annie Besant, the social reformer who championed the cause of the match girls during their famous strike, Eleanor Marx, daughter of Karl, and most important of all, Emmeline Pankhurst herself.

It was not long before Hardie was mentioning votes for women in his speeches – particularly after he was elected to Parliament as MP for West Ham in 1892. But during the 1890s the suffrage campaign was in the doldrums, and other issues cemented Hardie's relationship with the Pankhursts. He supported Emmeline during her struggle over the ban on public meetings at Boggart Hole Clough in Manchester, and was summonsed for his trouble. While he badgered ministers at Westminster over locked-out shoe workers in Leicester, the Pankhursts were on the streets there pleading the same cause. When Hardie, ousted from his West Ham seat in 1895, stood unsuccessfully at a by-election in Bradford, Emmeline rode over with her pony and trap to campaign for him. As Sylvia put it: 'Like the bit and brace, Keir Hardie and the Pankhursts seemed wrought to work in unison.'[3] Richard and Emmeline were early recruits to the Independent Labour Party, formed in Bradford under Hardie's inspiration in January 1893. The party would join with trade unions and other left-wing groups in 1900 to form the Labour Representation Committee, later renamed the Labour Party.

Hardie had become something of a hero in the Pankhurst household, and not just with the adults. The arrival of the *Labour Leader*, which he edited, was eagerly awaited each week, not least because Hardie wrote a column called 'Daddy Time' for its younger readers. Sylvia recalled her first sighting of the great man, sitting in the library at her parents' house, with something approaching awe: 'Kneeling on the stairs to watch him, I felt that I could have rushed into his arms; indeed it was not long before the children in the houses where he stayed had climbed to his knees. He had at once the appearance of great age and vigorous youth.'[4]

Although Hardie was not yet forty at this time he was already going grey. Indeed, a colleague had recently referred to him in passing as 'Old Hardie'. Hardie, despite a lifelong capacity for fun and even flirtation, seems to have been regarded as an old man for most of his adult life. He was never tall, though his years in the pit had strengthened him and his stature was upright. His dress was often considered eccentric. When he entered Parliament for the first time he wore a deerstalker and checked trousers with a red scarf – an outfit which excited much attention for its radical departure from the politicians' uniform of frock coat, silk top hat and winged collar.

Hardie's status as an almost God-like figure in the Pankhurst household was threatened in the early days of the WSPU. In her fury at the banning of women from the new Pankhurst Memorial Hall, Emmeline even withdrew her regular contribution to the Keir Hardie wages fund – MPs did not receive salaries and Hardie lacked the private means on which most lived. And while Hardie remained silent on the suffrage question for several months after the foundation of the union, his Labour colleagues did much to stir the women's discontent. Philip Snowden, the Independent Labour Party's national chairman, declared that women's suffrage could only help the Conservatives. John Bruce Glasier, who had taken over from Hardie as editor of the *Labour Leader* in 1903, recorded in his diary after a meeting with Christabel and Emmeline that he had derided with scorn 'their miserable individualist sexism' and that he had told them the ILP would not lift a finger to help them. 'C paints her eyebrows grossly and looks selfish, lazy and wilful. They want to be ladies and lack the humility of real heroinism,' he added.[5] The Marxist Henry Hyndman suggested that women who wanted the vote should be exiled to a desert island.

None of this did anything to reassure the Pankhursts of Hardie's continuing friendship and support. So it must have been with some trepidation that he made his next trip to Manchester. The meeting was a tense one, but it seems Hardie handled the situation with equanimity. And where his colleagues had had little positive to say about the new organisation, he seemed unable to deny its members anything, according to Sylvia: 'Votes for women? Of course! The party must be brought into line and a big campaign set on foot. A separate women's organisation? Excellent! A simple one-clause measure to give votes on the same terms as men? Certainly.'[6] Hardie even agreed to get the Independent Labour Party to publish a pamphlet by Christabel, and asked branches of the party to find out what proportion of women voters in their area would be likely to be working class – information needed to counter the argument that the WSPU aimed to enfranchise only middle-class women.

A question mark hovers over why the socialist Hardie, by now back in Parliament as MP for Merthyr, gave his unqualified support to such an organisation. The WSPU wanted votes for women on the same terms as men, and specifically *not* votes for all women. Even after the three great franchise reform acts of 1832, 1867 and 1884, just a third of all men had the vote in parliamentary elections.[7] The WSPU was avowedly a feminist organisation. Its demand went much further than a straightforward plea for enfranchisement, it was a demand for sexual equality. Was Hardie forward-thinking enough to attach himself to such a radical idea? On a theoretical level, he was. He argued it was valid to separate out the votes for women campaign from the struggle for full adult suffrage because it pushed the issue of gender to the fore. He also believed it was a good tactical move because it would be more easily achievable. But at heart, Hardie remained a traditionalist with his feet firmly planted in Marxist clay. If he had not had a close relationship with the Pankhursts, it is hard to believe he would have supported them in the way he did.

A gap of several months had elapsed between the birth of the WSPU and Hardie's visit to Manchester. In September 1903, after an August holiday with Lillie in Ireland, he had confessed to Bruce Glasier that all was not well with him. Hardie's troubles tended to follow a pattern: debt, family rows, ill-health, convalescence and then travel. This time Hardie's son Jamie, now living in Glasgow, had kicked off the chain of events. He had, Hardie discovered, run up substantial gambling bills. The sum amounted to around £45 – Lillie's annual household budget – and Hardie felt obliged to pay it despite his wife's strong objections. A month later he was discovered in a state of collapse on a train in London's Euston station. Many of his acquaintances diagnosed exhaustion or nervous collapse, but the doctors said Hardie was suffering from appendicitis. After an operation he was sent to Falmouth to recuperate, thanks to generous donations from party members. In February 1904 he ventured further afield, to Italy, where he spent a relaxing spring on the Riviera. But, he wrote to his secretary, Maggie Symons, Lillie was – not surprisingly – still 'out of sorts'.[8] So he returned home to face the wrath of the women.

Lillie was used to her husband's prolonged absences, though, and before long Hardie had settled back in his London home at Nevill's Court, just off Fleet Street. Here, as much as anywhere, he could relax and be himself. His quarters were small but not unpleasant, despite the piles of paperwork that tended to mount up. A cleaner came in once a week but Hardie did most of his own cooking and housework, such as they were. He had hung pictures of his heroes on the wall – Robert Owen, William Morris, Robert Burns – and on the mantelpiece was a little iron figure of Dr Johnson. There were fossils collected during his time in the pit, and a Union Jack captured from violent protesters who stormed one of his pacifist meetings during the Boer War. He worked by candlelight and usually had a coal fire burning in the grate. Apart from the bannocks and scones Lillie sent down from Scotland he lived mainly on bread and tea, scattering the leaves on cold water in a pan then taking it off as it came to the boil. There were leeks, too, grown alongside his favourite ox-eye daisies in the tiny garden. Hardie enjoyed eating out and often took acquaintances to the nearby Food Reform Restaurant. Once he even took a young admirer to dine at the Savoy. Later in life he became a vegetarian.

In the autumn of 1904 a new arrival gave Hardie a perfect opportunity to take a break. Sylvia Pankhurst, who had won a scholarship to the Royal College of Art, needed a chaperone. Sometimes alone and sometimes with her brother Harry, who was at school in London, she would visit on a Sunday afternoon. They would take tea at a Lyons Corner House or even have a day out in the country. Hardie, who enjoyed flirtatious relationships with a number of young women throughout his life, found Sylvia rather dour and earnest. While he would become playful, throwing stones in the air and catching them, she would look on bemused.[9] Her upbringing had been too serious, he told her. She should have had more opportunities for play. But sometimes Sylvia found Hardie strikingly unworldly. Once when she ordered coffee in a restaurant he told her he was as astonished as if she had called for a cigar – he had never tasted the drink himself. On another occasion she shocked the teetotal Hardie first by fainting in public and then by telling him he should have revived her by giving her a teaspoon of brandy.

When the WSPU sent Annie Kenney to 'rouse London', Hardie was happy to help by recruiting an audience of East End women to pack the union's first big London meeting in Caxton Hall. He also helped Sylvia and Annie Kenney get tickets for a Liberal meeting at the Royal Albert Hall, in the full knowledge that they planned to stage a noisy protest. Sylvia even credited Hardie with inspiring the suffragettes to their first acts of militancy. When a group of unemployed men were arrested for causing a disturbance in Manchester in the summer of 1905, Hardie applauded them. He told Sylvia they were 'poltroons' for agreeing to apologise to avoid imprisonment. The women noted, she said, that the government backed down soon afterwards and implemented reforms to ease their plight: 'It was only a question now as to how militant tactics would begin.'[10] There was support in the other direction, too. Sylvia spent many hours making big coloured posters to back the Unemployed Workmen's Bill: 'Workless and Hungry. Vote for the Bill'. During the general election of 1906, Emmeline campaigned in Merthyr, while the MP went on a grand tour around the country. Annie Kenney stayed on at Merthyr afterwards to work with women in the constituency.

Soon after the election Emmeline came to London to claim her reward for her part in his re-election – a place in Labour's list of favoured Private Member's Bills. But it was not to be. There was a stormy meeting, Hardie uncomfortable, grim-faced and silent, Emmeline voluble and angry. In fact there was little he could do – his hands had been tied by his parliamentary colleagues. Hardie promised that if he won a place in the ballot he would bring a bill for women's suffrage himself – something he could not do without resigning his new position as leader of his thirty-strong parliamentary party. When he failed to win a place he proposed instead to move a resolution that women should be given the vote – a procedural measure which would have no legal effect even if passed.

There was more trouble to come. Hardie had no problem with militancy at a distance, but he drew the line when it affected him personally. He was furious when Emmeline and a dozen of her suffragettes created a disturbance in the public gallery of the Commons as his suffrage resolution was debated. As she was dragged out, Sylvia saw Hardie turn angrily and stride from the chamber. But despite his fury he would not criticise the women in public. He even defended them on the grounds that the police were waiting for any excuse to throw them out.

Sylvia's reaction was telling. 'I knew … we had angered this generous friend,' she wrote. 'Hardie remained silent for a few days – they were an age to me.'[11] The young student, now aged twenty-four, had fallen for the fifty-year-old politician in a manner which went far beyond mere admiration or friendship. As the relationship developed, the complexity of these feelings became clearer. Sylvia saw Hardie as part political hero, part father-figure and part potential lover. Gradually he began to return her feelings. In the summer of 1906, when Sylvia was forced to leave the Royal College of Art because her grant had been withdrawn, Hardie helped her move into cheaper lodgings, soothed her furrowed brow and took her out for a cheering meal. From then on Sylvia often visited him at the House of Commons and the two walked together in St James's Park or spent the evening at Nevill's Court. Quite how they dealt with the fact that he was already married is not entirely clear. Sylvia later described his relationship with Lillie as 'tragic',[12] probably reflecting Hardie's own account. Nor was Sylvia the first woman with whom Hardie had had extramarital relations: in 1893 he had a brief but intense flirtation with Annie Hines, the daughter of a party worker in Oxfordshire.

Hardie seems to have possessed the ability to separate the different parts of his life and somehow not to recognise the potential conflicts they created. He described his views on marriage as 'conservative', and wrote in 1906 that he had 'kept to the straight path of duty' and had 'never yielded to the temptation to try the … easier way without having cause to rue it'.[13] This was no radical advocate of free love or the bohemian lifestyle. He remained rooted firmly in the nonconformist, teetotal soil from which both he and the early labour movement had sprung. In 1907 he wrote a pamphlet, 'From Serfdom to Socialism', in which he spelled out his romantic notion of the ideal woman: 'Oh, the pathos of those bright, clean, bien, couthie cottage homes, with the thrifty mother never idle, and never fussed … patching, darning, knitting.' He went on to write admiringly of the 'old fashioned woman' who was willing to bear eight or ten children, and said capitalism had much to answer for in replacing such females with modern ones who thought it a disgrace to have more than two or three children. His basic analysis was a Marxist one – at best the vote would be but a means to an end. Until both men and women had socialism, neither sex would be free.

Hardie was a traditionalist in his heart, but in his head he was a political pragmatist. In Parliament he continued to support the suffragettes, hoping for a continuation of their loyalty and backing for him personally if not for the Labour Party. When Sylvia was sent to prison he protested in Parliament that she had been convicted on the uncorroborated testimony of a single policeman. He wanted to know why Annie Kenney had been imprisoned by a magistrate who served as chief steward at the demonstration where she was arrested, and why Teresa Billington-Greig was arrested, convicted and imprisoned within a single day. Philip Snowden complained that Hardie's leadership of the party was 'a hopeless failure. Hardie never speaks to me. He seems completely absorbed with the Suffragettes.'[14]

Other colleagues, too, judged Hardie's performance as party leader harshly, and he did not enjoy the work. The Labour Party was always a broad church, bringing together disparate groups from the Liberal to the Marxist, and Hardie struggled to manage the inevitable divisions within it. At Labour's 1907 conference in Belfast, the suffrage question brought these tensions, and the question of Hardie's position, to a head. Much of the party wanted to keep to its belief that votes for women should mean votes for all – universal suffrage. Despite Hardie's pleadings, the conference voted for such a measure rather than supporting the WSPU's more narrowly focused aims. Fearing that the decision would force him to vote against a narrow women's bill in Parliament, Hardie used his closing speech to the conference to drop a bombshell. He threatened to resign from the party if its resolution was used to limit his support for the WSPU.

Back in Westminster the parliamentary party met to discuss the crisis, and in the end a compromise was struck. A free vote would be allowed should the issue be put to a division in the Commons. But the controversy did not abate. In the *Labour Record*, Fred Pethick-Lawrence wrote that the conference decision meant 'the final severance of the women's movement from the labour movement'. Within a few months, all the leading figures in the WSPU had withdrawn from the Independent Labour Party. Hardie's stance had not won him friends within the union, which later accused him of backsliding, and that spring he felt friendless and depressed. As usual when under stress he became ill, and after several weeks at St Thomas's nursing home in London he returned to Scotland to recuperate. So dire was his condition that Sylvia believed he was dying and called her mother down from Manchester to see him off at Euston. By July, though, he had recovered enough to set off from Liverpool on a tour of the Empire. Local socialists sang 'The Red Flag' at the docks as his ship sailed. Hardie stayed away for eight months, visiting Canada, Japan, Malaysia, India and South Africa, possibly funded by a wealthy philanthropist named Joseph Fels.

He sent almost daily postcards home, many addressed to his son Duncan and daughter Nan. In January 1908 he sent Lillie a card from New Zealand: 'Were we 20 years younger I would ask you to come out here. Everyone is well off. The climate too is delightful. Jamie.'[15] Hardie could never have given up British politics, but it is interesting to note that his disillusionment had grown deep enough for him to reflect on the possibility.

Hardie arrived home refreshed to find Lillie ailing. She had had a lot to try her during his absence, he wrote to Bruce Glasier, and 'her nerves have given way under the strain'.[16] Within a few months Hardie was off abroad again – this time to America, with Lillie and Nan in tow. This was just a short trip, though, and he was back in the Commons in October 1908, raising questions about the treatment meted out to suffragette prisoners.

As the suffrage struggle intensified, so did Hardie's emotional engagement with it. In September 1909, when the news came that Mary Leigh and Charlotte Marsh had been force fed in Winson Green prison, he became increasingly concerned, not least because Sylvia felt she should return and go to jail herself to support them. That summer he had suggested she rent a cottage in Penshurst, Kent, and had visited her there as often as his schedule permitted. During one of these interludes he begged her not to go back to prison. The thought of the feeding tubes and the violence with which they were used was already making him ill – how much worse would it be if it were her? In Parliament Hardie protested that the action was 'a horrible, beastly outrage'. Some MPs laughed. Shocked by their response, he wrote to the press:

> That there is difference of opinion concerning the tactics of the militant Suffragettes goes without saying, but surely there can be no two opinions concerning the horrible brutality of these proceedings? Women, worn and weak by hunger, are seized upon, held down by brute force, gagged, a tube inserted down their throats and food poured or pumped into the stomach. Let British men think over the spectacle.[17]

Despite the reactions of his colleagues, he continued questioning the government on the subject almost daily.

Hardie received a rare plaudit from the suffragettes for his efforts over force feeding: *Votes for Women* carried a leading article by Christabel in which she wrote: 'Mr Keir Hardie's magnificent protest in the House of Commons against force feeding will be remembered when much that occurred in the late Parliament has been forgotten.'[18] There was little time for him to bask in this praise, though, for a general election was called in January 1910. In Merthyr an Anti-Socialist Union was set up to campaign against Hardie, and claims were made that he was a rich man with a castle in Scotland. In response Hardie published his annual income: a total of £210, £120 of which was spent on political work and lodgings in London; £90 for Lillie and the children. Hardie had his own press to counter such allegations – having relinquished the editorship of the *Labour Leader* he had started a paper called the *Merthyr Pioneer*. Among those who bought shares in the venture were a local party supporter called Ted Davies and his wife, Rose, with whom Hardie had a warm and flirtatious friendship. She visited him often in London, and once he suggested to her that they might take a trip together with some friends, 'a merry party of four: discreetly and judiciously paired, crossing the mountain in delicious darkness'.[19] It seemed Hardie craved such dalliances: now that his relationship with Sylvia had matured it probably offered fewer opportunities for such light-hearted banter. There was no sign of their closeness abating, though. 'I am in splendid condition and thoroughly enjoying the work,' he wrote to

Sylvia from Copenhagen during a foreign trip that year, signing the note 'with affection and bundles of kisses'.[20]

With militancy suspended, Sylvia turned her attention to helping Hardie lobby for a new National Health and Unemployment Insurance Bill which would provide a safety net for the sick and the workless. The suffragettes opposed this bill on the grounds that any legislation on domestic matters should wait until women could participate fully in the debate. Hardie included some of Sylvia's suggested amendments to the bill with his own. Others received less favourable responses. A request from the Female Mission to the Fallen that 'in the interests of morality' maternity benefit should not be given to the mothers of illegitimate babies drew a curt note from Hardie to his secretary: 'Can't some reply be sent to these pious prigs?'[21]

Such interludes could be only temporary diversions from the business of the suffrage struggle, which was about to come to the fore again. In November 1911 the WSPU lost patience with the government over the non-appearance of its long-awaited Conciliation Bill. Hardie was pictured in the *Daily Sketch* looking on as 220 women were arrested at the opening of Parliament: 'Labour Leader watching the women rioters', the caption read.[22] The government's announcement that it intended to introduce manhood suffrage – seen as the final act of betrayal by the suffragettes – eased Hardie's often tense relations with Christabel. Now she began declaring that if all men were to have the vote all women should have it too, and in January 1912 she even appeared at a public meeting with Hardie to demand adult suffrage. Nor apparently was Hardie deterred when militancy took a new departure with stone-throwing raids in March 1912. Three days after the first incident Hardie protested in Parliament that visiting rights had been withdrawn from Suffragette prisoners in Holloway. The Home Secretary, Reginald McKenna, replied that the women were being punished because they had rioted in support of the stone-throwers.

With Christabel in Paris and her mother and the Pethick-Lawrences in prison, Sylvia had a freer rein than she had been given for some time. She busied herself organising what was to be the suffragettes' last big Hyde Park rally, with a theme recalling the radical movements of the early nineteenth century. Women dressed in white and held up poles with scarlet caps of liberty on top, and Hardie wore a white suit and red plaid tie, specially chosen to fit in. There were twenty platforms, and he spoke for both the ILP and the Fabians.

It would not be long before Hardie again upset Christabel. With the government's electoral reform bill making its way through Parliament without any promise of votes for women, he made a rare departure from the WSPU line. The union now wanted MPs to vote against all government bills until women had the vote, but this would mean opposing Home Rule for Ireland and several other much needed measures. Hardie refused. From her sanctuary in Paris, Christabel declared war. It was 'preposterous and insulting' that Labour should put Ireland before votes for women. 'A women's war upon the Parliamentary Labour Party is inevitable, a war which could have been averted if the Labour Party had agreed to use their power to compel the introduction of a government measure giving votes to women,' she wrote in *The Suffragette*.[23] A month later the paper launched a personal attack on Hardie, claiming he had sacrificed his principles for the sake of party unity.

Even while the women vilified him, Hardie continued asking Parliamentary Questions on their behalf. The very issue of *The Suffragette* that carried the attack also reported that he had raised the case of Gladys Evans, a WSPU activist released from prison in Dublin after trying to set fire to the Theatre Royal and then repeatedly rearrested for failing to report to the authorities. At the beginning of December Hardie was heckled at a meeting in Wales by suffragettes wanting to know why Labour was not opposing the government with sufficient vigour. A week later, the same thing happened again in York. Now he became rattled, according to the paper: 'Mr Hardie turned to two of his women questioners and shouted angrily, "I will have you turned out!"' He accused the women of attacking their friends, *The Suffragette* said, adding that, when one of the hecklers pointed out not all Labour MPs were friends of the suffragettes, he replied: 'Just like a woman!'[24] There was even worse to come. In February 1913 *The Suffragette* ran a front-page cartoon bearing a picture of Hardie with a fat cigar, pushing aside a woman in his eagerness to have a friendly chat with the Prime Minister. Underneath was the comment: 'The Labour MPs have betrayed the cause of working women … They cannot be friends of the Government and friends of women too.' By now, Hardie was being heckled regularly at meetings: in Newcastle and in Edinburgh in February, Leeds in March. Other Labour MPs were suffering the same fate. But when the government introduced its Cat and Mouse Act in March, Hardie protested vigorously. Just six of his Labour colleagues joined him in the 'No' lobby, while fourteen of them voted for the bill. For a while, the heckling stopped.

Hardie's forbearance in the face of the WSPU's hostility seems to have been almost saintly. But he had one very good reason to keep haranguing the government on behalf of the women: Sylvia. She had abandoned her promise to Hardie to stay out of prison and was arrested three times in the spring of 1913. On the first two occasions her efforts were thwarted when her fines were paid and she was released – the first time she blamed WSPU officials, the second time her mother. Finally, in February, she managed to get a two-month sentence and went on hunger strike. She was force fed, then released on Good Friday in a terrible state. Her eyes blood red, almost unable to walk, she was taken to a WSPU nursing home where Hardie found her a few hours later. He had hardly slept during her imprisonment and she blamed herself for the pain she had caused him, 'his face haggard and seamed with sorrow and insomnia, his hair long and unkempt.'[25] Even this could not deter her, though. Back in prison again in July, she refused food, drink and sleep. Now she was placed under the Cat and Mouse Act, repeatedly released and then rearrested. With the nation in uproar and arson attacks escalating around the country, Sylvia was determined to do her bit. And this, finally, caused Hardie's patience to snap.

During one of her releases from prison, Sylvia had been invited to speak at a meeting of the Free Speech Defence Committee, set up to protest against bans on militant suffrage demonstrations. Frank Smith, Hardie's closest aide, asked Sylvia to promise she would not create trouble at the meeting. She refused. When Hardie visited her next, she accused him of 'dragging the party's banner in the mud' by becoming too close to the Liberals. Although Hardie did not respond, Sylvia said the meeting became 'almost a quarrel'.[26] She told Hardie not to visit her again, and indeed she did not see him again until the following year. 'I had told him it was too painful, too incongruous he should come in the midst of the warfare waged against him and the Labour Party by the orders of my sister,' she wrote later.[27] On the day after this meeting, Emmeline visited Sylvia. She had planned to come the day before, she said, but had changed her mind when she learned Hardie was there. 'She spoke as if he were a person a Suffragette should be ashamed to meet,' Sylvia remarked.[28]

It was, in effect, the end of Hardie's relationship with Sylvia, though the two continued to write to each other. In the summer of that year, when Sylvia left England to tour Scandinavia, he sent her off with a list of contacts and an affectionate farewell. Confessing that he had been thinking of her and hoping she was better, he concluded: 'Go then ... and come back strong to me after.'[29]

Again, the strain was taking its toll on Hardie. As had happened ten years earlier, a colleague found him slumped in his seat on a train at Euston. It was feared he had had a stroke, but he recovered relatively quickly and was able to attend an ILP summer school in Keswick only a few days later. None of this stopped Hardie from touring the country making speeches. Nor, surprisingly, did it stop him from agitating on behalf of the suffragettes.

In February 1914 a short notice appeared in *The Suffragette*, under the heading: 'One Policy, One Programme, One Command'. It noted that Sylvia's East London Federation of Suffragettes was 'a distinct organisation independent of the WSPU' and added that this was merely a restatement of a situation which had existed for some time: 'Viz, that Miss Sylvia Pankhurst prefers to work on her own account and independently.' Sylvia had been thrown out of the union. Hardie had just questioned the Home Secretary about hunger strikers, of whom she was one. Not long afterwards, he asked about the rearrest of Emmeline in Glasgow. As the war between Christabel and the Labour Party continued, Hardie's support was unabated. At the ILP conference that year, a party rally had to be stopped while a crowbar was fetched to separate a suffragette from the seat to which she had chained herself. When Ramsay MacDonald got up, bags of flour were thrown and the fire alarm went off. Hardie, who was in the chair, remarked mildly that he could better endure such behaviour from women than from men.

Just before this conference Hardie had re-established contact with Sylvia, who had been almost continually either in prison or evading rearrest – apart from a short spell abroad – during almost all of the previous year. In June 1914, in a state of collapse after repeated hunger strikes, she asked her supporters to carry her to the House of Commons. Hardie was there to meet her, and while she lay prostrate under Cromwell's statue he went to find Asquith and persuaded him to agree to a meeting with a group of her supporters. Again, Hardie began raising questions related to Sylvia's concerns in Parliament. Just a few days after her trip to Parliament he rose to defend one of her East End friends, Melvina Walker, who had proclaimed apropos of the suffragettes' arson campaign that if there had been mansions to burn in the East End 'they would have been hot long ago'.

Sylvia even managed to engineer a weekend in the country with Hardie that summer, though it was but a sad echo of their previous breaks together. Accompanied by her friend Norah Smyth, she arranged to meet Hardie at Penshurst in Kent, where she had spent such a happy time in 1909. The meeting was constructive, and as a result Hardie agreed to press his party colleagues to include a call for both manhood and woman-hood suffrage in their next election manifesto. But other events were about to intervene. The prospect of war was looming, and the harrowing thought of it threatened to bring Hardie down completely. And if the treatment meted out to him by the suffragettes seemed cruel, it would be as nothing to what he would now have to endure from his own colleagues.

As war broke out, Hardie rose in the House of Commons to speak of the hardships that were bound to follow for the poorest people. As he did so, pro-war Labour MPs began to sing the national anthem. Even in Merthyr, where Hardie was less a hero than a God-figure, jingoists broke up a meeting he had called to condemn the declaration of war. Relief committees set up to counteract the worst effects of the war in the area declined his offers of help. One supporter of the war asked Hardie: 'Where are your two boys?' Hardie replied that he would rather see them put against a wall and shot than see them go to war.

At Christmas of 1914, Hardie wrote to a young female admirer that his arm had failed him. He had had a stroke. By February, although he was little better, Hardie was back in Parliament voicing his opposition to the war. But his health was failing fast. He had lunch with Bruce Glasier, who reported that his colleague kept falling asleep. More than once that spring he was taken ill in the House of Commons. At the end of May he admitted defeat, packed up his belongings from Nevill's Court and returned to Scotland. Sylvia came to see him for the last time to collect some of her belongings, and left, she said tellingly, 'orphaned and widowed at heart'.[30] Despite a spell in a sanatorium, Hardie continued to sink. His friend Frank Smith told Sylvia he had been suffering from delusions, and his family reported that he had been increasingly difficult and had developed a violent antipathy to the family dog.

Hardie died in hospital in Glasgow on 26 September 1915. The ILP paid for his funeral, at which the cortège was a quarter of a mile long. Although Sylvia sent a wreath in suffragette colours there were few other tributes from the women of the WSPU for whom he had toiled so long and tirelessly. It fell to Isabella Ford, a leading constitutional suffragist, to pay tribute to the work Hardie had done to promote women's suffrage:

His extraordinary sympathy with the women's movement, his complete understanding of what it stands for, were what first made me understand the finest side of his character. In the days when Labour men neglected and slighted the women's cause or ridiculed it, Hardie never once failed us, never once faltered in his work for us. We women can never forget what we owe him.[31]

By modern standards, Keir Hardie was not a liberated man. His old-fashioned romanticism and his admiration for his Victorian mother left him ill-equipped for the more radical sexual politics espoused by some of his contemporaries. But he was in many ways a man ahead of his time. His devotion to the cause of women's suffrage is just one example, along with his opposition to the Empire and his internationalism. He was also a man who, once attached to a belief, clung to it with a tenacity that had sometimes to be seen to be believed. For that, if for nothing else, the members of the suffragette movement had much to be grateful for.

Mary Augusta Ward.

VII

Mary Ward – True Victorian

It is time that the women who are opposed to the concession of the parliamentary franchise to women should make themselves fully and widely heard. The matter is urgent. Unless those who hold that the success of the women's suffrage movement would bring disaster upon England are prepared to take immediate and effective action, judgement may go by default and our country drift towards a momentous revolution, both social and political, before it has realised the dangers involved.

Manifesto of the Women's National Anti-Suffrage League, July 1908

One warm day at the height of the suffrage struggle, H. G. Wells was sitting in the woods reading the letters page of *The Times* with his lover Elizabeth von Arnim. So outraged and amused were they by the views of one contributor that they stripped naked, laid the open newspaper on the ground with her letter uppermost, and made love on it. Then they lit a match and burned it.

It was not surprising that Wells should have found this funny – so much so that he chose to write about it later.[1] For Mrs Humphrey Ward was fast becoming a national joke among the liberal intelligentsia. No reader of *The Times* could have been left in any doubt that the famous novelist had no hunger for the vote, so frequent and vehement were her tirades on the subject. Indeed, she had already put her name to the new Women's National Anti-Suffrage League – an act which in itself had provoked much hilarity among suffrage campaigners. After all, was there not something ridiculous about women starting a political campaign to argue that their sisters should not be involved in politics?

As a result of her anti-suffrage activities the many achievements of Mary Ward, as she was known to friends and family, were largely erased from the history of the late nineteenth and early twentieth centuries. She came to be regarded as a dinosaur, a relic of the Victorian age, who had somehow stumbled on after she should have quietly faded away. And to some extent, she was. For the latter half of the nineteenth century was a time of great and welcome reform, of big ideas and of an unswerving belief in man's ability to change the world for the better. Mary Ward was very much a part of that.

Mary Ward was a pioneer of women's education, founder of special education and play schemes across England and a major contributor to the post-Darwinist debate on the role of organised religion. She was also a woman with little formal education who never lost sight of her role as a wife and mother and who believed passionately that men and women should stick to their allotted places in the world. But there is no contradiction here. Mary was a Victorian to the core, and her life should be celebrated in that context.

Mary was born to greatness, for her family had made themselves illustrious in the fields of education, literature and politics. Thomas Arnold, famous headmaster of Rugby, was her paternal grandfather. The poet Matthew Arnold was one of her uncles, while another, William Forster, achieved fame as the architect of the 1870 Education Act, which provided schooling for the masses. Mary herself was born in 1851 in Tasmania, then known as Van Diemen's Land. Her father, Thomas Arnold the younger, was Inspector of Schools on the island and there had met and married Julia Sorrell, granddaughter of its governor, in 1850. Julia was according to her granddaughter, 'the favourite and pet of Hobart Town society, much admired by the subalterns of the solitary battalion of British troops that maintained our prestige among the convicts and the "blacks" of that remote settlement'.[2] There was only one cloud on the horizon – Julia's family were protestants, descended from Huguenot refugees, and Thomas had leanings towards Catholicism. In 1856, when Mary was five years old, he converted. Anti-popist feelings ran high in the colonies at the time, and Julia had threatened to leave him if he did such a thing. She ultimately failed to carry out her threat, but the Arnolds' life in Hobart was at an end. The couple were forced to set sail for England with Mary and her two younger brothers, Willie and Theodore.

Mary was not the easiest of children. Passionate and wilful, she was quick to lose her temper. Her father wrote to his mother in the Lake District that he was 'having a regular pitched battle with her about once a day … her domineering spirit makes even her kindness partake of oppression'.[3] Later she described herself as a child 'caught in the toils of a hot temper and a stubborn will'.[4] She was displaying little of that fiery temperament on her arrival in England. Miserable with toothache, she spent her first night in her father's native land in a dreary inn near the London dock where the family had landed. Soon she was rescued by her grandparents, and though her parents moved first to Dublin then to Birmingham in pursuit of her father's career, she stayed in their Lakeland home for much of her childhood. Mary's memories of their house, Fox How, were all happy ones, though her description of it also betrays the affluence of her background: 'It is a modest building with ten bedrooms and three sitting rooms. Its windows look straight into the heart of Fairfield, the beautiful semi-circular mountain which rears its hallowed front and buttressing scaurs against the north, far above the green floor of the valley.'[5] As a child Mary spent much of her time wandering about the Cumbrian countryside, often alone and lost in daydreams.

The Arnolds' house was filled with books and they were often visited by the great and good of the literary world. Charlotte Brontë dined there the year before Mary arrived, and the little girl was taken to Rydal Mount to meet Mary Wordsworth, the poet's widow. William Wordsworth had been a good friend of Mary's grandfather but had died in 1850, the year before she was born. Mary's father had been one of nine children, so her childhood was populated by many aunts, uncles and cousins. Among them was her father's sister Jane, who had married William Forster.

Mary's brothers were educated at the Oratory in Birmingham and later at Rugby, but she went first to a school at Eller Howe near her grandparents' home. It was a small, friendly establishment run on liberal lines by Jemima Clough – so much so that one of the other teachers thought it disorderly and tried during one of the headmistress's absences to arrange the children's desks into straight lines. Miss Clough was full of ideas on education, and would later become principal of Newnham Hall, Cambridge. She gave evidence in 1866 to the commission of inquiry on education, which also heard the views of Elizabeth Wolstenholme Elmy.

But this cheery interlude lasted just a few years, and at the age of ten Mary was sent away to board at the Rock Terrace School for Young Ladies at Shifnall in Shropshire. It was not a happy time, and she later fictionalised some of her experiences at the school in her novel, *Marcella*. Mary was always short of pocket money and she found that her illustrious family name counted for little. She suffered constantly from colds and other minor ailments. She was moved in 1864 to a school at Clifton, near Bristol, and though she was happier there she later wrote that her years in education had been 'practically wasted': 'I learnt nothing thoroughly or accurately, and the German, French and Latin, which I soon discovered after my marriage to be essential to the kind of literary work I wanted to do, had all to be relearnt before they could be of any real use to me.'6 Her brothers' education at Rugby was much more thorough, she believed. The experience was a formative one for her, though, in that she became a firm advocate of women's education.

Mary was sixteen when a change in her parents' fortunes released her from the rigours of boarding-school life. In 1865 her father had reconverted to Anglicanism, and this allowed him to start his own school in Oxford. Mary left Clifton in 1867 and embarked on a richer, informal education in Oxford which would do much to shape the rest of her life. By now she had seven younger siblings, and those who were not away at school were housed in a large residence in the Banbury Road. Mary loved Oxford. Soon she had enrolled for music lessons and had attached herself to the rector of Lincoln College, Mark Pattison, and his wife Emily, known universally as 'Mrs Pat'. Mary was in an evangelical phase, but the Liberal Pattisons took to her and she became a fixture at their relaxed Sunday dinner parties. There were no women students at Oxford but Pattison procured for Mary a pass to the Bodleian library. There she began to study Spanish history with a view to publishing a book on the subject. This gave her access to many more Oxford drawing rooms, for she had now become a 'clever girl' and therefore a desirable adornment for any gathering.

Mary had always harboured an ambition to be a novelist, and it was during this time that she set to work on the project. Much of her early writing remained unpublished but one piece, 'A Westmorland Story', was published in *The Churchman's Companion* in 1870. In the spring of that year Mary had dined at the Pattisons' with George Eliot, who sat chatting to her about Spain for twenty minutes.

In her late teens Mary Arnold was a vigorous girl, easily interested and never shy, and she quickly picked up the rules of the elite society in which she mingled. As it was largely male – fellows were not allowed to marry – she was much in demand at parties where it was necessary to invite women. Although her features were a little on the severe side and her tendency to bookishness could be intimidating, she caught the eye of more than one academic. In 1871 she met Thomas Humphry Ward, a 25-year-old tutor and newly elected fellow at Brasenose College known to his friends as Humphry. While Mary spent her days engrossed in medieval Spanish, Humphry's diary from the period suggests he had a rather more dilatory lifestyle: 'Even the milder pleasures of the punt on the Cherwell passed into the riper charms of the lawn and the luncheon pleasant party ... There was little to do save read, and bathe and fish.'[7] Humphry's approaches to Mary were a little dilatory at first, too. Indeed, he seemed for a while unsure whether to marry her or another striking young Oxford woman named Louise von Glehn, but Louise made his mind up for him by marrying his friend Mandell Creighton. Mary had no such doubts, and accepted Humphry's proposal as soon as it was offered. Ever forthright, focused and determined, she eventually become her family's main breadwinner while Humphry, first a don, then a journalist on *The Times*, drifted along cheerfully but less profitably.

The Reverend Charles Dodgson – Lewis Carroll – had used Mary's younger sisters as child models, and now took Mary and Humphry's engagement photographs. The wedding was conducted by the dean of Westminster Abbey, Arthur Stanley, and the couple started married life in a substantial house with Morris wallpaper, blue-and-white china and a vegetable garden – like Emmeline Pankhurst, seven years her junior, Mary was much influenced by the arts and crafts movement. Mary's social rise continued: she became known as the best croquet player in Oxford, a fashionable hostess and a more than tolerable pianist. There was still time for writing, though: 'It became plain very soon after our marriage that ours was to be a literary partnership ... our three small children arrived in 1874, 1876 and 1879 and all the time I was reading, listening, talking and beginning to write in earnest – mostly for the *Saturday Review*.'[8] Early in his married life Humphry began publishing *Ward's Poets*, an anthology of English poetry in several volumes, which continued to appear until 1918. Some of the critical essays it contained were written by Mary, who spent her mornings in the Bodleian and wrote for three hours every evening after the children went to bed.

The couple were not entirely conventional. Their children were once chastised for hissing at a picture of Queen Victoria, and afterwards explained that they were 'not loyal'. They were also sceptical of the Church. Mary published a pamphlet called 'Unbelief and Sin', which railed against the restriction of free thought by organised religion. It was withdrawn from sale after a cleric complained it had no printer's name on it. Mary had a new interest too – the education of women. In 1873, the year after her marriage, she became joint secretary of Oxford's Lectures for Ladies committee. This was so successful that in 1877 an Association for the Education of Women was formed with the aim of providing a women's 'hall' – a residential

establishment without full collegiate status – for Oxford. While the Anglican community pushed forward the founding of the Anglican Lady Margaret Hall, Mary's faction worked, agitated and fund-raised for a
non-denominational centre: 'My friends and I were all on fire for women's
education, including women's medical education, and very emulous of
Cambridge, where the movement was already far advanced.'[9] Mary chose
the name Somerville Hall after Mary Somerville, a self-taught astronomer
who had died in 1872. The new college opened in October 1879, a month
before the birth of Mary's younger daughter Janet, and her friends feared
the strain might be too much for her. She was also much occupied with her
mother, who was seriously ill. Louise Creighton wrote to Mary: 'Do not lay
on yourself a burden which is more than you can bear; hard mental work,
a house full of family, the anxiety of a sick mother, is too much strain for
you to bear continuously without break. You … work too hard.'[10]

Through her educational activities in Oxford Mary had met Millicent
Fawcett, a leading suffrage campaigner. Although they were friendly, Mary
had never been a suffragist herself, she said, and neither were most of her
friends: 'Hardly any of us were at all on fire for woman suffrage … the majority … were at that time persuaded that the development of women's
power in the state … should be on lines of its own.'[11] A suffragist she never
was, but neither was Mary Ward ever a simple, old-fashioned advocate of
the view that women should stay at home and concentrate on their embroidery. Her belief, which changed little throughout her life, was that
women's concerns had little to do with the business of running an empire
– something which at the time formed one of the major activities of government. Furthermore, she argued, women had little to say about organising or fighting a war. There were other and more appropriate ways in
which women could exercise political power, she felt. She was a firm
believer that women should be more involved with local politics, for example: 'We believed that growth through local government and perhaps
through some special machinery for bringing the wishes and influence of
women of all classes to bear on Parliament, rather than the Parliamentary
vote, was the real line of progress.'[12]

For Mary and her set, life was full enough without the vote. In 1881
Humphry was offered a job with *The Times* as a leader writer, and the Wards
left Oxford. Mary departed with a sense of loss, for some of her happiest
and most fulfilling years had been spent in the university city, but she retained links with it through a seat on the Somerville council. In the follow-

ing seven years she would also serve twice as an examiner for a Spanish scholarship at Oxford, becoming the first woman examiner of men at either of the ancient universities. At the same time, the Wards settled into the frenetic social whirl London had to offer. They took a house in Russell Square and were soon hosting smart soirées for the literati. They were guests at the weddings of Alfred Lyttelton, where Gladstone made a speech, and Herbert Asquith. The earnest Mary loved to talk, and her dinner parties tended to turn into seminars. It was at one such in 1882 that she met the novelist Henry James, who soon became a friend, and who gave her the idea for her first published novel. The two went together to the theatre to see an American actress with whom they were both unimpressed. Mary decided to write a story whose main character was an actress with charm but no technique, and who was forced to learn that hard work was the best route to success. *Miss Bretherton* was dashed off in six weeks and appeared towards the end of 1884. It received mixed reviews and its sales were unexceptional.

Mary was not deterred, though. She set to work on her next novel, *Robert Elsmere*, which tackled the strictures of organised religion. The book took almost three years to write and after drastic cuts it came out in three volumes. It told the story of a young clergyman who lost his faith, decided to stay on to help the poor, but then achieved 'synthesis' through a belief in eternal goodness. Despite its unwieldy length and heavy subject-matter, the book was a sensation. Gladstone wrote a 10,000-word review of it for the journal *Nineteenth Century*, and suddenly queues formed outside London bookshops. Libraries held long waiting lists for the book, which had touched the doubts of a whole generation about organised religion. Where *Miss Bretherton* had sold 1,150 copies and made a loss of £22, *Robert Elsmere* sold half a million copies within a year in the US alone and several hundred thousand more in the UK, netting its author £3,200. It was the publishing sensation of the century.

Mrs Humphry Ward was soon a household name. In the next decade, her works would make her a fortune. Mary completed a new novel every couple of years for the remaining thirty years of her life, and her publisher's accounts reveal phenomenal sales. *Sir George Tressady*, published in September 1896, sold 102,000 copies in its first six weeks; *Helbeck of Bannisdale*, published in June 1898, sold 108,035 copies in a similar period.[13]

This phenomenal success played a major part in drawing Mary into the suffrage struggle. The idea that women should have the vote was becoming accepted wisdom in the smart drawing rooms through which she moved, yet Mary remained certain her acquaintances were wrong. The first sign that she was about to speak out publicly came in January 1889, while Mary was still savouring her newfound celebrity. In a letter to Louise Creighton she mentioned she had been talking to James Knowles, editor of *Nineteenth Century*, at a function at the French Embassy. Mary had given him an idea. An appeal by men against women's suffrage would be counterproductive but an appeal by women, headed by one currently so fashionable, could only be a good thing. He had pressed her to devise an anti-suffrage manifesto, to be published in his journal and signed by a number of eminent women. Mary, ever busy, in turn pressed Louise to collect names: 'Keep a little book, as I mean to do!' she urged.[14]

The reason for the 1889 call to arms was a Private Member's Bill on Women's Suffrage being brought that year by an MP named William Woodall. The manifesto duly appeared in the June 1889 edition of *Nineteenth Century* and bore the signatures of 104 women. It was clearly Mary's work. Its main thrust, namely that women were not concerned with the mechanics of empire-building, was straight from her heart. The manifesto also welcomed the advent of greater feminine influence outside Parliament, on school boards and on the boards of guardians who ran the workhouses. But it also added a line which seems unlikely to have come from her: 'We believe that the emancipating process has now reached the limits fixed by the physical constitution of women.' It seems Mary was being pushed further than she would naturally have gone, for she did not believe womankind had reached its limits, nor did she feel her personal constitution was being overstretched. This line was probably the work of Frederic Harrison, recruited by Knowles to help with the manifesto. So hard-line an anti-feminist was he that he believed the women who signed the petition were sullying their femininity by doing so.

Why Mary allowed herself to be cajoled into this exercise is something of a puzzle. Her sisters, Julia and Ethel were in favour of votes for women, along with her father's sister, her favourite 'Aunt Fan'. Some of those who signed the appeal – for instance Beatrice Potter, later Beatrice Webb – would eventually regret doing so. Mary's most recent biographer gives three reasons for her decision – a horror of militancy, a fear that women might look ridiculous as political figures, and a tendency to be easily flattered by powerful men such as the ones who persuaded her to take part in this exercise.[15] None of these, in itself, is adequate to explain her actions. Militancy did not begin until seventeen years later, and it is hard to see why national politics would have made women look more ridiculous than local politics – or, for that matter, the sort of notoriety that comes with being a famous novelist. It is probably true that Mary was flattered by the approaches of James Knowles. She was not a political animal, but a literary and intellectual one, yet she allowed herself to be cajoled into believing she was essential to the anti-suffrage movement. However, a fourth explanation should be added: an excess of self-belief. While her friends were beginning to admit they had been wrong on this issue, Mary was not a woman who suffered from self-doubt. Supremely self-confident and highly intelligent, she formed her ideological landscape in the Oxford of the 1870s and saw no need for any major mental upheavals later. This was often remarked on by those who met her. During a trip to Italy she was called on by Gertrude Bell, female mountaineer, archaeologist and inveterate traveller, who wrote to her mother that Mary was remarkably sure of herself: 'She showed me her preface to Jane Eyre, very good I thought – so did she! "Now this is so true," she said, pointing to a passage in an impersonal way! Never mind, she was a great dear.'[16]

The *Nineteenth Century* appeal drew an immediate response. In the journal's July 1889 edition Lydia Becker wrote that in twenty years of campaigning for the vote she had never before seen such public opposition from women. She dismissed the signatories as married women who would not, under the terms of the current bill, get the vote. Her response also contained a comment on one of the appeal's oddest propositions – that the enfranchisement of female lodgers would give votes to immoral women. Lydia Becker, herself rather prim, countered that most lodgers were not fallen women but governesses or music teachers. It would be most unfair to exclude them on this basis. In any case, she added, the unfortunate derelicts might be lifted by the franchise into positions of personal power which would free them from their 'partners in sin'. In August *Nineteenth Century* published a list of 1,200 women who had signed a petition in favour of the suffrage.

Meanwhile Emmeline Pankhurst, residing at the time a few doors away from the Wards in Russell Square, had none of Mary's qualms about the dignity or otherwise of 'personal struggle and rivalry'. She was in that very month gathering her own group of women to protest about the Woodall bill – in flagrant rivalry with other suffrage campaigners including Lydia Becker, who supported it. Emmeline's objection was quite different from Mary's, of course – she wanted it to pass but only after the erasure of a 'couverture' clause which would stop married women from voting. The Pankhursts and the Wards were close neighbours for more than two years, from late 1888 until early 1891, but there is no evidence they were friendly. Mary and Emmeline apparently kept their separate salons, the one largely literary, the other tied firmly to the world of radical politics, a few doors from each other without ever touching one another's world. We do not know whether Mary popped into Emmeline's homewares shop, Emerson's, to buy a painted arts and crafts milking stool or some blue china, but probably she did not, for her tastes were a little grander now than they had been in her Oxford days.

Over the following decade Mary had little time for suffrage, which in any case was making few headlines. In 1890 she launched a new venture which, along with her literary work, kept her fully occupied. Since moving to London she had increasingly been concerned at the lack of further education facilities, particularly for the working classes. Her impulse was in the mould of many a Victorian philanthropist but it had a modern flavour, as she explained later in her memoirs: 'A spirit of fraternisation was in the air, an ardent wish to break down the local and geographical barriers that separated rich from poor, East End from West End'.[17] Following a pattern already set by the Toynbee Hall in East London, she founded a centre where male students could live cheaply in return for giving evening lectures and doing social work. Funded partly by a Liberal Peer, Lord Carlisle, and partly by the Unitarian Church, the venture was a great success. At first the settlement was based in a shabby hall in Bloomsbury's Marchmont Street, but eventually a new centre was built in Tavistock Place, funded mainly by a wealthy philanthropist, John Passmore Edwards, after whom it was named.

In this building Mary started two projects which would prove to be major developments in British educational history. The first was a school for children with physical disabilities, the 'Physically Defective School'. Mary became a high-profile campaigner on behalf of these 'physically weak but often intelligent and artistic children', as she called them in one of her many letters to *The Times* on the subject. This became the first special school to be adopted by a local education authority, and by 1906 it was one of twenty-two across the capital. Mary also lobbied and fund-raised for an industrial training scheme on to which these pupils could move once they finished their basic education.

The Passmore Edwards Settlement also hosted the first permanent play scheme in England, giving children from the slums a place to go in the evenings. In a letter to *The Times* in 1906, Mary described movingly how many such youngsters were often forced to spend their leisure time.[18] Many were turned out from overcrowded houses on to the street, where they played a fantasy game in which henpecked mothers were attacked by drunken fathers, or where they amused themselves by throwing cherry pips at passers-by. She quoted an East End head teacher, who had told her: 'We teach these boys the 3Rs during the school day and then by sending them out to spend idle evenings in the streets we turn them into packs of pariahs.' At the settlement these children were offered the chance to learn cooking, crafts, games, painting, drawing and dancing. In 1906 it played host to 1,700 children a week. By 1908 there were twelve such play centres in London, attended by 242,000 children in a three-month period.

In the early 1890s the Wards were forced by building works to leave Russell Square, and moved to a new London home in Grosvenor Place. Soon afterwards, buoyed by Mary's financial success, they also took on a handsome manor house near Tring in Hertfordshire. At first Stocks was rented but in 1896 they bought it, later carrying out extensive renovations. By then the family was living a very grand lifestyle, with winter 'seasons' in London and summers in the country. There were regular foreign holidays and Arnold, the only boy, was educated at Uppingham, Eton and Oxford. Family life seems generally to have been happy, though Humphry's spell as a leader writer on *The Times* was not a success and he was soon moved to the job of art critic. In this role he amused himself by buying paintings, only occasionally selling them for a profit. Humphry's sister Gertrude lived with the Wards for some years and helped to run the household, but in 1895 she emigrated to Zanzibar to become a missionary nurse. At that point Mary's older daughter, Dorothy, then twenty-one, took over the role.

Of the Ward children Arnold was both the brightest hope and the most trouble. While Humphry reacted to his wife's success by buying expensive pictures, Arnold's vice was bridge, and on several occasions his mother was forced to bail him out when he ran up debts. She was less unhappy when he asked for financial help with his main goal in life – or possibly his mother's main goal for him – entering Parliament. This he finally achieved in 1910 as Unionist MP for West Hertfordshire, a seat a few miles from Stocks. Arnold, like his sister 'darling Dot', seems to have found it hard to emerge from his mother's shadow. He was friendly with the Asquiths and in 1907 contemplated asking their daughter Violet to marry him, but for reasons that remain obscure nothing came of it. Maybe she turned him down, maybe he lost courage and never asked her. Mary's other daughter,

Janet, was the only one of the three to escape, by marrying the social historian George Macaulay Trevelyan, though she remained close to her mother
and later wrote a biography of her.

Mary Ward had several means of maintaining control of her loved ones
apart from her sometimes tenuous grasp on the family purse strings. As
one biographer put it, her medical history would have made a full-length
study in itself.[19] From writer's cramp to depression, from eczema to
toothache, she seemed to wallow in every ailment known to man. In the
last thirty years of her life she was a near-invalid, though ill-health did little to stem her prolific output of novels and political pronouncements.
What it did, though, was to keep the rest of her family, particularly
Dorothy and Humphry, in close proximity and with their attention firmly
focused where it should be – on Mary. Being at the centre of her family,
though, in no way meant that Mary considered herself a housewife. Although she was always known in public by her husband's name, it was
probably the only manner in which she felt herself subservient. The fashionable view among anti-suffrage women was that they should exercise
'the iron hand in the velvet glove' on the domestic front. Laurence Housman, a key member of the men's campaign for women's suffrage, reported
a conversation with 'a very prominent anti-suffragist' who told him: 'When
my husband consults me on any important point and I advise him as I
think best he always says at once, 'Oh no dear that would never do at all.'
But after a time he goes and does it.'[20] Mary certainly endorsed the view.
She wrote in the *Evening Standard* that 'exceptional women' were always
able to influence their men by stealth.[21]

And it was by stealth, if at all, that Mary co-operated with the anti-suffrage movement in the last years of the nineteenth century. She does not
appear to have protested publicly in 1897, for example, when a bill brought
by an MP named Faithfull Begg passed its second reading in the Commons. But privately she was furious, mainly because she believed many
members had voted in favour to keep their constituents quiet, in the full
knowledge the bill would never become law. She wrote to her father:

> I don't know when I have felt so angry about anything. The tone of the
> Conservative members in private is the most cynical thing you ever heard
> … there are not six men in the whole House who want the change and yet
> there they all go and vote to rid themselves of what they are pleased to call
> their 'pledges' to a 'pack of women'.[22]

It was characteristic that Mary could not remain silent for ever. As the suffrage movement grew during the early years of the new century she began to waver. As usual her desire to express herself, to make a mark, was at war with her fear of looking ridiculous. In March 1907 she cracked and on the 8th wrote to *The Times* – adding in an aside to her son that she feared her effort would 'convince nobody and offend many'. In her published letter Mary admitted she knew her views brought her into conflict with many of the women she most respected and admired. 'But the matter seems very urgent, and I feel driven to write in spite of reluctance ... But a wholesale move towards women's suffrage now would add hugely to the "ignorant unstable vote" which is already too large,' she complained. For the time being, though, she was able to maintain relations across the political divide. During 1907 she was made president of the Society of Women Journalists, and her guest at the society's annual dinner was Lord Lytton, whose sister Constance was a militant suffragette and who was soon to become prominent in the cause of women's suffrage himself.

The following year, however, such friendly relations ceased when Mary was dragged further into the anti-suffrage camp. The movement's two leading lights, Lord Curzon and Lord Cromer, persuaded Mary to take her place on the committee of a new Women's National Anti-Suffrage League – designed to counter the argument that it was only men who were against votes for women. Gertrude Bell, the mountaineer and archaeologist who had found Mary so self-assured in Italy, was secretary, while Mary was chairman of the literature committee. Although the title sounded minor she became closely associated with the movement, partly because she was its most famous backer.

Although she complained in private letters that the anti-suffragists were taking up too much of her time – 'I am trying to think of Diana [her latest novel, *Diana Mallory*] but have been pursued by letters ... about the Suffrage,' she wrote to Arnold[23] – she now took the plunge into public speaking. It was not an instant success. Lord Cromer complained to Lord Curzon that she had arrived at one meeting with a 'written essay, full of commonplaces and platitudes ... Women are quite unfit to speak at public meetings.'[24] But Mary rarely reported even the stormiest of meetings without claiming some success. After two debates in Cambridge she wrote to Dorothy that although she had found the audience 'really too chilling' at Newnham, at Girton some of the noisy crowd were clearly on her side. 'I really got through the heckling very well and the Antis were delighted. But the fire and the rage were immense, and considering that the staff is hotly suffrage at both colleges, I should think discipline will soon suffer,' she added starchily.[25] After a similar experience at the Free Trade Hall in Manchester she concluded the meeting was 'of course carried by the suffragettes, who packed the galleries with young girls who vote en bloc against the resolution – but the body of the hall was very evenly divided … and altogether we felt we hadn't done badly'.[26]

In Bristol she had to wait while Annie Kenney and another suffragette were flushed out of the organ, where they had hidden themselves in order to shout slogans during her speech. But even in the face of such adversity Mary did sometimes manage to get her message across. With 13 million people on the verge of hunger, the male franchise had clearly failed to achieve much needed social reform, she told the Bristol crowd. Progress depended on much more than mere votes, and women should trust the forces which had already led to so many great changes in the past century. Soon the anti-suffragists were claiming 1,700 members in the city. In 1910 they had 15,000 supporters across the country, aided by the rise of militancy. But this was tiny in comparison with their opponents, who by Mary's figures had 290,000 supporters at the time. While she took tours around the country before retiring back to her Hertfordshire estate, many suffragettes gave up their entire lives for their cause. In the week that Mary Ward quoted these figures the Women's Social and Political Union held 250 meetings in London and its suburbs alone. Still, the antis could muster a good platform. At one meeting in the Albert Hall they had five dukes, fifteen earls, five viscounts, forty-four barons and seven cabinet ministers ranged before the crowd.

Unlike some of her companions in arms, Mary Ward was never completely against votes for women. She had always believed women should get more involved in local politics, and now she began to campaign actively on that front, founding a Local Government Advancement Committee with the specific aim of getting more women on to local councils. To Lord Curzon's fury, the committee even pledged the support of the Anti-Suffrage League to a woman who was standing for election in West Marylebone. Worse, the woman's opponent was an anti-suffragist. Cromer wrote to Curzon: 'I have not the health, strength, youth, or I may add the temper to go on dealing with these infernal women.'[27]

Mary's leap into the political world had had just the effect she feared it might – it had led to a loss of dignity, the puncturing of her rather overblown public persona. Reading Mrs Humphry Ward, Virginia Woolf opined, was like catching the 'flu. Lytton Strachey wrote to his brother that he saw her as 'that shapeless mass of meaningless flesh – all old and sordid and insignificant'.[28] Arnold Bennett imagined her heroines being gang-raped by an army of 'brutal and licentious soldiery'. Max Beerbohm even started a club in which she was reviled as 'Ma Hump'. The suffragettes, not unduly perturbed by the anti-suffrage campaign, made less of a fuss, though their 1909 exhibition at the Prince's skating rink in Kensington had a coconut shy with Mary Ward's face on one of the coconuts.

It was small wonder that Mary was not being taken seriously, for her comrades' pronouncements were becoming increasingly outlandish. In 1912 she felt impelled to distance herself from an eminent pathologist, Sir Almroth Wright, who wrote to *The Times* to explain that the actions of the militant suffragettes were caused by menopausal madness:

> The woman of the world will gaily assure you that of course half the women in London have to be shut up when they come to the change of life … no doctor can ever lose sight of the fact that the mind of woman is always threatened with danger from the reverberations of her physiological emergencies. It is with such thoughts that the doctor lets his eyes rest upon the militant suffragist. He cannot shut them to the fact that there is mixed up with the woman's movement much mental disorder.[29]

This was too much for Mary, not least because the leadership of the Anti-Suffrage League had decided to circulate it among members. The militants could not have made such an impact if they had merely been mad, she wrote to *The Times* in reply: 'I have always refused to underestimate either the power or the numbers of the extremists … I strongly disapprove of Sir A Wright's odious letter and of our action in regard to it.'[30]

Feelings were running high, for the suffragettes had just smashed hundreds of central London shop windows. Mary wrote again to *The Times* to complain that suffragettes should not be allowed to be teachers. But, with a complacency that betrayed a remarkable level of political misjudgement, she claimed the suffragettes had become a spent force as a result of the raids. The arrests of the movement's leaders and the exile of Christabel Pankhurst must surely be the end of the affair, she said. She wrote to her son Arnold from Paris, where she had made a stopover on the way to her spring break in Italy: 'I can't help feeling that the position of the Government is stronger than it was six months ago – what with … the elimination of the suffrage apple of discord.' Her feelings had been reinforced by a chance meeting with the sister of Emmeline Pankhurst's friend Ethel Smyth, who was in Holloway after the stone-throwing raids. Ethel's sister, Mrs Charles Hunter, had recently seen Emmeline and thought her a broken woman, unlikely to continue the fight. 'One would be very sorry for her but for the thought of what she has brought on others,' Mary concluded.[31]

Mary would soon find herself on the same side as Emmeline Pankhurst after the First World War broke out. As an author she was called on to make her own special contribution to the war effort – a book aimed at persuading Americans their nation should join the war. So while Emmeline made propaganda efforts to the east, in Russia, Mary set her literary cap westwards, towards the United States. The episode began with a call to arms from the former American President, Theodore Roosevelt, whom she had met in the US during a visit in 1908. He suggested she should write a series of articles in support of the British campaign to bring the Americans in. The British War Office approved and Mary was sent with Dorothy to view the allied efforts in France, where they even watched a battle through field-glasses. She described it as 'a wonderful day … I was looking over ground where every inch was consecrated to the dead sons of England'.[32] It was the high point of her war. The low point was fast approaching.

News had already reached the family in England that Arnold had got himself into trouble in Cairo, where he was stationed, by running up gambling debts. The amount was around £6,000, and Mary agreed to pay it in instalments of £500 every six months. There were only two possible means of finding such a huge sum – sell Stocks, or hold on to it but sell off its contents to survive and pay the bills. Mary and Humphry, believing they would not live long, chose the latter option. Although Mary's wartime work, *England's Effort*, was a success she knew she could no longer rely on her novels to make her the kind of money she now needed to earn. It was a depressing end to a glorious career.

Mary still found the energy for one last fling, though, when the bill which would finally enfranchise women was put before Parliament. In many senses she was resigned to having lost the suffrage war – she had written to Cromer as early as 1915 that she sometimes 'wondered in my secret thoughts whether we are not already beaten'.[33] In fact the war had changed her views on the subject and she, like the suffragettes, felt the women's roles on the 'Home Front' had changed them. A statement by the Anti-Suffrage League, which she signed, concluded that some people might rightly think 'the experience gained during the war has introduced some new elements into the case which will require careful consideration'.

But Mary and her colleagues were not going to give in without at least a semblance of a fight, so the Anti-Suffrage League issued a statement saying it would oppose the measure. In January 1918 Mary led a deputation to the House of Lords to point out the 'injustice' of introducing women's suffrage without first holding a consultative referendum. But the tone at the league's final meeting in Central Buildings, Westminster, was one of resignation. Mary spoke, claiming the antis might have won the day if they had started actively campaigning sooner. But she also looked to the future with the hope that the war might have had a positive effect on those who would benefit from the vote: 'More life – more opportunity – more leisure – more beauty! – for the masses of plain men and women, who have gone so bare in the past, and are now putting forth their just and ardent claim on the future'.[34] Lord Weardale, presiding, paid tribute to her energy and generosity, saying she had done 'everything that even a woman could do in circumstances of this kind'. To add insult to injury Lord Curzon, as leader of the Lords, was forced to pilot the bill through the House.

Mary Ward died in March 1920 and was carried by hand on a bier to the local church at Aldbury, near Stocks. Her funeral address was given by her friend Dean Inge, who described her as 'perhaps the greatest living English-woman of our time'. Buckingham Palace sent condolences. The liberal literary establishment was less fulsome.[35] Virginia Woolf wrote in her diary: 'Poor Mrs Humphry Ward, it seems she was merely a woman of straw after all – shovelled into the grave and already forgotten.'

In his book on the anti-suffragists, *Separate Spheres*, Brian Harrison suggests that while Mary Ward's faction helped to curb the worst excesses of people such as Sir Almroth Wright, their main problem was that they were too dull: 'There was a heaviness and seriousness … which invited ridicule from generations … it lacked the vigour, humour and spice of the WSPU.' It would be easy to say the same about Mary Ward – although only a few years older than Emmeline Pankhurst, she certainly did not have the same capacity to enjoy herself. But it would be easy, too, to underestimate this indomitable woman. Perhaps the fairest assessment of her was that of one of her political opponents, Millicent Fawcett. Mary Ward was, she said, simply 'a social reformer who somehow wandered into the wrong camp'.[36]

May Billinghurst.

VIII

May Billinghurst – Fighting Spirit

Going to Cannon Row between 9.30 and 10 I found arrested women being brought in there every few minutes. The numbers in that station alone had reached 180 by 9.50. Just at that time as I was returning to Whitehall I met Miss Billinghurst, that indomitable cripple, being carried shoulder high by four policemen in her little tricycle or wheel-cart that she propels with her arms. Amid immense cheering from the crowd she followed the rest into the police station.

Henry Nevinson reports in Votes for Women *on a demonstration at*
Westminster, 24 November 1911

May Billinghurst does not feature prominently in the histories of the suffragette movement. She is not mentioned among its leaders, nor is she celebrated as one of its most notorious militants. Yet her image will be familiar to those who have studied the many photographs taken at suffragette parades and demonstrations. Partially paralysed since childhood, she is often placed at the forefront of the picture with the purple, white and green colours flying proudly from her wheelchair.

May Billinghurst played two important roles within the movement to which she devoted her life for seven years. First, she was one of the many workers who kept the local branches of the Women's Social and Political Union running from day to day. Her duties ranged from organising bazaars and acting as assistant in the local WSPU shop to ensuring a good turn-out for all-important national demonstrations. In later years they even extended to pouring noxious substances into letter-boxes. But her second and perhaps more intriguing function was the one for which she was known to her comrades, in the parlance of the times, as 'The Cripple Suffragette'. May Billinghurst was no fool. She knew full well, and so did the leaders of the WSPU, that her hand-propelled invalid tricycle gave her a special advantage in the propaganda battle they were waging. It made it difficult, if not impossible, for the media to portray May as a howling harridan with little care for the safety of others. At its least effective the sight of her at a demonstration was a picturesque one, commented on lightly along with other aspects of the pageantry of the day. At best, it served to underline in bold the brutal tactics of the police and the vulnerability of the suffragette demonstrators.

A close look at the way May Billinghurst's disability was used by the WSPU, with her full and informed acquiescence, can tell us much about the movement's skill with spin. For although her appearance of physical frailty was accentuated by her wheelchair, the message she carried was essentially the same as those of other suffragette demonstrators: 'Look at us. We are compromising both our delicate physiques and our ladylike demeanour for our cause. We are doing this because we have been left with no alternative.' In committing acts which were socially unacceptable the suffragettes asked the public to recognise their desperation, their vulnerability.

This convenient line represented only a partial truth, for as has been demonstrated through the stories of other stalwarts there was also a great sense of fun, even of liberation from the strictures of Edwardian social etiquette, about the suffragette movement. May Billinghurst was no exception to this. Not only did the movement give her opportunities she might otherwise not have had, it also gave her the chance to 'laugh a defiance', in the words of a famous suffrage song,[1] in the face of a world which had not always given her cause for joy.

When Rosa May Billinghurst was born into a comfortable home in Lewisham, Kent, in 1876, the portents for her future seemed good. Her mother had grown up in London as Rosa Ann Brinsmead, daughter of a wealthy piano manufacturer named John Brinsmead. He had been born in Devon but had married in London and set up shop in Hampstead. When Rosa Ann married, aged thirty, in April 1873, her two brothers, Edgar and John, were working for the family firm, then renamed John Brinsmead and Sons. In 1883 they would win the right to label their goods: 'Pianoforte makers to HRH the Prince of Wales'. At the time of the wedding at All Souls church in Marylebone Rosa's groom, Henry Farncombe Billinghurst, was forty-one and working for a consortium of banks in London. The son of a bookseller from Tonbridge, Kent, he had begun work in Lambeth as a bank clerk during his late teens. A journal which survives shows he had a taste for travel – by the age of twenty-two he had been on a ramble through Belgium with friends and had spent a summer walking from Oxford to North Wales.[2] There is little trace of him between that time and his marriage and it is possible he went further afield, maybe to Australia. By the 1870s he was in London, working as secretary to the London Committee of Ten Associated Australian Banks.

Rosa and Henry gave their own names to their first two children, Henry, born in 1874, and Rosa May, born in 1876. They then produced Walter in 1877, Alice in 1879 and Albert in 1880. May, as she was known, was a healthy child at birth but when she was five months old disaster struck. She suffered an illness which left her whole body paralysed, and although she regained the use of her hands and arms she would never walk unaided. In later years she would use either a pair of sticks or, when outdoors, a tricycle whose wheels she could turn with her hands. Throughout her life she would wear irons on her legs. During her childhood May's parents took her to a series of doctors in both London and Paris, to little avail. All agreed her nervous system was 'most peculiar and unusual', according to her mother, but none had a solution to her ailments.[3] In addition to problems with her legs she also suffered from chronic hay fever and in her late teens she fell prey to what seems to have been a paralysis of the throat. For a year she could not drink any liquid without it flowing out through her nose. However, her home was a happy one and May grew up with a positive, even ebullient, attitude to life. It is unlikely she had the chance to go to school, for special education in England was not even in its infancy at the time of her childhood. However, it was not at all unusual for middle-class families to educate their children at home and May gained a good basic education. There was political awareness, too. In the early 1880s the Billinghursts took an interest in the prison treatment of the Irish leader Charles Parnell, keeping a sheaf of newspaper cuttings about him.[4]

May's disability, along with her gender, was bound to limit her options in life. By 1901 May's father had retired from banking. May, then twenty-five, was the only one among her siblings who had not managed at least in part to flee the family nest.[5] Her older brother, Henry, twenty-seven, was in Hampstead working as company secretary to John Brinsmead and Sons. Walter, twenty-four, was still at home but studying to be a doctor and Albert, twenty-one – known as Alf – had left home and was pursuing a desire to become an artist. By this time Alice, twenty-two, was living in Albury in Surrey, and it seems it was she who showed May the way to a life outside

the family. During the early years of the twentieth century Alice became involved in 'rescue' work among the poor and also worked as superintendent
of a children's home, and May soon found opportunities to accompany her
on her rounds. Sensing a chance to do something worthwhile, May began
taking on regular work at the Greenwich and Deptford Union Workhouse,
a vast structure stretching to four separate blocks and housing up to 1,000
people, more than 600 of whom were chronically sick or infirm. It was a
salutary experience, and one which began gradually to politicise the young
woman.

Having spent much of her own childhood and youth in an environ-
ment in which her own health was a focus for attention and concern, she
now found others whose disabilities, both physical and economic, were
much more severe. In Greenwich she met women who had spent their days
working in ghastly, unhealthy factories and who were condemned through
poverty to sit 'listlessly and hopelessly' waiting for death. 'My heart ached
and I thought surely if women were consulted in the management of the
state happier and better conditions must exist for hard-working sweated
lives such as these,' May would say later in explanation of how she became
a suffragette.[6] She was soon carrying out a variety of work among the
poorer inhabitants of Lewisham and Greenwich, teaching in a Sunday
School and in a Band of Hope, a temperance organisation set up by the
Methodists to help children from working-class families. She loved children, and it seems they loved her too. Her wheelchair served both as a curiosity and as an ice-breaker, and throughout her life she would often go
about followed by a small entourage of youngsters. In the homes of those
South London children she found conditions which both shocked and impressed her. Their mothers, often deserted by their husbands or coping
with violence and drunkenness, struggled to feed them and to send them
out on to the streets properly clothed. May began to question not just the
economic system which kept these women on starvation wages, but also
the marriage and divorce laws that placed them in thrall to their abusive
husbands. May's sister Alice reinforced these feelings by telling her stories
of girls aged twelve or thirteen arriving pregnant at the home where she
worked; the men who had abused them were rarely brought to account:

> It was gradually unfolded to me that the unequal laws which made women
> appear inferior to men were the main cause of these evils. I found that the
> man-made laws of marriage, parentage and divorce placed women in every

way in a condition of slavery – and were as harmful to men by giving them power to be tyrants.[7]

Seeking a political outlet for her anger at these conditions, May joined her local Women's Liberal Association. Increasingly, though, her desire for change would be focused on the need for women to have the vote in parliamentary elections. She followed with interest the activities of constitutional campaigners such as Millicent Fawcett, Charlotte Despard and even Emmeline Pankhurst, all of whom had been engaged for years in lobbying MPs and writing petitions. But she shared their growing frustration that the votes for women campaign had remained an academic rather than a political question, one which had simply failed to become a burning issue of the day. Then quite suddenly everything changed, she remembered later: 'I wondered how the public could ever be made to think about it. In the midst of the hopelessness of it all Christabel Pankhurst sounded the war note of militancy and was imprisoned for her boldness, and the subject of votes for women was on every tongue.'[8] As soon as the opportunity arose, May joined the Women's Social and Political Union. The first ever issue of the suffragette newspaper *Votes for Women*, published in October 1907, recorded that she had pledged a shilling to the union and her sister Alice had done the same. In November she gave £5, in December £1 and in January a further £5 – hefty sums for a young woman without paid employment. May had thrown herself into the cause with gusto.

May was among the first members of the Lewisham WSPU, which later split into three branches covering Lewisham, Woolwich and Greenwich. There were constitutional societies she could have joined – Blackheath London Society for Women's Suffrage, Lewisham Women's Franchise Club, or Church League for Women's Suffrage, for example – but she had been deeply impressed by the militancy of Christabel and Annie Kenney.[9] May's papers contain a leaflet published by the Women's Freedom League in 1908 but there is no other sign she became involved with this breakaway group of former WSPU members, which included Charlotte Despard. Not only had May and her sister joined the WSPU but their mother, Rosa, had done so too, making their Lewisham house available for 'at homes' and herself donating £5 in February 1908. May's father also gave money to the cause and her brother Alf became an active member of the men's campaign for women's suffrage.

Soon the union was sending May round the country to help with its campaigning. In April 1908, while in Manchester working on a by-election,

May wrote to the *Manchester Guardian* that she had withdrawn her active support from the Liberal Party, of which she had been a member for many years: 'I feel that the present government is not acting in accordance with the first principles of Liberalism, by refusing the right of representation to women taxpayers. I have joined no other party and I still claim to be a Liberal woman but a Liberal woman on strike.'[10] Her stance reflected the line of the Women's Liberal Federation, which had been putting intense pressure on its party leadership over the issue of votes for women.

The by-election at which May was working had been caused by the resignation of Henry Campbell-Bannerman as Prime Minister. Herbert Asquith had replaced him and the ministers who changed jobs in the subsequent reshuffle were required to face re-election. The suffragettes' campaign centred on North West Manchester, the seat of Winston Churchill, and Christabel had settled there for the duration. The women had enormous fun, holding a series of meetings which consistently drew bigger audiences than Churchill's.[11] May stayed at the Waverley Hotel in Oldham Street, campaigning till late each evening then adjourning to the nearby Lockhart's café with her comrades for hot coffee and cakes. One of the local newspapers reported that she was a star attraction of the militants' campaign: 'Miss Billinghurst excited much interest in Ancoats yesterday when she went through the streets propelling her hand-driven tricycle and distributing "Votes for Women" literature and canvassing votes for "anyone but Churchill".'[12] Churchill was defeated and his victorious Tory opponent, William Joynson-Hicks, acknowledged the suffragettes' contribution in his acceptance speech.

Back in Lewisham there was plenty of work to do. At a by-election that year in Peckham a Women's Freedom League protester – who became known as 'La Belle' Maloney – had regularly scuppered Churchill's speeches by appearing at his outdoor meetings with an enormous bell and ringing it constantly. Now May's mother, Rosa, took up a similar tactic to attract an audience to the WSPU's meetings on Blackheath. In *Votes for Women* the Lewisham organiser, a Russian widow named Eugenia Bouvier, recorded that up to 300 people could be drawn in by the ringing of Rosa's bell, even in a freezing April wind.[13] By then the South London suffragettes were attracting major speakers. They were disappointed in May 1908 when Emmeline Pankhurst and Christabel were both forced to cancel, but instead they had Emmeline Pethick-Lawrence and Flora Drummond. At the end of the month Christabel did appear, and 'got an excellent hearing in spite of the noisy youths who jingled bells and gave snatches of songs, and succeeded in inducing these same youths to practise our great shout for June 21'. The 'shout' in question was a huge cry of 'Votes for Women', being practised as the finale to a forthcoming national demonstration in Hyde Park.

May made herself busy on this front, too. On 13 June the *Evening Standard* reported that she had attended a constitutional suffragists' march of 10,000 women from the Thames Embankment to the Albert Hall, with the express purpose of distributing leaflets for the WSPU's own demonstration. The union had decided, contrary to its former practice, not to ask other suffrage organisations to take part in its event. On the day of the WSPU procession May's tricycle chair, decked out in purple, white and green, attracted a great deal of attention. It was at events such as this, as well as at by-elections, that she came into her own. She knew her appearance provided a small tableau which would be picked up in the press the following day, and she enjoyed the attention. She kept a comprehensive file of press cuttings of the events she attended, each little mention of her appearance boldly marked in black pen.[14] Like many of her contemporaries May had devoted herself body and soul to the cause, but May's body had a propaganda value which went beyond that of most suffragettes. Others could, and did, emphasise their vulnerability by hunger-striking or being photographed helpless in the grasp of a burly policeman. May's appearance in her chair pushed the same message on to a new plane. Her very appearance at suffrage events was a statement simultaneously of frailty and of cheerful defiance, and it was a statement she was more than happy to make.

May achieved the same result again in July, at a by-election in Haggerston. She travelled there daily by train from Lewisham to Cannon Street and onward under her own steam, propelling herself two miles along Bishopsgate and the Kingsland Road. Eugenia Bouvier reported in *Votes for Women* on 30 July 1908 that May had again proved a hit: 'Miss Billinghurst won the hearts of the children of Haggerston, who followed her tricycle chair through the whole constituency singing our new song to the tune of the Absent-minded Beggar, and cheering our prisoners.' During the by-election fifteen WSPU members were released from Holloway and were borne around the constituency in seven gaily decorated brakes, each bearing its own inscription: 'It's Dogged is as Dogged Does it'; 'Through Thick and Thin We Never Give In'. The *Evening Standard* noted on 31 July 1908 that May, who followed these carriages in her tricycle, was one of the suffragettes' most tireless workers. 'Notwithstanding her infirmity she has carried on a systematic house-to-house canvass and has even addressed meetings in the street … Last night several little children from the slums of Haggerston got behind her chair and pushed it all the way to Cannon Street,' the paper said. This cutting bears the first mention of a public speech by May. Throughout her work with the WSPU she rarely appeared on the union's platforms as a speaker, though she would occasionally chair a meeting when there was no one else available. Acquaintances do not describe May Billinghurst as being a shy or reticent person – one would later say she was 'completely fearless' and openly frustrated at the limits placed on her militancy by her disability – but she was never eager to push herself forward with a speech.[15]

The Haggerston by-election over, May went on holiday to Westcliff-on-Sea, in Essex. But she had no intention of taking a break from her suffrage activities. In common with other WSPU activists she devoted a part of each day to propaganda work and the sale of literature. Mrs Bouvier reported she had raised a great deal of interest and firm pledges of support from a number of fellow holidaymakers.[16] She returned to Lewisham in time to welcome home Edith New, a former Greenwich teacher who had been imprisoned for two months with Mary Leigh for breaking the windows of Number 10 Downing Street – the first stone-throwing incident, which was not sanctioned in advance by the union leadership but which was emulated to great effect later.

Events such as this first stone-throwing marked an increase in militancy and though May did not immediately become directly involved, demonstrations became increasingly fraught. On 13 October 1908 May was at Westminster with thousands of others to answer Emmeline Pankhurst's call to 'Rush the House of Commons!' Emmeline had been arrested that day for incitement along with Christabel and Flora Drummond, and Keir Hardie's secretary, Maggie Symons, had invaded the floor of the House of Commons shouting suffrage slogans. Outside, the atmosphere was cheerful if more than a little lively. 'One quaint sight was that of a lady flying the colours in an invalid cycle-chair, wheeling herself through the cheering mass near Caxton Hall. Pickpockets seized their opportunity and one was chased and arrested amid great excitement at the corner of Great Smith Street,' one paper reported.[17] When May returned home to Lewisham that night it was with a smaller band of comrades than she had arrived with. One of the key members of her branch, Mary Aldham, was among the forty-two arrested, charged with disorderly conduct.

Such excitements were only occasional events at this time, though, and the day-to-day work of the local unions continued unfettered by them. In the spring of 1909 the Lewisham members were much engaged with preparations for a WSPU exhibition at Kensington skating rink, for which they organised a 'guess the weight of the cake' competition. The cake had eventually to be split into six, the winners including Christabel Pankhurst. Rosa Billinghurst donated a large cache of Bruges pottery, which was sold from a separate stall and raised £15. The Lewisham branch had been offered the free rent of a local shop for three months, and when the venture proved a success it moved to permanent premises in the high street. From then on the weekly notes written by May or Eugenia Bouvier for *Votes for Women* were dominated by pleas for extra volunteer help behind the counter.

Increasingly, though, militancy and violence were intruding into this comfortable world. In June 1909 Eugenia Bouvier was arrested on a deputation to Parliament and went on hunger strike in prison. In October a WSPU meeting addressed by Emmeline Pethick-Lawrence at Blackheath was invaded by medical students who sang songs, threw fruit and destroyed the furniture. Eventually the police removed them but the union had to pay for the damage. But there were compensations. Militancy put the suffragettes in the public eye, and the weekly open-air meetings on Blackheath were attracting crowds of thousands where once there had been just a few hundred. When Christabel came to Ladywell Baths early in 1910, her arrival heralded by the WSPU's own drum and fife band, the crowds were so huge the traffic had to be stopped. 'There was a small element of opposition present and one or two fireworks were discharged, but members of the Men's League acted as stewards and at no time were the speakers seriously injured,' the local paper reported.[18]

May was not unduly perturbed by such events, and in November 1910 she had her first direct taste of the violence which often characterised suffragette demonstrations. A truce called during negotiations on a suffrage bill had ended when the political process stalled, and the WSPU's demonstration at the opening of Parliament was a particularly angry one. The police met the demonstrators with much greater force than previously, and May found herself in the thick of the fray. Several women sustained serious injuries and three subsequent deaths, including that of Emmeline Pankhurst's sister Mary Clarke, were later attributed to the brutality meted out on what became known as 'Black Friday'. May was one of 159 people arrested, though she was later released without charge and apparently without injury. There were two quite different versions of what happened, one public, one private. They serve to demonstrate clearly the propaganda game being played to good effect by the WSPU, which made much of its treatment that day. The public account, produced by May for the press, emphasised her frailty and the heartless response of the police:

> At first the police threw me out of the machine on to the ground in a very brutal manner. Secondly when on the machine again they tried to push me along with my arms twisted behind me in a very painful position. Thirdly they took me down a side road and left me in the middle of a hooligan crowd, first taking all the valves out of the wheels and pocketing them so that I could not move the machine.[19]

All this may well have been true, but the young daughter of one of May's comrades later recorded how the tales were told and re-told around the suffrage tea-tables in Lewisham:

> I remember hearing startling stories of her running battles with the police. Her crutches were lodged on each side of her self-propelling invalid chair and when a meeting was being broken up or an arrest being made she would charge the aggressors at a rate of knots that carried all before her. When the police retaliated and tried to control this she ran the risk of being ejected on to the ground, where she was quite helpless. Of course she took the risk with her eyes open and when this happened, as it did on occasion, made full and unscrupulous use of her infirmities so as to obtain the maximum publicity for the cause.[20]

It is clear from this account that May was quite aware of what she was doing and was indeed proud of her ability to manipulate the press in this way. If it did the cause good, it was something to celebrate. And, in the genteel surroundings of Lewisham, celebrate she did.

As her comrades testified, May was also frustrated by her disability. It was hard for her to watch her friends arrested and imprisoned but to find the police always gave her a wide berth – possibly with a keen eye to just the sort of publicity May excelled at. But finally, at the 1911 opening of Parliament, May was sentenced to a term in prison. The scene was similar to that of a year earlier. The truce, reinstated after Black Friday, had finally ended. Wave after wave of women attempted to storm the House of Commons, and were pushed back by police. The arrests totalled 156, and May was among them. The press reported that May had 'set her chair going at full tilt towards the police'.[21] She tried to force her tricycle through their cordon and when they failed to turn her round, they lifted her bodily, chair and all, and carried her to Cannon Row. She was charged with obstruction and sentenced to five days' imprisonment or a five shilling fine.

It seems someone must have paid May's fine, for there is no record of her having gone to Holloway on this occasion. It was not long before she did, though, and this time her arrest was carefully planned in advance. May agreed, along with more than 100 other women, to take part in the mass window-smashing raids which devastated London's main shopping thoroughfares in 1912. On such occasions her tricycle had a very practical use, for implements of destruction could easily be hidden underneath the rug covering May's knees, and the sight of a woman in a wheelchair tended not to excite suspicion – even despite the purple, white and green metal flag which always flew behind it. May took part in the first of two waves of raids, on 1 March. It was a Friday, and as she and her comrades made their way into central London the rain which had been falling all day gave way to pale sunshine. Regent Street was heaving, as usual, with shoppers and homeward-bound office workers. At 5.45 p.m., according to *Votes for Women*, the street erupted: 'In front, behind, from every side it came – a hammering, crashing, splintering sound unheard in the annals of shopping … At the windows excited crowds collected, shouting, gesticulating. At the centre of each crowd stood a woman, pale, calm and silent.'[22]

May received a longer sentence this time – one month's hard labour, though in reality the 'hard labour' part was not enforced. According to one acquaintance who gave testimony to May's impish sense of humour she viewed arrest, as she did much else in life, as an opportunity to have some fun.[23] After being sentenced she declined to be taken from the court to Holloway in the prison van, insisting that the only possible way for her to travel was to use her wheelchair. Uncertain how to deal with this unprecedented demand the authorities gave in and detailed a policeman to push May to her destination. The pair had not travelled far before May noticed she was passing a friend's house. She asked the policeman to stop for a moment: could he just wait while she popped in to say hello? As soon as he had agreed May got out of her chair and walked, with the aid of her sticks, into the house, leaving the policeman to mind the tricycle. She emerged twenty minutes later – though she then returned the favour by waiting while the policeman then paid a visit of his own to a convenient hostelry.

May's first experience of Holloway was not arduous. In fact the prison became known among suffragette inmates during this period as 'Liberty Hall'.[24] While some of their number were on hunger strike and enduring appalling treatment, many others found their incarceration surprisingly jolly. The authorities had given in to some of their demands for special status and had begun allowing far more freedom than in previous days. Though not officially in the 'first division' they were able to wear their own clothes and most were in one wing with their cell doors unlocked so they could come and go as they pleased. A dancer who had been on a window-smashing raid ordered her ballet skirts to be brought in and put on a performance for both prisoners and warders, while other inmates spent their time doing amusing drawings or writing humorous sketches about the prison. Ethel Smyth, Emmeline Pankhurst's composer friend, was once seen leaning from her cell window while the others were at exercise, conducting them with a toothbrush as they sang her suffragette anthem, 'March of the Women'. During these halcyon days before the final, gruelling two years of the struggle friendships were made and cemented, and May was no exception. A fellow prisoner, Alice Ker, a doctor from Liverpool who had smashed Harrods' window, wrote to her daughters in early April: 'Miss Billinghurst, the tricycle lady, is going out on the 11th and will take this. She is quite lame, wears irons on her legs and walks with crutches when she is out of her tricycle. We shall miss her very much when she goes out.'[25] A suffragette 'at home' was held in Woolwich to celebrate May's release. During her absence one of her local comrades had undertaken double newspaper-selling duties to make up for her absence, and members had raised extra funds by stepping up their 'self-denial' efforts.

May's experience did not deter her from further acts of rebellion and it was not long before she became involved in a new type of action ordered by Christabel: secret militancy. There were various forms of this, including setting fire to empty buildings and making false calls to the emergency services. May was asked to commit a third, which involved destroying the contents of pillar-boxes. This was done with red ochre, jam, tar, permanganate of potash, varnish or phosphorus. By December 1912 the government said 5,000 letters had been damaged in this manner, many of them, we now know, by May.[26] According to Lilian Lenton, a fellow suffragette who had been in Holloway with May that year and who later used the Billinghurst home as a safe house while hiding from police after committing arson, May was quite blatant about this activity and was bound to be caught sooner or later.

She would set out in her chair with many little packages from which, when they were turned upside down, there flowed a dark brown sticky fluid, concealed under the rug which covered her legs. She went undeviatingly from one pillar box to another, sometimes alone, sometimes with another suffragette to do the actual job, dropping a package into each one.[27]

It seems this routine was a frequent one throughout the last three or four months of 1912. She must have been given the sticky substance by a WSPU aide who was assigned full time to the task of stirring up secret militancy, for when asked what it was she had to admit she did not make it herself. A narrow escape would always amuse her and give her a story to tell later. Once, going down Kingsway near the WSPU headquarters, a businessman who was about to post a bundle of letters noticed her coming along and spied the suffrage flag on her chair. 'I'm not going to post these until that woman's past!' he joked loudly. With a cheeky smile May sailed past him just before he posted his letters. Then her companion, following unobserved with the substances, dropped her little package in on top of them.[28]

In mid-December 1912 the inevitable happened. May and two other suffragettes, Grace Mitchell and Louisa Gay, were spotted on Blackheath preparing for a pillar-box raid. They were followed, the police were called and all three were arrested. At the police station a bag was found in May's tricycle containing a number of packages wrapped in white tissue paper. Each was filled with an unidentified black fluid, probably varnish. May told the officer she had been disappointed by the response to her activities: 'With all the pillar boxes we've done, there has been nothing in the papers about it – perhaps now there has been an arrest there will be something,' she chirruped.[29] Although the men who reported the offence said they had seen Grace Mitchell post the package, she denied having done so. May, who must have agreed beforehand to confess if necessary, simply responded: 'All right, let my mother know.' She was given bail and remanded for trial at the Old Bailey in January, and spent Christmas contemplating the difficult times ahead. By now suffragettes were hunger-striking routinely, and May was determined to do the same once back in Holloway.

The WSPU leadership were delighted with her and letters of congratulation flooded in during the weeks before her trial. Her Lewisham comrade Dora Gregory enclosed a gift of a silver hammer – she owned one like it and May had asked her for one – and thanked May for her own gift of anti-suffrage toffee, which had been devoured by Liberal teachers at the school where she worked. Emmeline Pankhurst wrote from Paris, where she was spending Christmas with Christabel: 'I cannot tell you how deeply I feel your splendid courage and endurance. All my heart will be with you during the ordeal that lies before you.'[30] Emmeline suggested May should see the WSPU solicitor, which she did – but she was reluctant to follow his advice that she should conduct her own defence. Such heroics were fine for the union leaders, who were used to making eloquent speeches under stress, but May did not feel confident of her own ability to do so. A fellow inmate from the previous March, Agnes Kelly, wrote to reassure her:

> As to your idea that you cannot speak in words as well as in deeds why that is (forgive me!) the veriest nonsense. Of course you can speak and even if you could not still you remember the words of one of the Lenten hymns – 'And all three hours his silence spoke.' Your silence will speak even if your tongue refuses to be eloquent.[31]

In the end May did defend herself, but she neither cross-examined witnesses nor gave evidence on oath. There were no full reports of her speech – the WSPU shorthand writer was excluded – but May's notes suggest she read out an eloquent defence of her position.[32] She explained how she came to the suffrage movement through her rescue work with impoverished families, and went on to say that she would never have committed her militant acts if she had felt there was an alternative. 'The government authorities may further maim my body by the torture of forcible feeding as they are torturing weak women in prison at the present time. They may even kill me in the process for I am not strong, but they cannot take away my freedom of spirit or my determination to fight this good fight to the end,' she concluded.[33]

The judge was impressed. Usually such speeches from the dock were dismissed as propaganda, but in summing up the recorder told May:

> No one could, I think, doubt for a moment – as mistaken as I think you to be – that you were animated by the highest and purest motives in what you did … you do not belong to the class of hysterical women, many of whom are associated with this movement, who appear to be animated mainly or at any rate in some measure by a desire for notoriety.[34]

He sentenced May and Louisa Gay to eight months but Grace Mitchell, who suffered from curvature of the spine, gastritis and rheumatism, was bound over in view of her poor health. May was placed in the first division, which presented her with something of a dilemma. She had been determined to hunger-strike but the usual pretext for this was the suffrage prisoners' lack of special status. Now May became the first suffragette to be awarded such a privilege. She wrote to her mother after the trial that she intended to continue as planned: 'I shall be out quite soon but a bit ill I have no doubt. If I do not fight for this the next lot of women will have *years* in the first division … I am the one who must fight for *no* division.'[35] She added an exhortation to her mother, who had just made a £50 donation to the cause, to keep harassing the Home Secretary about her case: 'Save the papers for me and worry the life out of McKenna.'

May's family did as she asked, instituting a formidable letter-writing campaign on her behalf to plead for her exemption from forcible feeding. Her health would not stand it, they said – particularly her throat, which had been paralysed during her youth. Sympathetic MPs sent helpful replies – George Lansbury promised to do all he could, while Keir Hardie put down parliamentary questions and suggested Alf should write directly to the Home Office. Emmeline Pankhurst wrote to Rosa to tell her that she had just seen a friend who had influence with Reginald McKenna, and that she was arranging for the Home Secretary to see Rosa's letter voicing her concerns.

May's first few days in prison were relatively peaceful. A suffrage choir sang 'The Women's Marseillaise' outside the gates each night and she could hear them from her cell in the infirmary wing. There was little contact with other prisoners and although someone managed to smuggle notes from Louisa Gay, she soon began to feel lonely and isolated. Gradually her hunger strike started to have an effect. In a long letter smuggled out of Holloway she told her mother that she had been in bed ever since she started the strike: 'I just laid on my back and endured it all – on Sunday I was very weak and on Sunday night I tried to get out to the bell because my head was swimming round so I fell on the floor and fainted.'[36] There was worse to come. On the third day prison doctors tried to force feed her but withdrew when she resisted. The following day, May continued, they made a far more determined attempt:

> My head was forced back and a tube jammed down my nose. It was the most awful torture. I groaned with pain and I coughed and gulped the tube up and would not let it pass down my throat. Then they tried the other nostril

and they found that was smaller still and slightly deformed, I suppose from constant hay-fever. The new doctor said it was impossible to get the tube down that one so they jammed it down again through the other and I wondered if the pain was as bad as child-birth. I just had strength and will enough to vomit it up again and I could see tears in the wardresses' eyes.[37]

The doctor in charge, Irwin Forward, then forced May's mouth open using iron pincers, which broke a tooth, and poured liquid down her throat before leaving her weeping with rage.

The news of May's treatment was soon made public and caused outrage in the Liberal press. Albert Dawson, editor of the *Christian Commonwealth*, sent a messenger to Rosa's house with a request for a picture of May 'preferably on her tricycle',[38] to accompany an article about the case. In it he pointed out that as the purpose of forcible feeding was to prevent prisoners from determining their own sentences, it could be justified only if it then allowed the sentence to be completed in full. 'Otherwise, obviously, the process becomes torture, pure and simple, naked and confessed; the pretence that the object is to protect the prisoner against herself being abandoned,' he wrote.[39]

And so it was with May. On 18 January she was released into the care of an aunt, considerably thinner and suffering from soreness in her nose and throat as well as a broken tooth. The prison doctors were by now concerned about her health, for her heart was showing signs of stress. Back at home, May spent a couple of weeks recovering and enjoying the congratulatory messages of her friends. Dora Gregory wrote to tell her she was to have the place of honour at a meeting with Emmeline Pankhurst on 4 February, sitting beside the leader on the platform. Eleanor Penn-Gaskell wrote from North London to say she had been lobbying on her behalf: 'I know that man Forward is a double-dyed brute – I went to the Home Office and denounced him to the under-secretary and I have spoken against him in public again and again – we must act and I will consult with others.'[40]

There was adverse reaction too. An anonymous letter addressed to Rosa Billinghurst warned that neither she nor May should leave home alone.

Do not allow your daughter to go out in the neighbourhood of Blackheath alone or she will be a worse cripple than she now is – as she will be treated as a coward (which she is considered to be) for not taking her punishment.

If you can leave the neighbourhood do so as sooner or later she will be attacked (and possibly yourself as you are much disliked for being the mother of a coward).[41]

At demonstrations in Lewisham that spring police twice had to rescue suffragettes from angry crowds. This ill-feeling was more due to national events than to May's imprisonment though. At one meeting there were shouts of 'Let Mrs Pankhurst die' and suggestions the protesters 'ought to be boiled and horsewhipped'.

The controversy over May's treatment rumbled on for months, and she visited a variety of medical specialists – partly for treatment, particularly to her broken tooth, and partly to gain testimonies of the damage done to her nose and throat. McKenna himself was drawn in after a WSPU supporter raised the issue in a speech in the Home Secretary's Pontypool constituency and he felt obliged to deny such brutality had been used. May wrote a statement saying that in her doctors' opinion no one should have attempted to feed her through a nasal tube if they had examined her first.[42] Meanwhile she continued to be in demand at meetings where she was asked to give an account of her experience in Holloway. In November 1913 she spoke at an 'inquiry' into force feeding at the Kingsway Hall, having apparently by then overcome her dislike of public speaking. *Votes for Women* recorded that she produced 'a roar of cheering' when she recalled how the prison doctor had tried to dissuade her from hunger-striking by asking her what her mother would say if she were brought home a wreck or worse. Her reply – that her mother would sooner have her brought home a corpse than a coward – delighted the audience.

At around this time May's family opened their home to suffragettes who were out on licence under the Cat and Mouse Act and were evading rearrest. One of those who stayed with them was Lilian Lenton, a dancer who had resolved to burn down two buildings each week – including the tea pavilion at Kew Gardens – and who was released from Holloway in a state of collapse in February 1914 after doctors accidentally forced food into her lungs and caused pleurisy. Lilian's presence appealed to May's sense of humour, she recalled later, and she made a point of taking her around the neighbourhood: 'It amused her greatly to go about in that chair, proclaiming her faith, with me, badly wanted, walking by her side and pushing when necessary. She took great pleasure in introducing me to all and sundry as a "budding suffragette".[43] On one occasion May even asked a policeman to push her chair up a particularly steep hill with Lilian, heavily disguised, walking alongside.

May's final major act of militancy was, as it turned out, the WSPU's last big raid before the outbreak of war.[44] Emmeline Pankhurst had announced that as ministers had degraded themselves by cruelty to the suffragettes, they would now talk directly to the King. He refused to meet them and a 'deputation' to Buckingham Palace was organised for 21 May 1914. The event was widely advertised and a large crowd, some of them hostile, assembled near the palace along with 1,500 police. The suffragettes, who in the past had only rarely used weapons at such demonstrations, came armed with clubs or with red or green powder. The police responded with equal violence. One woman was struck on the head by a truncheon and another claimed she had heard one constable advising another to grab a demonstrator by the breasts. Arms were twisted and hair was pulled. In the thick of this fray May drove her tricycle into the line of mounted policemen, according to Charlotte Drake, one of Sylvia's East London suffragettes:

> I was beside her. They threw us back, but we returned. Two policemen picked up the tricycle with Miss Billinghurst in it, turned it over and dropped her to the ground. The excitement gave me strength – I picked her up bodily and lifted her back. We straightened the machine as best we could, rested a little to take breath and struggled on again.[45]

At that point Charlotte lost sight of May, but photographs taken on the day show that she managed to chain her chair to the Buckingham Palace railings. *The Suffragette* reported that her chair was broken up by the police, though there is no record of her being arrested or charged.[46] Charlotte Drake's account suggests May tried hard to get arrested but the police declined.

After the outbreak of war May remained loyal to the WSPU, and in 1917 she attended a meeting on 'Russia and the War', addressed by Emmeline Pankhurst after her trip to the East. In 1918 May went to Smethwick to support Christabel's election effort, and in an echo of former days the papers noted her presence in a gaily decorated tricycle. She also attended Emmeline Pankhurst's funeral and the unveiling of her statue in 1930. But she now had time for other interests. In 1922, having moved to a basement flat at Alf's home near Regent's Park, she got a car and was able to travel long distances with much greater ease. She also became a regular visitor to the theatre. Monica Pittman, the young daughter of one of her suffrage friends, would often accompany her on these trips.[47] May had a particular passion for the Russian Ballet and when the Al-Hambra reopened after the war she went to as many performances as she could, befriending the pit attendants to obtain their help in getting to her seat. May always enjoyed the company of children and Monica remembered being given the run of her pretty garden in Regent's Park as well as being fed wonderful teas, even in wartime. She may even at some time in the 1930s have fostered a child – there is a letter in her papers from St George's Training School in Stonebury, Gloucestershire, to which she had written for help or advice about a girl named Beth who was causing her some distress. When the Second World War broke out May moved to Weybridge in Surrey, where she lived for fourteen years until her death in 1953.

When May died Lilian Lenton, who had kept in touch with her over the years, wrote an affectionate obituary in the journal of the Women's Freedom League, of which she was by then editor:

> Despite her frustrating affliction I have known her always as full of life and courage, not to mention jollity, not bitter as she might have been, sustained, I think, by her belief in re-incarnation. She thought of this life as but one of many. She hoped for and expected better luck next time, and this, I trust, will be hers.[48]

It would be easy to characterise May Billinghurst as a woman whose disabilities were cynically used by the WSPU for the purposes of propaganda. Indeed, they were. But to leave it at that would be to do May a grave disservice. Better to say that she was a woman who shamelessly used *her own* disabilities for the purposes of propaganda, and who was proud to do so in the service of a cause for which she would cheerfully have given her life. The work May Billinghurst did for the WSPU in Lewisham and the surrounding area was as valuable, as tireless, as that of any other volunteer. With no full-time employment and a secure financial background she was able to devote more time to it than most. But her disability gave her a special extra talent, and her own efforts and those of the union ensured it was exploited to the full.

Emily Wilding Davison

IX

Emily Wilding Davison – First Martyr

The glorious and inscrutable spirit of liberty has but one further penalty written in its power: the surrender of life itself. It is the supreme consummation of sacrifice, than which none can be higher and greater. To lay down life for friends, that is glorious, selfless, inspiring! But to re-enact the tragedy of Calvary for generations yet unborn, that is the last and consummate sacrifice of the militant! Nor will she shrink from this Nirvana. She will be faithful 'unto the last'.

> Essay by Emily Wilding Davison, 'The Price of Liberty', circa 1912

The name Emily Wilding Davison is seared on the public imagination as a summation of all that was radical, daring and desperate about the militant suffragettes. To record the details of her life seems almost perverse for it is the very public, very violent nature of her death which is remembered. The grainy, jerky film of Emily's diminutive figure rushing on to the Epsom race-course, her split-second transformation from protester to prone, limp mound of clothing, still makes shocking viewing. Its impact in the early days of newsreel, when such a dramatic event had rarely, if ever, been screened, was momentous. Thousands of people watched the scene played and re-played in picture houses across the country and it horrified, thrilled and divided them in equal measure. Emily Wilding Davison went down in history as the woman who threw herself under the King's horse at the 1913 Derby.

Emily's death was as public as it could possibly have been, and yet she remains one of the more obscure figures among the handful of suffragettes whose names are still familiar today. Indeed, the very manner of her death makes it hard to see her properly. What could cause a woman to run to her death under the hooves of a galloping horse? It is as if the act itself had formed a sort of distorting lens, through which from that day on the world

has been forced to view everything that led up to it. Who was Emily Wilding Davison, we want to know? What was there in her early life, in the way
she conducted herself as a young adult, to suggest that something like this
might happen? Apart from the obvious – the undisputed fact of her extreme militancy in the suffrage cause – there is not much to go on. If Emily
had married early into middle-class respectability and never been heard of
by the world at large, no one who knew her would have raised an eyebrow.

Though seen by posterity as a Northumbrian, Emily Wilding Davison
was born into comfortable circumstances in Blackheath, in London. The
Davison family had made money before leaving their Northumbrian roots
behind. Emily's great grandfather had been armourer to the Duke of
Northumberland in the early nineteenth century, her grandfather had set
up successful gunmaking businesses in Newcastle and Alnwick. Her father,
Charles Edward Davison, had been articled to a firm of solicitors in Morpeth but as a young man he left the family home for India. There he met
and married Sarah Siton Chisholm. The couple returned to England, where
they had nine children in fifteen years before Sarah died, aged forty-four.
Charles, then aged forty-five and mainly occupied by an investment in the
London Tram Company, married again in 1868. His new wife, Margaret
Caisley, was from Longhirst in Northumberland and was just nineteen. The
following year she gave birth to Alfred, who was followed by Emily on
11 October 1872. The youngest of Charles' first family was eight years old
when Emily was born. While she was still a baby the Davisons moved to
Gaston House in Sawbridgeworth, Hertfordshire, a big, three-storey Georgian building with ample room for their large and still growing family.[1]

Despite being among the youngest of the brood, Emily was a determined child and a leader among her playmates. When she was very young
her older half-brothers and sisters would send her as an emissary to her
mother to ask for sweets – to the point where she earned the pet-name
'Weet', for she could not pronounce the word. It stayed with her for life. According to Gertrude Colmore, a friend and fellow suffragette who interviewed Emily's mother while writing a eulogy to her soon after her death,
the child loved to play military games and had some of the 'disciplinary instincts of the martinet'. On one occasion she lined up the other children to
take part in a military funeral for all the flies that had died in the house.
Everything had to be perfect – the child soldiers in the correct marching
order, flags in position. When they objected to this tyranny Emily took
herself off to play alone, allowing the flagless, straggling procession to go

on without her rather than take part in a substandard operation. An un-named childhood friend told Colmore Emily was a high-spirited, daring child who delighted in 'treading on forbidden ground'. She could also be difficult. She often gave her nurse trouble, and she hated the affectionate teasing of her older brothers and sisters.

When Emily was eleven her family moved back to London and in her teens she attended the Kensington High School, where she thrived. Her headmistress, Miss Hitchcock, liked her bright young pupil so much that she continued to write to her and follow her progress long after she had left: 'She was rather a delicate looking child, fair-haired and without much colour, but with bright, intelligent eyes, and a half shy, half confident way of looking up with her head a little on one side and smiling at one which won my heart at once.'[2] Emily was not as fragile as she looked. At school she was a hard-working, active girl who excelled at French, English litera-ture and drawing.[3] Emily was not the most brilliant or the most inspiring pupil in her year, but she had originality and a habit of doing better than expected in exams. Determined to do well, she must have devoted a good deal of her spare time to study. But she was also an active girl who enjoyed swimming – she once won a gold medal in a swimming championship at Chelsea Baths – cycling, skating and the theatre. Her tastes embraced everything from Shakespeare or Shaw to musical comedy. Nobody re-membered her having any interest in politics.

Emily was treated to a year in Switzerland before she left school, but she was not the kind to drift along waiting for a suitable husband. She was al-ready thinking ahead, and when she visited an old schoolfriend who was studying at Holloway College she knew what path she should take. In 1891, aged nineteen, she won a bursary to study English at the college in Egham, Surrey, which had been opened five years earlier by Queen Victoria. The college was not admitted as a school of the University of London until 1900, and so Emily studied for the Oxford Honour School qualification. Here she was able to blossom, enjoying the grand and spacious surround-ings of the college, which was modelled on a French château. Then, two years into her studies, her father died.

The loss came as a shock in more ways than one: 'I do not know if I can stay on after this term, as we do not know how matters are yet, so I must make the best of this term. Mamma is very anxious to keep me at college for my exam if it is possible,' Emily wrote to a friend just after the funeral, which had taken her to Morpeth for the first time.[4] It soon became clear the family's finances were in a poor state. Emily was forced to leave Holloway College and take a job as a governess, though she made it a condition of her employment that she should have time free in the evenings to study. By borrowing notes from friends who were still at Holloway and by saving enough money to spend a term at St Hugh's Hall, a women's college recently founded in Oxford, she managed to gain a first class degree. She then went on to study for an honours degree from London, which she also took while working as a governess. A glimpse of Emily's more exuberant side can be seen in an account of her reaction to learning she had been awarded a first. She received her results while staying with her mother, who had moved back to Longhorsley, near Morpeth and opened a bakery and confectionery in the village. Emily was so overjoyed to learn of her success that she grabbed a jar of sweets from the shop, ran out on to the village green and began distributing them among the children playing there.[5]

Having gained her honours degree in English language and literature Emily, then aged twenty-three, took a teaching job at the Church of England College for Girls in Edgbaston, Birmingham. It was not a success, for she found it difficult to discipline the children and she left after a year. In a testimonial the head teacher, Miss Landon Thomas, said she had let her go because although she had needed someone to prepare candidates for the Cambridge Higher Local examination in English, she later decided she needed a science tutor instead. 'I consider Miss Davison better suited for girls in the middle and upper school than for quite young ones,' she said.[6]

By all accounts Emily was a sunny but determined individual with a mobile face, an attractive manner and a quizzical way of looking at her companions, head to one side and a half-smile on her lips. Miss Hitchcock, who continued to see her regularly, said she always seemed cheerful: 'I never heard her complain or express anxiety about her future or that of her mother. I never heard her utter a word against anyone under whom she worked, and no-one ever had less thought of adopting a "misunderstood" pose.'[7] Sylvia Pankhurst would later describe her as tall and slender with unusually long arms, a small narrow head and red hair – though others described her hair, her most striking feature, as reddish or golden blonde. 'Her illusive, whimsical green eyes and thin, half-smiling mouth bore often the mocking expression of the Mona Lisa,' Sylvia wrote.[8]

Emily was deeply religious, and this must provide some clue to the events of her later life. She kept a Bible by her bed, attended church regularly and would often sing hymns to keep herself cheerful at difficult times.

A friend recalled that before going to bed each night Emily spent a strikingly long time saying her prayers. In her mind everything she did was done hand-in-hand with God, and she would later tell her mother that her acts of militancy were committed while 'under the influence'. If there was one slight oddity in her character, it was this. It was not unusual, of course, for a young late-Victorian woman to take on such religious fervour, but Emily's capacity for devotion would carry her into hitherto unimagined crusades. For in her, this quality was combined with a much more less exalted attribute – the desire to win. Emily had to be more religious than her friends, more earnest in her displays of adoration. Later, she would compete to be the most daring militant, to prostrate herself more fully than any other before the altar of the suffrage cause.

From Birmingham Emily moved to Seabury School in Worthing, where she spent two years. She seemed to be coming to terms with the job, but then she decided school teaching was not for her. Her headmistress, Miss Carr, gave her a more glowing testimonial. Emily's work had given her 'entire satisfaction', she said. 'I have found her a most capable teacher, a conscientious worker and a good disciplinarian.'[9] Emily went back to working as a governess in the employment of Edward Moorhouse, a Yorkshireman, and his New Zealand-born wife, Mary Ann. The 1901 census-takers found the family living in Spratton, Northamptonshire, with Emily in charge of their three children – Ann, aged fifteen, Mary, aged eleven, and Edward, aged seven.[10] Mr Moorhouse, who was sixty-six at the time, recorded his occupation as 'living on own means', which were substantial. Emily enjoyed the work and had a happy relationship with the Moorhouse children, but as time went on a problem began to emerge: politics.

Not much is known about Emily's early WSPU activities, but it seems she noted the publicity in the autumn of 1905 when Christabel Pankhurst and Annie Kenney were imprisoned in Manchester, and soon afterwards began attending meetings. She went first with a sense of curiosity and then with a growing zeal for the women's cause. Emily was forced to keep a low profile, though, because her employers were firmly opposed to the activities of the union. Mary Ann Moorhouse did not want her daughters indoctrinated into views she did not share. When it became impossible to continue this double life, Emily opted to give up her job rather than her extramural activities. She went briefly to work for a more sympathetic family in Berkshire, but felt the need to be where the action was – in London. She found work as a coach and teacher for university extension classes, but from 1908 the real focus of her life was to be the suffragette movement.

Emily's family had left London and so she lodged with a succession of different families, some of them suffrage supporters. Her first recorded address during this period was Titchborne Street, Hyde Park, the home of a Mrs Elizabeth Elsmore.[11] Emily probably did not spend much time there. With the London suffrage movement growing apace, she spent most of her evenings at meetings, and began to draw to her a close circle of suffrage friends. One old acquaintance with whom she now re-established contact was Rose Lamartine Yates, who had been at Holloway College just after Emily and who was also becoming involved with the suffrage movement. There were new contacts, too, including Mary Leigh, a fellow militant and teacher who became one of Emily's closest friends.

Even now, Emily's life was not all protests and speeches. She always maintained contact with old friends and much mystery has been made of the existence of a close companion called Miss Morrison whose exact identity remains obscure. Miss Morrison knew Emily's family well and was in their carriage at Emily's funeral. In one letter she is described as 'Miss Morrison the singer', and is mentioned as having visited Longhorsley with Emily during summer holidays.[12] Winifred Stobbart, whose family knew Emily's mother well, clearly remembered these visits.[13] Miss Morrison was a frequent visitor to her house for musical parties, she said, and as a girl she knew her as 'Auntie Daddy'. In their book on Emily's life, Ann Morley and Liz Stanley suggest obliquely that this may have been a lesbian relationship. They suggest Miss Morrison may have been the 'Loving Aberdeen Friend' who sent an engraved marble book to rest on Emily's grave, and that she may in fact have been a suffragette called Edith Jane Douglas Morrison. But it seems more likely Emily's Aberdeen connection was Katherine Riddell, with whom she stayed during visits to Aberdeen. Miss Morrison was probably an old schoolfriend or a friend of the family. Among Emily's papers is a letter from her sister which mentions she is sending sweets and adds: 'Don't tell the Morrisons as I don't think I've enough boxes.' Colmore refers frequently to this 'constant companion' and says Emily had known her since her schooldays. It was with her that Emily visited the old school fellow who inspired her to apply for Holloway College, and with her she gained her taste for the theatre.

Emily was close to her mother, wrote to her frequently and visited at least twice a year, at Christmas and during the summer. Norah Balls, a Newcastle suffragette, knew Mrs Davison well because she used to cycle out with friends for one of the 'teas' offered in her shop. 'I think she felt her daughter was rather too much for her. She was a typical countrywoman, a very fine woman who worked very hard to keep herself – fiercely independent,' she said in a later interview.[14] Norah Balls knew Emily only slightly, and described her as 'higher grade in a way because she was a born militant'. But while the WSPU was active in Newcastle, in rural Longhorsley the suffrage cause was not winning a great deal of sympathy. Winifred Stobbart's mother allowed Emily to hold a meeting at her house and wrote later to a friend that she found her 'a fool'.[15] Sometimes Emily would stand on a barrel at the gate of a local farm and preach the cause; sometimes she would ask Winifred Stobbart's father to give her a lift to Morpeth, where she would jump on the back of his open car to make a speech.[16] When one heckling farmer suggested she should be at home helping her mother to darn stockings, she promised to display hers if he would do the same. Needless to say, hers were perfect while his were full of holes.

There are only rare glimpses of Emily's sense of humour, and she does not seem to have been adopted by the WSPU as one of its regular speakers. But she was full of enthusiasm for everything she did. In one early letter to Mary Leigh she exclaimed: 'Thanks ever so much for your jolly letter … What ages since I have seen you all!' In a postscript she added: 'NO SURRENDER. Bravo! Mrs Leigh!' Perhaps more surprisingly Fenner Brockway remembered Emily as 'a charming and serene woman, quite attractive, feminine and sweet'.[17]

Emily's life as a militant grew from small beginnings. In June 1908 she was chief steward at Marylebone station for the WSPU's big rally in Hyde Park, charged with meeting the special trains as they arrived and ensuring that each contingent of marchers set off at the right time and in the right formation. During 1909 she spent time working for the union in Manchester and it was there that she volunteered, during a meeting held by Emmeline Pankhurst to mark the end of a tour of Lancashire, to go on a deputation to the Prime Minister. The expedition followed a 'Women's Parliament' rally and was led by Georgiana Solomon, widow of the former Governor General of South Africa. Emily was among twenty-one people arrested while trying to gain entry to the House of Commons. She was charged with obstruction and imprisoned for a month after refusing to give an undertaking not to repeat the offence.

Emily would spend many days looking at the walls of prison cells over the next four years, and just three months later she was arrested again. She had volunteered, with Mary Leigh and Alice Paul, among others, to interrupt Lloyd George's meeting on 30 July 1909, and was sentenced to two months. In a letter to a schoolfriend written after her release, she described her exploits with all the girlish joy of one who has recently discovered a delightful new talent. She also displayed her competitive spirit:

> When I was shut in the cell I at once smashed seventeen panes of glass ... Then they rushed me into another cell in which everything was fixed. I broke seven panes of that window, to the matron's utter astonishment, as I had a *hammer*. I could not have done it otherwise, and I don't think any of the others were able to do that. Then they forcibly undressed me and left me sitting in a prison chemise. I sang the second verse of 'God Save the King' with 'Confound their politics' in it![18]

Despite this upbeat tone, the rest of her spell in Holloway was grim. Emily was moved to one of the worst cells, 'very dark, with double doors,' where she found an earlier suffragette incumbent, Lillian Dove-Willcox, had inscribed 'Dum Spiro Spero' – While I breathe I hope – on the wall. Emily added her own inscription, which was to become her battle-cry: 'Rebellion against tyrants is obedience to God.' There she began her first hunger strike, the women having all resolved to do so if they were not treated as first class prisoners. Emily fasted for 124 hours before being released, and lost one and a half stone. The experience seemed to strengthen the religious zeal of her militancy, and she wrote in *Votes for Women* that through her suffrage work she had 'come into a fullness of joy and an interest in living which I never before experienced'.[19]

Emily quickly became one of the movement's most active militants. On 9 October 1909, after a spell of recovery in Longhorsley, she tried to throw a stone at Lloyd George's car in Newcastle but was grabbed by two plainclothes policemen before she could do so. On 14 October she was in Lancashire, writing to WSPU headquarters that she was staying with a Mrs Murphy in Radcliffe, 'once more acting almost as organiser here ready for a certain person'.[20] Although she never held an official post with the union she was a useful foot-soldier, always available to go to prison, anywhere in the country. This, in the view of the union's leadership, was the high tide of Emily's militancy. She was in favour. Indeed, what would long be regarded as her finest hour was now upon her. In September 1909 Emily's friends Mary Leigh and Charlotte Marsh, arrested in Birmingham after a rooftop protest, became the first suffragettes to suffer force feeding. Emily, facing arrest for protesting at the meeting of this 'certain person', a Liberal ship-ping magnate named Sir Walter Runciman, knew she would be next.

Emily had been in Strangeways gaol just one day when the prison doc-tors entered her cell. When she resisted, they resorted to violence. 'The scene which followed will haunt me with its horror all my life and is almost indescribable. While they held me flat the elder doctor tried all round my mouth with the steel gag to find an opening,' she recalled afterwards.[21] Emily developed a genuine horror of force feeding, partly prompted by her own experience and partly by her concern for Mary Leigh, and when she was moved to a cell with two beds she seized the opportunity to barricade herself in. The warders spent several hours trying to persuade her to open the door, then they took radical action: they brought a hosepipe, pointed it into the cell and doused Emily with icy water for fifteen minutes. Then, having failed to persuade her to move, they used crowbars to break down the door. As the warders finally burst in one of them told Emily: 'You ought to be horsewhipped for this.'

The WSPU leadership was thrilled by Emily's stand against force feed-ing. Keir Hardie asked questions in Parliament about the prison authorities' actions and the government was forced to announce an inquiry. Emmeline Pethick-Lawrence, echoing Emily's own religious turn of phrase, praised her as a member of the Calendar of Saints of the Church Militant. 'Emily Wilding Davison attained on Thursday last … the triumph of the spirit over physical force. This day should be henceforth a red-letter day in the annals of the union,' she said at a meeting in the Albert Hall. On 5 November 1909 *Votes for Women* described Emily as one of the most devoted voluntary workers in the union who had 'given up her whole life' for the cause. The union brought an action against the Visiting Justices of Strangeways gaol on her behalf and in January 1910 she was awarded forty shillings' compensa-tion.[22] Emily wrote to Mary Leigh in triumph that she had 'had an ab-solutely unique chance and did not miss it. My star was in the ascendant.'[23]

Although Emily never received a salary from the WSPU, she was now given regular work writing articles for *Votes for Women*. These were usually eulogies on great women in history or reviews of plays to which a suffrage angle could be found, such as *No Surrender*, by Constance Elizabeth Maud, or *Pains and Penalties* by Laurence Housman. She also continued to de-velop new and novel methods of protest. Three times during 1910 and 1911 she spent the night in the House of Commons. On the first such occasion, armed with a guide to Parliament, two bananas and some chocolate, she spent more than twenty-four hours in a tower which housed a heating system before she was discovered by a policeman. She hoped her offence would have to be tried at the bar of the House, but instead she was released without charge. Despite this she repeated the escapade twice, once on census night in 1911 and once more later that year. On both occasions she was discovered but released.

Emily went to prison twice in 1910, in June for breaking a pane of glass in the Crown Office and in November for breaking a window inside the House of Commons. She then spent her longest trouble-free spell during these last turbulent years of her life – a whole year during the WSPU truce. During this period, she found other work. Hardly a week passed when she did not have a letter in one newspaper or another on the suffrage question. No publication escaped her attention. Editors from the *Daily Graphic* to the *Stratford-Upon-Avon Herald,* from the *Finsbury and City Teachers' Journal* to *New Age,* became the targets of her prolific pen. Every subject was turned to the advantage of suffrage campaigners. Pit brow women campaigning for better conditions? The answer: the vote. Wages for housework? If women had the vote they would no longer need to discuss such questions. In a letter to the *Sunday Chronicle* she revealed something of her attitude to marriage – she was then thirty-eight and resolutely single: 'There is undoubtedly a marked tendency among the intelligent middle-class women not to enter matrimony readily … these women, having had their eyes opened by independent work and education … hesitate to exchange freedom for possible slavery.'[24] Such concerns do not seem to have worried her unduly. She was surrounded by a small clique of suffrage friends and they, along with her Christian zeal for the cause, left little room for other emotional attachments.

In November 1911 Emily instigated a new type of militancy – incendiarism. That month Mary Leigh and Constance Lytton, both friends of hers, were arrested for window-smashing in Whitehall. Constance, an aristocrat, was sent to prison for two weeks but Mary, a working woman, was sentenced to two months. Emily, furious at the injustice of this, took a package soaked in kerosene, set light to it and dropped it into a pillar-box in Fleet Street. She then had lunch in a Lyons Tea Shop before phoning a news agency to tell them what she had done. After that she went to the Parliament Street post office and did the same thing again in front of a policeman. Sylvia Pankhurst claimed that as a result Emily was condemned by the union's leadership for acting without instructions, but if this was true she was soon forgiven.[25] The incident sparked a new departure, and such attacks became a major plank of the union's militancy.

After a Christmas on bail Emily returned to Holloway in January 1912 for a six-month sentence. It was a miserable time. Although she claimed she was not on hunger strike she barely ate and lost a great deal of weight. During the early weeks of the year all her fellow suffrage prisoners were released, and Emily was left alone and increasingly depressed. Friends were concerned about her and tried to visit, but few were admitted. According to prison records Mary Leigh tried without success to pass herself off as Miss Morrison to gain access, because convicted prisoners were not allowed to visit unless they were close family.[26] Another friend, Eleanor Penn-Gaskell, was allowed to visit but was later excluded because she was suspected of passing Emily a copy of *Votes for Women*. By 19 February she had been force fed twice through a nasal tube and had offered 'violent resistance' on each occasion. On 29 February a report to the prison commissioners added that she was 'generally surly'.[28] In early March 114 new suffragette prisoners were admitted after West End window-smashing raids. Emily's conditions became a little easier, but more drama was to come.

In May Emmeline Pankhurst and the Pethick-Lawrences were convicted of conspiracy, and the suffragettes in Holloway decided to protest. In Emily's words, a 'regular siege' ensued.[29] The women barricaded themselves in their cells, and one by one the doors were broken down in order that they should be force fed. Emily recorded that when her turn came she fought like a demon but was not strong enough to resist. The doctors tied her to a chair and carried out their work. As soon as she could get up she smashed the few panes remaining in her already badly damaged window. Then she decided to go one better than her friends. She pushed her protest to the limit in a way that was to have an irreversible effect on her place in history.

Sitting alone in her cell, boiling with fury at the treatment she and her friends had received, Emily began to meditate on what would happen if she were to die. Gradually she became convinced that such an event would cause such anger and grief that the government would have to treat the women with more humanity. She began to form a plan to do herself harm. 'The idea in my mind was "one big tragedy may save many others", she wrote afterwards.[30] The minute her cell door was opened Emily rushed out and threw herself straight over the nearby balcony. The result was more farce than tragedy, for there was netting stretched between the walkways and she landed spreadeagled on it, livid but unharmed. When the warders pulled her back she struggled free again and made a second attempt, throwing herself from the top of an iron staircase. This time she was more successful, hitting her head and injuring her spine in two places. But despite her protests that she was hurt, the prison authorities continued to force feed her twice a day. She was eventually released more than a week later, just a few days before the end of her sentence.

Much has been made of this incident in the light of later events and in the light of an essay written by Emily, published only after her death, in which she extolled the virtues of martyrdom. This article was read as a suicide note by many people, among them some of Emily's closest friends. It has been suggested that her words revealed a settled desire to die for the cause, and that from 1912 onwards it was merely a matter of time before she would find an effective means of killing herself. Perhaps she was unclear in her own mind about whether she could really commit such an act. Certainly she was reckless with her life on more than one occasion. And certainly, from the evidence of her article, she believed it would be a glorious thing to die for the cause.

After her release Emily went to Longhorsley to recuperate, but her recovery was slow for she had cracked two vertebrae in her spine and lost more than two stone. Later in the summer she was well enough to visit Brighton, where she stayed at Sea View, a guest house often used by suffragettes recovering from hunger strikes. Whether this interlude, which extended into late September, was purely recreational is not clear. It seems possible that at around this time Emily was engaged in secret militancy, and committed a number of undiscovered crimes on behalf of the WSPU. Sylvia Pankhurst claimed Emily was involved in the bombing of Lloyd George's new house at Walton-on-the-Hill in February 1913,[31] though Home Office records show police suspected other suffragettes rather than her.[32] Years later Emily's friend Edith Mansell-Moullin, who was planning a memoir of her, wrote to ask a friend if she should 'leave out the bombs'?[33] It has also been suggested that Emily tried unsuccessfully to blow up the coronation chair in Westminster Abbey – an act later carried out successfully by another suffragette in 1914.[34] Certainly she had the opportunity to try this, for in 1913 she received and accepted an invitation to a ceremony at Westminster Abbey for London University graduates, and in January that year she had her university gown altered in preparation.[35]

Emily's last known act of militancy but one was more public, though the circumstances surrounding it are obscure. In November 1912 she was arrested and imprisoned in Aberdeen for attacking a Baptist minister with a dogwhip. When questioned she said she had mistaken the man for Lloyd George. There were several odd things about this incident. First, it was the only occasion on which Emily is known or believed to have committed violence against another person. Second, it is the only occasion on which she is believed to have used an alias – when arrested, she said her name was Mary Brown, which was Mary Leigh's maiden name. Third, quite how she could have mistaken a solitary man on a station for a government minister who would surely have travelled with aides and a certain fanfare is not clear. What is clear is that she went to prison for the offence, and spent four days on hunger strike before being released. She then went to stay with her friend Katherine Riddell, who lived in a large house on the outskirts of the city. From there she wrote to the newspapers protesting at claims she had been released because a suffragette had anonymously paid her fine. She would have objected strongly to such a move: 'The truth is that Bonnie Scotland will not adopt the barbarity of forcible feeding!'[36]

Emily spent Christmas and the early part of 1913 in Longhorsley, again recovering from her hunger strike. She wrote to her old schoolfriend: 'This last four days' hunger strike in Aberdeen, of course, found out my weakness … While here I busy myself writing my experiences and doing what I can to help my mother. I wish I could hear of some work though.'[37] The lack of money was becoming a problem. Emily's tendency to act without reference to the WSPU leadership seems to have led to her being barred from a paid position, though suggestions she was completely out of favour with the leadership are exaggerated. In February 1913 a WSPU official wrote on Emily's behalf to the *Manchester Guardian* to ask if someone there could see her to talk about the possibility of literary work,[38] and in the same month she received a letter from union headquarters asking her to send in her suffrage prisoners' medal so an extra bar could be added to commemorate her Aberdeen hunger strike.[39] She also received a personal invitation from Emmeline Pankhurst to a reception at union headquarters on 1 March 1913. Her family felt the union could be doing more for her, though. At around this time Emily's half-sister in France sent her two postal orders – one of which Emily promptly handed over to the union's 'self-denial' fund – with the comment: 'I hate to think of you without work and feeling as you do. I do think the militants might remember you and give you something.'[40]

By then Emily was back in London and living with some friendly militants – a Mrs Green and her daughter Janette – in Clapham Road,

Stockwell. She spent much of April and May in a fruitless search for paid journalistic work. A letter from the *Daily Citizen* in early May was typical: 'Thanks for the manuscript which I am glad to have seen but am compelled to return. There is plenty of good stuff in it but it has two faults – first, it is too long by a great deal; and second it is too late ... But still you can write: there is no doubt of that. You must only learn the rules of journalism.'[41] There were some glimmers of hope. At the end of April she had a letter from the *Nursing Times* suggesting she should come in for a chat, and a different editor at the *Daily Citizen* also invited her to come in and see him. In early June she applied for a job as a secretary with the Women's Tax Resistance League.

In late May Emily paid a visit to Longhorsley, during which she received a parcel from her friend Katherine Riddell, from Aberdeen, enclosing some cakes as a gift. Emily had sent Katherine a synopsis of a proposed book, but Katherine's efforts to find a publisher for her had failed. She had shown it to a 'good man', she wrote, but he felt Emily would need to publish the book herself.

A great deal of local mythology has grown up around this visit of Emily's to Longhorsley, and this is now difficult to disentangle. Interviewed by local radio in 1986, Winifred Stobbart said Emily received a telegram soon after she arrived there, and subsequently told her mother she would have to return to London sooner than planned. She said the local Morpeth suffragettes saw Emily off on the train and that it was clear she did not want to leave.[42] On the same programme, Betty Jobson described how her grandmother had seen Emily watching horses in training at Longhorsley racecourse, and claimed she had run out and attempted to grab a horse's bridle. These stories may or may not be true but it is quite possible Emily was planning her Derby Day escapade by then. A Newcastle suffragette with whom she stayed on her way south, Cissie Wilcox, said she had discovered Emily tying a flag around her dress with a reel of cotton and trying out the effect in front of the mirror. She said Emily was secretive about what she was planning.

Several pieces of evidence have been produced to 'prove' that Emily could not have been planning to die on Derby Day. First, that she did not give her mother any indication that something so terrible was likely to happen. Second, she told friends in London that although she would be busy on 4 June she would see them at a suffrage fair the day after the Derby. And third, that she bought a return train ticket to Epsom – suggesting she fully intended to come back in one piece. None of this is conclusive. For one thing, Emily might not have known whether she was going to die but she certainly knew there was a strong possibility she would be arrested – in which case she could neither use her return train ticket nor fulfil her promise to be at the suffrage fair. What we do know is that on 3 June she visited the fair with Mary Leigh, and that while there she spent some time standing before a statue of Joan of Arc. She told Mary she was going to the Derby the following day but when asked what she planned to do she simply put her head on one side, as she was wont to do, smiled enigmatically and said: 'Ah!' Mary should read the evening paper the next day, she said.[43]

On the morning of 4 June 1913 Emily took the train to Epsom Downs with a suffrage flag wound around her under her coat and another rolled tightly in her hand. She got to the course in time for the first race, at 1.30 p.m., and carefully marked on her race-card that it was won by Honeywood, with King's Scholar in second place. The second race, she recorded, was won by Marco Prunell followed by Sweet Slumbers. The Derby Stakes was at 3 p.m. From that point on, Emily's card remained unmarked.

An eyewitness account in the *Manchester Guardian* the following day recorded that Emily ran out as the horses rounded Tattenham Corner:

> All had passed but the King's horse when a woman squeezed through the railings and ran out into the course. She made straight for Anmer, and made a sort of leap for the reins. I think she got hold of them but it was impossible to say … The horse fell on the woman and kicked out furiously, and it was sickening to see his hoofs strike her repeatedly. The horse struggled to its feet – I don't think it was hurt.

Anmer's jockey, Herbert Smith, escaped with concussion and a cracked rib but Emily was gravely wounded. She was taken to Epsom Cottage Hospital where her friend Charles Mansell-Moullin, a surgeon, operated to try to relieve bleeding inside her head from a fractured skull. For several days she remained in a coma while her family and friends clung to the hope that she would survive. Rose Lamartine Yates and Mary Leigh were among those who kept vigil by her bedside. The Queen, who had seen what happened, inquired several times about her condition.

On 8 June Emily died without regaining consciousness. She never saw the furious newspaper articles raging that the horse and jockey could have been killed, or the hate mail sent to the hospital. 'I hope you suffer torture until you die,' one letter read. Nor did she see the anguished letter sent by her mother, who was being comforted in Northumberland by Emily's landlady, Mrs Green, and another suffragette friend, Ada Wright. 'I cannot believe that you could have done such a dreadful act,' Mrs Davison wrote, 'even for the cause which I know you have given up your whole heart and soul to. It has done so little in return for you. I can only hope and pray God will mercifully restore you to life and health and that there may be a better and brighter future before you. I know you would not wilfully give me any but happiness.'[44]

An inquest held at Guildford on 10 June decided that Emily's death had been accidental, but made it quite clear where blame should be apportioned. The cause of death had been a fractured skull 'caused by being accidentally knocked down by a horse through wilfully rushing on to the race course at Epsom Downs Surrey on the 4th June 1913 during the progress of a race', the coroner recorded.[45]

Christabel Pankhurst, in exile in Paris, had already decided to see Emily's death in quite a different light. 'Miss Davison has died for women,' she wrote on the day of Emily's death for an article in the *Daily Sketch*:

> She has died to call attention to their wrong, and win them the vote. The Government's refusal to grant the vote drove her to make her protest. Argument has not convinced Mr Asquith of the seriousness of the position, but perhaps a woman's death will. Miss Davison's memory will live in women's hearts and in history for all time. There will be a public funeral in honour of this soldier fallen in a war of freedom.

Why Christabel chose Emily to be the suffragettes' chief martyr has never been made clear. The decision seems to have had as much to do with the timing of the death as its manner. Indeed, other candidates might have laid earlier claim to the crown that Emily now held. Emmeline Pankhurst's sister Mary Clarke, for example, died of a brain haemorrhage just after being released from prison in the wake of the 'Black Friday' protest in November 1911. Henria Williams and Cecilia Haig both took severe beatings at the same demonstration and died within a year. But at that time the WSPU truce, called during negotiations on the Conciliation Bill, had still been holding. That had not been the time for martyrdom or for furious displays of emotion. Now the right opportunity had presented itself. Militancy was reaching its height, and there was a growing feeling that something tragic needed to happen. Mrs Pankhurst had just been released from prison in an emaciated and exhausted state, and there were genuine fears that even she might die. Announcing Emily's funeral arrangements, the WSPU described her death in heroic terms: 'With her clear and unflinching vision she realised that now as in days of old, to awake the conscience of people, a human life would be needed as sacrifice – a human life freely given under circumstances of tragedy, the shock of which would travel round the world … She heard the call, and made answer, "I come."'[46]

The full might of the WSPU machine was devoted to giving Emily's funeral all the pomp of a state occasion. It was, as it turned out, the suffragettes' last major spectacle and they did not waste a minute of it. Thousands of women marched four abreast through London led by a banner which read: 'Fight on and God will give the victory'. The procession was divided into eleven sections, each with its own group captain. At St George's church in Bloomsbury the mourners sang 'Nearer My God to Thee' and 'Fight the Good Fight' before marching to King's Cross station to dispatch the coffin, accompanied by a suffragette guard of honour, to the Davison family grave in Morpeth, Northumberland. Those who could not gain access to the church waited outside in Russell Square.

On 16 June Emily's half-brother, Captain Henry Jocelyn Davison, told *The Suffragette* he did not believe she intended to die: 'I look upon it entirely as an accident and I think she did it hoping she would be saved from the possible results. She wished merely to draw as much attention as possible to the movement.' But whatever was going through Emily's mind as she stood by the railing at Tattenham Corner with her race-card in her hand, she showed, as always, a quite extraordinary lack of fear. If Emily Wilding Davison possessed a personal quality which made her stand out from the militants among whom she spent her last five years, it was this nervelessness. If she had a fatal flaw, it was that she lacked some power of imagination that would have deflected her from that final, headlong rush. Throughout her life Emily had acted with a single-minded determination that distinguished her from her fellow militants. When she resolved on a course of action, no sense of danger or of possible consequence could deflect her. She was swept up like all her close circle in the movement's rushing tide, its unstoppable magic, yet somehow she retained some essential element of separation. When she committed a militant act, even one in which she worked in concert with her friends, in some sense she acted alone. Whether she was picked out by some unseen hand for her final triumph, or whether she drove herself to it, she was the right woman for the job.

Millicent Fawcett.

X

Millicent Fawcett – Pacifist Warrior

Before the bedroom fire, the girls were brushing their hair. Emily was twenty-nine, Elizabeth twenty-three and Millicent thirteen. As they brushed, they debated. 'Women can get nowhere,' said Emily, 'unless they are as well educated as men. I shall open the universities.' 'Yes,' agreed Elizabeth. 'We need education but we need an income too and we can't earn that without training and a profession. I shall start women in medicine. But what shall we do with Milly?' They agreed that she should get the Parliamentary vote for women.

Louisa Garrett Anderson describing a conversation at the family home in Aldeburgh between her mother, Elizabeth, and Emily Davies, in 1860. Elizabeth became the first woman on the medical register; Emily founded Girton College, Cambridge.

Arguably, Millicent Garrett Fawcett did more than any other individual to win the vote for women. Unquestionably she worked longer and more consistently at the heart of the struggle than anyone else involved. When Emmeline Pankhurst first joined the Manchester National Society for Women's Suffrage in 1880, Millicent had already been campaigning steadily for more than a decade. When Emmeline was on the verge of ditching women in favour of votes for soldiers in 1917, Millicent was contemplating the progress made during more than a year of wartime ministerial lobbying. Yet it was Emmeline, not Millicent, who was honoured with a statue outside the Houses of Parliament. It was Emmeline, not Millicent, who entered the public consciousness as the architect of votes for women. In some respects, it is fitting that this should be so. For as leader of the non-militant suffragists, Millicent Fawcett was never a woman who demanded public adulation. Her memorial, in contrast to Emmeline's, stands in the calm shade of Westminster Abbey. What she lacked in glamour she amply made up in understated efficiency. She was the measured, respectable Dr Jekyll to Emmeline's furious, passionate Mr Hyde.

There was nothing dull about Millicent, though. To suggest that her natural milieu was the polite drawing room or even the dusty corridor of power would be unfair. Indeed it is hard fully to explain why she ended up in such surroundings at all, for her birth and childhood presaged a life in much closer touch with the elements. Born in 1847, the eighth of the ten children of Newson Garrett, a wealthy Suffolk merchant, she spent her early years on the wild east coast. She rode, she walked home unperturbed when her carriage overturned in the snow, she watched from the shore when her father went out with the Aldeburgh lifeboat to the aid of a storm-distressed ship. She recalled with great joy the windy day when she was allowed to accompany the lifeboatmen herself on a practice trip.[1]

Millicent believed her mother, a strong and steadfast character, could successfully have run a large business if she had been born in more enlightened times. But it was not from her conventional, God-fearing mother that she gained her pioneering spirit. Her father, a self-made businessman who started life as a publican and pawnbroker in London, could claim more of the credit for his daughters' pioneering spirits. A meteoric character who could be as impossible as he could be charming, he treated his daughters almost exactly as he treated his sons and always took a keen and delighted interest in their achievements. Although not a political radical – he switched his allegiance from Tory to Liberal as his family were growing up – he took a lively interest in world events and expected his children to do the same.

Even the dynamic Newson Garrett cannot be given the main credit for Millicent's political enlightenment, though. The biggest portion of that honour must be handed to her older sister Elizabeth – later Elizabeth Garrett Anderson – whose battle to become the first woman on the medical register was observed at close quarters by the teenage Millicent. Millicent felt she had been a suffragist 'from the cradle', and Elizabeth must have been key in ensuring that this was the case. She also played an important part in broadening the education of her younger sisters, which had been patchy despite the efforts of a governess and of a school in Blackheath, London, which Millicent left at sixteen. Elizabeth held regular 'Talks on Things in General' for her younger siblings, which covered anything that might be on her mind at the time: Garibaldi and events in Italy, Carlyle's *Cromwell,* Macaulay's *History of England.* They must certainly have included women's rights, for Elizabeth's own enlightenment had gone much deeper than a straightforward desire to train as a doctor. While still at school she had become acquainted, through friends, with the early feminist Emily Davies, and she carried that influence back to her family in Aldeburgh. Millicent, a bright though unexceptional pupil, quickly began to absorb these ideas and to take note of the narrowness of her female acquaintances' lives. Once, while preparing for a party, she listened to two slightly older women discussing a friend's troubled marriage. 'I cannot see what she has to complain of. Look how he dresses her!' one of them remarked. Millicent, who had never been taught to think of such trivialities as central to her existence, was horrified.

The Garrett girls were brought up to expect more from life than a regular supply of pretty frocks, but their family was conventional enough to stick with the received wisdom that they should all aim to make a good marriage. Millicent set to work on this project early. She was only eighteen when, in the spring of 1865, she caught the attention of Henry Fawcett, a Cambridge professor and MP. The date was a significant one, for the news of Abraham Lincoln's assassination had just reached London – where Millicent was visiting her eldest sister Louie – and there was talk of little else. Millicent was probably barely aware, when she expressed her own opinion that the death would have deeper ramifications than if it had been that of any of the crowned heads of Europe, that she was not behaving as most girls of her age would. Fawcett was impressed, and resolved to inveigle an invitation to Aldeburgh in order to become better acquainted with Millicent. In 1866 they were engaged and in the spring of 1867 they were married.

Marriage to the 33-year-old Henry Fawcett would have been demanding for a 20-year-old country girl in any circumstances. Not only did Millicent have to adjust to being a wife and running homes in London and Cambridge, with their attendant population of servants, but she also had to learn the appropriate way to mix in both academic and political society. That would have been enough for any young bride. Life with Henry, though, had an added complication. Several years earlier he had been involved in a shooting accident which had left him blind. Clearly a man of extraordinary determination, he resolved almost immediately that the catastrophe should not be allowed to change his life plans. By the time he met Millicent he had successfully entered academic life and, even more remarkably, had persuaded both Liberal Party grandees and electors in Brighton that his blindness would not impair his ability to represent them as their MP. Millicent's role as spouse would include the additional duty of acting as Henry's 'eyes', accompanying him around London and reading to him almost incessantly.

Despite these apparent drawbacks the marriage seems to have been an unqualified success. Henry's determination to live life to the full extended to horseriding, skating and fishing – the latter being the only activity Millicent did not share. Acquaintances would often comment on how radiant the couple looked. Henry constantly demanded that his other companions tell him how Millicent was looking: Did she seem well? Did her latest new frock suit her? For although Henry could not see his young wife, he was always anxious to know if she was well dressed. Millicent, despite her personal lack of interest in fashion, responded by ensuring he always received a positive answer. This does not seem to have posed a problem. Although she was tiny by comparison to her very tall husband, descriptions of her suggest she always carried a certain calm beauty.[2] She had a smooth complexion, masses of shining brown hair and a serenity of appearance which throughout her life would continue to impress both those who met her and those who heard her speak.

Politics, though, was the pivot on which the relationship turned. Henry had long been a devotee of John Stuart Mill, and during his engagement to Millicent had suggested his colleague should raise the issue of women's suffrage in Parliament, which he did in 1867. Henry also encouraged Millicent to take up politics. In 1868 her Cambridge drawing room was the venue for a meeting at which a series of lectures for women was announced. In later life Millicent was proud to have played a part in the venture which led ultimately to the founding of Newnham College. In the same year she made her debut as a political speaker at the first women's suffrage meeting ever to be held in London. The venue was the Gallery of the Architectural Society in Conduit Street, a far cry from the rowdy outdoor meetings at which Emmeline Pankhurst would make her early speeches almost three decades later. In the 1860s the very idea of a woman standing on a public platform was considered shocking. According to one of Millicent's early biographers she was 'clear, logical, self-possessed and pre-eminently "ladylike",[3] but a few days later she and the other female speaker, Clementia Taylor, were accused by an MP in the House of Commons of having 'disgraced themselves' by their action. A few weeks later an amused Millicent found herself seated next to this MP at a Cambridge dinner. When she jokingly asked the horrified man if he would prefer a more respectable companion, he gallantly declined and henceforth mellowed towards her. Millicent's ability to see the funny side of such abuse was to serve her well, and she delighted in teasing those who were shocked by her activities. Once, during one of the European trips she liked to take while Henry fished, she listened with apparent sympathy while a fellow traveller described her disgust for women who 'unsexed' themselves by speaking in public, and who then went on to ask rhetorically if Millicent could think of a woman doctor to whose scalpel she would submit. To her challenger's surprise Millicent responded mildly that yes, she could certainly think of one – her sister.

Soon Millicent was travelling the country speaking at suffrage meetings as the movement began to spread, with committees in existence by then in London, Manchester, Birmingham, Bristol and Edinburgh. Although she always maintained an air of calm while on the platform, she professed not to enjoy this aspect of the work. She was so nervous before a speech that she was often physically ill, she said. She restricted her speaking tours to the months when Henry was able to spare her, usually in early spring and late autumn, and she refused to speak either more than once a day or more than four times a week.

While her devotion to the cause would always remain steadfastly at the centre of her existence, she would never rival the physical or emotional extremes scaled by so many of the militants. Millicent's steady nature did not admit of the evangelical fervour experienced by Emily Wilding Davison, nor did it tend towards the all-consuming energy with which Emmeline Pankhurst tackled her speaking tours. In Millicent's political life, an earnest desire to pursue the path of political righteousness took the place of the extravagant displays of others. She never questioned her ideals, which she saw strictly in black and white, and so for her the way forward was almost always clear. 'Things did not really perplex Milly, nor depress her. She could be sad but she would not be discouraged; for she truly believed, without any effort of faith, that all was for the best and that good must triumph over evil,' one biographer wrote.[4]

The Garrett Fawcett household seemed destined to follow a steady path towards success. In 1874 Henry lost his Brighton seat but was elected again for Hackney, and the couple moved to a house in Vauxhall with a large garden. In 1880 Gladstone made Henry Postmaster General, and Millicent was presented to Queen Victoria at court. Newson Garrett, proud as ever, bought her a deep cream dress for the occasion. Henry must have made an impression on the Queen on this and other occasions, for when he became ill in 1882 with diphtheria and typhoid, she telegraphed more than once a day to inquire about him. Politically, though, Henry's support for women's suffrage did not help his career. In 1884 William Woodall proposed a women's suffrage amendment to an electoral reform bill, and Henry found himself caught between conviction and duty. As a member of a government which opposed the measure he could not vote for it; as a keen supporter of reform he could not vote against it. In the end he abstained. The measure was roundly defeated but Gladstone was furious with Henry, and wrote to him saying his action had been tantamount to resignation. Henry was reprieved only because the Prime Minister wanted to avoid the bad publicity which would inevitably accompany a ministerial sacking. The incident had far-reaching effects. First, according to Millicent, Gladstone's opposition caused real anger among the women campaigning for the vote. 'That division probably sowed the seed of the militant movement,' she wrote.[5] Sadly, it may also have contributed towards Henry's early death. Still weakened by his illness two years earlier he decided to forgo a holiday to cope with the increasing demands of his political role – and possibly because of anxiety about his position. By the autumn he was exhausted and in early November he became ill again. A cold quickly developed into pneumonia and within days he was dead. Elizabeth Garrett Anderson, who attended him, telegraphed to Agnes Garrett: 'We have lost our dear Harry. Millicent is asking for you.'[6] It was a loss from which Millicent, then thirty-seven, never recovered. It seems appropriate that Queen Victoria, herself a long-standing and very public widow, should have been among those who sent condolences after Henry's death. Millicent lived for thirty-five years as a widow and even decades later she would be visibly distressed by the mention of her husband's name.

After Henry's death Millicent gave up both their homes and moved, with her sixteen-year-old daughter, Philippa, to the house in Gower Street where her sister Agnes lived. At first she could bring herself to do little. Within weeks of her bereavement she was offered a job, as Mistress of Girton, but she confessed she was not ready to take on such a project.[7] It was not long, though, before the suffrage recaptured her attention and by February 1885 she was writing long letters to her nephew Edmund Garrett on the subject of whether married women should have the vote or not. She hoped they would, she explained, but believed the franchise for single women would be easier to win and 'half a loaf is better than no bread'.[8]

In the following two decades Millicent's suffrage work was supplemented by involvement in a range of other causes. Less than a year after

Henry's death she gave her support to W. T. Stead, who had gone to prison for 'procuring' a young girl from her mother during a journalistic exposé on prostitution in London. Ironically, one injustice Stead hoped to expose was the fact that to purchase a child from her father for prostitution was quite legal. His own action was illegal because the mother had no legal status and therefore no right to sell her. Millicent wrote to Sir Henry Ponsonby, the Queen's private secretary, to ask that Stead be given first division status in prison. Ponsonby responded by contacting the Home Secretary, but by then Stead had already been placed in the first division. The incident sparked what was perhaps the only militant phase of Millicent's political career. By 1886 she had become involved with the Vigilance Association, which took an active role in exposing men who preyed on vulnerable young women. Once, in December 1886, she was involved in a physical assault on an army major who had been pestering a servant of a friend of hers. The two women, accompanied by some burly male friends, engineered a meeting between the girl and the major outside the British Museum, where they set upon him and denounced him loudly.[9] A July 1890 article in W. T. Stead's *Review of Reviews* celebrated their action:

> They threw flour over his waxed moustache and in his eyes and down the back of his neck. They pinned a paper on his back, and made him the derision of a crowded street … in the sequel he was turned out of a club, and cut by a few lady friends – among them a young lady of some means to whom he was engaged at the time when he planned to ruin the country lass. Mrs Fawcett had no pity; she would have cashiered him if she could.

A few years later Millicent waged a long and vigorous campaign against a young parliamentary candidate named Henry Cust, who had seduced a young woman and been forced to marry her. Under assault from Millicent's ever-vigorous pen, he eventually abandoned his political ambitions.

To the modern mind some of these activities may be hard to comprehend, but the women's movement in the late nineteenth and early twentieth centuries tended towards the espousal of family values and, at its most radical, to the denunciation of men for their lascivious natures. Witness, for example, Christabel Pankhurst's 'Great Scourge' of 1913, which publicised the prevalence of venereal disease, and its battle-cry: 'Votes for Women and Chastity for Men!' The feminist movement at the time also often opposed moves to exclude women from heavy work, and Millicent was no exception. In 1891 she wrote to *The Times* to protest at plans to restrict women's work in industry: '[The legislation] will have the effect of preventing girls from doing work in the nail and chain trade before the age of 16 ... This, in the opinion of many competent persons, means that women are to be kept out of the trade altogether.'[10]

On these matters, Millicent had been in step with many of her liberal contemporaries. Sylvia Pankhurst, for example, later championed the right of the 'pit-brow lassies' to continue their heavy coal-moving work. 'There is no hardship so great ... as being without work and without means,' she wrote.[11] However, a further campaign in which Millicent became involved during this period is harder to see in a positive light. In May 1898 a newspaper called *The Star* ran an article headlined: 'They Profit by Phossy Jaw! An Appeal to Bryant and May Shareholders.'[12] Among the named shareholders of the firm, which was supposed to have improved working conditions after the famous match girls' strike a decade earlier, was Millicent Fawcett. The paper went on to describe the plight of Cornelius Lean, a 22-year-old match 'dipper' who had died a slow and horrible death after poisonous phosphorus fumes had afflicted him with 'phossy jaw', a form of cancer which caused the bone literally to rot away. Factory inspectors subsequently discovered eleven similar cases at the East End plant, all of which had been covered up. The simple solution, campaigners suggested, was to replace the deadly yellow phosphorus with the less poisonous red variety. Clearly concerned, Millicent set out on a fact-finding trip to the factory, accompanied by a senior official of the firm. She then wrote to campaigners and to the *Evening Standard* to say how impressed she had been. She even met a group of workers who told her 'phossy jaw' was the result of carelessness by their colleagues. One foolish man had had a rotten tooth extracted by a dentist in his lunch hour and had been poisoned on his return, she explained. Millicent received a warm letter of thanks from Bryant and May for her support. The firm continued using yellow phosphorus until 1901, when it finally withdrew it in the face of further protest.[13]

There were personal campaigns, too. Millicent became actively involved in pressing for the rights of women to earn degrees, at around the same time as her own daughter Philippa was studying at Cambridge. Although Philippa was not able to collect her mathematics degree her brilliant performance in the 1890 Tripos examination led to jubilant celebrations. She was placed 'above the Senior Wrangler' at the top of her year and was invited to take up a post teaching maths at the university. This did not match Millicent's fierce ambitions for her daughter. The life of a Cambridge academic would be far too tame, she decreed. What about the law? Or engineering? Millicent clearly felt Philippa should grow up an Amazon. After an anxious period of indecision she stayed on at Cambridge for a time but later became involved in education, first in South Africa, where she had travelled with her mother during the Boer War, and later in London.

The suffrage still took up much of Millicent's time, though, even during these despondent years when little progress was made. In 1888 a split in the Central Committee of the National Society for Women's Suffrage led her, along with Lydia Becker, to part company with the Pankhursts and their more radical companions. The following year when Lydia Becker's health began to fail Millicent took on much of her work. From this time on she came to be regarded as the leader of the non-militants in the suffrage cause. It fell to Millicent to take head-on the activities of anti-suffragists such as Mary Ward, who published her ladies' appeal against the suffrage in the *Nineteenth Century* magazine in June 1889. In her reply, published in the same magazine in July, Millicent deployed an argument she would use many times in the future against this group:

> The very same ladies ... who deprecate in the *Nineteenth Century* the introduction of women into political controversy are, as presidents and vice-presidents of political associations, urging upon their fellow-countrywomen the duty of mastering difficult and complicated political problems ... with the view of influencing the verdict of the country at the next general election.

She went on to add that women would be bound to be more intelligent voters than some men. 'Women who would be enfranchised cannot be held to be less fit to vote than the chimney-sweeps and labourers who vote already,' she argued.

The National Union of Women's Suffrage Societies, of which Millicent formally became president in 1907, came to be seen chiefly as the group representing suffragists who were opposed to militancy. Despite this, the growth of the Women's Social and Political Union would bring about a marked change in its fortunes. As 'Votes for Women' climbed up the political agenda, the National Union grew steadily. By 1909 it had seventy affiliated societies with 13,000 members, and by 1914 it had 600 branches and

53,000 members. Although large and well organised, it would never quite rival the income or the effectiveness of the Women's Social and Political Union.[14] In 1910 its national funding stood at £5,500 in comparison to £18,000 pulled in by the WSPU in subscriptions alone, though the National Union's affiliated societies had additional income of £14,000. In 1909 the circulation of *Votes for Women* stood at 30,000 per week, while the National Union's paper, *Common Cause*, managed only 10,000 by 1912. It became a substantial body, though, and at its head, leading almost without appearing to do so, was Millicent Fawcett. At committee meetings she said little, sometimes even seeming unaware of the internal squabbles that were brewing.[15] But when a debate became heated she had a knack of chipping in with an anecdote which would make everyone laugh – something she had learned from her husband – or if she could not think of one she would bring down the temperature by talking about something apparently quite irrelevant.

At first the activities of Mrs Pankhurst and her daughters, far away in Manchester, gave Millicent and her National Union little cause for concern. It was only when the WSPU became active in London that anxiety began to ripple through the organisation's ranks. When Annie Kenney invaded one of the Prime Minister's election meetings at the Albert Hall in December 1905, Millicent felt forced to issue a statement saying the National Union had not been involved.[16] Her friend Lady Frances Balfour wrote to her that they should not even acknowledge the militants' existence. 'Surely we should do or say nothing. These women never quote us. We might … write privately to Campbell-Bannerman but don't lets us do anything in public,' she suggested.[17] Privately, though, Millicent was impressed by the militants' actions. She heeded her friend's advice and rarely spoke or wrote of them at all, but in truth she could see the difference they were making even while she felt uncomfortable with their methods.

During the years between 1905 and 1908, the militant and constitutional wings of the suffrage movement worked far more closely together than is popularly supposed. In May 1906 both the National Union and the WSPU were among twenty-five organisations in a deputation to Henry Campbell-Bannerman, during which Annie Kenney appeared in her mill girl's attire and jumped on a chair to make her presence felt. Indeed, Millicent would later argue in her autobiography that during those years the WSPU's campaigners endured much violence but committed none: 'If there was great vehemence in their demonstrations, there was also great restraint,' she argued.[18] When a man at a dinner party told Millicent he would never again do anything for women's suffrage because of the way the WSPU had behaved, she merely smiled and politely asked him what he had done already. Many supporters – and critics – made little distinction between the two organisations and where previously the National Union's donations had come in in half crowns and shillings, now the £5 and £10 notes began to arrive. When Millicent ordered bulbs for her garden they came free of charge with a request that she should donate the money 'to those good women who are persecuting the Government'. She admitted later that she had seriously considered leaving the National Union and joining the WSPU instead. 'I asked myself this question very insistently ... I was before all things desirous that we should keep our artillery for our opponents and not turn it on one another,' she explained.[19] She did not do so, partly because she did not feel she could join a 'revolutionary' movement and partly because she found Emmeline's leadership style too autocratic.

In her own quiet way, though, Millicent gave considerable support to the militants. When Jane Cobden-Sanderson, a lifelong friend, was imprisoned with a group of prominent WSPU women after a House of Commons demonstration in 1906, she visited her in prison and even wrote to Lord Knollys, private secretary to King Edward VII, to petition for the women to receive first division treatment. It is not clear whether her letter had a direct effect, but a few days later Lord Knollys replied that all the women had been placed in the first division. On their release she organised a banquet for them, and wrote to NUWSS members that their action had touched the imagination of the country in a manner which quieter methods did not succeed in doing. Many of the National Union's members disapproved strongly of her action, but slowly the organisation was to change its methods and to move closer into line with the WSPU. The drawing-room gatherings and public meetings in hired halls continued, but now they took place alongside more flamboyant street demonstrations adorned with banners and bands. The first such demonstration, in 1907, was dubbed the 'Mud March' by dismissive militants after 4,000 women were soaked to the skin as they marched through London on a rainy February day.

The harmonious relations between the two groups were not destined to last. On 22 June 1908, a week before a major WSPU deputation to the Prime Minister, Millicent's niece Louisa Garrett Anderson wrote to tell her she had had a long talk with Emmeline Pethick-Lawrence 'about the next step.' 'I do very much wish that the National Society could combine in it – the WSPU are sending up a resolution to Mr Asquith. If [his answer] is unsatisfactory more militant action will be necessary according to the WSPU and I think they are right.'[20] Asquith's answer was unsatisfactory, and the WSPU called a public meeting in Parliament Square for the evening of 30 June. It was clear beforehand that there would be trouble and Louisa, who with her mother Elizabeth was far more sympathetic to the militants than her aunt, visited Millicent to discuss whether she should take part. Millicent, after some deliberation, said she should not. Louisa wrote to her joking that she could see advantages in staying out of prison: 'I shall revel in a comfortable bed and strawberry ices and everything else not provided for 2nd class "criminals".'[21] But Elizabeth, then aged seventy-two, had decided to go on the deputation. Concerned for her safety, Frances Balfour petitioned the Home Secretary, Herbert Gladstone, asking that she should not be treated roughly. He replied that he had issued 'special instructions' about her, and that in any case the police were being ordered to arrest only when strictly necessary. Elizabeth was not arrested, but during the demonstration Mary Leigh and Edith New made their way to Downing Street and flung stones through the windows, taking militancy on to a new plane. From that day on, Millicent said later, she could not support the WSPU's methods. Such demonstrations were designed to attract 'the lowest classes of London roughs', she believed. The demonstration was followed later that year by one at which women were invited to 'Rush the House of Commons', and at which many arrests were made. Millicent wrote to a supporter the following year that although she had not condemned the stone-throwing publicly she thought it 'dastardly'. 'The House of Commons, for all its faults, stands for order against anarchy, for justice against more brutality … It became evident to me then that our organisation must separate itself entirely from all co-operation from the people who would resort to such methods as these.'[22]

Over the ensuing three years the issue of militancy would be an increasingly thorny one for Millicent, both in political and in personal terms. Her sister Elizabeth and niece Louisa had both thrown in their lot firmly with the Women's Social and Political Union. Elizabeth opened a WSPU exhibition in 1909 and went on a speaking tour of the West Country with Annie Kenney that year, as well as taking part in several demonstrations. At the 'Black Friday' demonstration in November 1910, condemned afterwards for the brutality of the police, she stood on the steps of the House of Commons for two hours alongside Emmeline Pankhurst. Louisa went further in her support of militancy, taking part in the 1912 window-smashing raids on the West End of London and serving four weeks of a six-week prison sentence as a result. Although family relations remained cordial, they were strained. In December 1911, as the Conciliation Bill around which a two-year truce had been woven teetered on the brink of collapse, Millicent felt compelled to let Elizabeth know her feelings: 'We have the best chance of Women's Suffrage next session that we have ever had, by far, if it is not destroyed by disgusting masses of people by revolutionary violence.'[23] In her reply Elizabeth revealed that she, too, had now parted company from the WSPU and from her daughter: 'I am quite with you about the WSPU. I think they are quite wrong. I wrote to Miss Pankhurst … I have now told her I can go no more with them.'[24] A few months later, with Louisa in prison, Millicent wrote to her sister again to express her sympathy. Elizabeth was clearly losing patience with her daughter. 'I am in hopes she will take her punishment wisely, that the enforced solitude will help her to see more in focus than she always does,' she wrote.[25] She had, she added, just received a large cheque 'for the cause', which she intended to send to Millicent: 'I certainly do not intend to give it to Mrs Pankhurst.'

Even within the National Union, there was controversy over the usefulness of militant methods. Some of its members wanted it to take on a more radical policy, while others were determined that it should not. Up until this point there had been a cross-over between the two wings of the suffrage movement, with many women joining both their local constitutional suffrage society and their WSPU branch.[26] In 1909 a group of militants within the London Society had tried without success to take it out of the union altogether, and Millicent had spent more than one national council meeting fighting a rearguard action against moves to take a harder line by standing shoulder-to-shoulder with the WSPU in a show of unity. Millicent's response, that the most striking example of unity she could think of was the tale of the Gadarene swine, was acid. Despite these upheavals her view prevailed within the union, and as militancy escalated the militants were excluded from membership of National Union branches. The union continued to concentrate its efforts on the 'antis' as much as on the government, and its younger members regularly attended their meetings to hand out badges and literature. In 1909 Millicent took part in a head-to-head debate with Mary Ward, after which the defeated novelist admitted to having been shaken by the audience's animosity towards her.

The best efforts of the National Union to distance itself from the Pankhursts were often ineffective. On more than one occasion Millicent found her organisation tarred with the brush of bad publicity. Once, she even found herself accused by an anti-suffragist of the unlikely sin of promoting 'pornous vices' at her meetings, and when she inquired further was told by the self-confessed slanderess that she had really meant to aim the accusation at the militants.[27] Emmeline, on being informed of the problem, responded loftily that she intended to 'forget all about it'. 'The lives of women in this union are open to inspection,' she added.[28] Millicent was usually able to employ her sharp tongue to good effect in such circumstances. Once, while waiting in an anteroom during a deputation of mostly elderly constitutional suffragists to Herbert Asquith, she was approached by a rather nervous-looking secretary. 'I want you, Mrs Fawcett, to give me your personal word of honour that no member of your deputation will employ physical violence,' he quavered. 'You astonish me,' Millicent replied. 'I had no idea you were so frightened.'[29] She confessed later that she had taken no pains to conceal her amusement. On another occasion Lloyd George told Millicent the government could do nothing for women while the outrage of militancy continued.[30] Millicent, who had recently seen Conservative Club windows smashed in Lloyd George's constituency on election day by his triumphant supporters, inquired what punishment had been inflicted on *them*. Lloyd George was forced to admit that there had been none.

Such exchanges aside, relations between the National Union and the government remained reasonably cordial throughout the years leading up to the First World War, even though Millicent entertained a growing sense of frustration. The National Union was left open to the accusation that it was too friendly with ministers who claimed to be sympathetic but who in fact were not. Both Lloyd George and Sir Edward Grey wrote letters to Millicent suggesting they were making vigorous efforts within government on the women's behalf. Their task would be so much easier, they suggested, if only the militants could be persuaded to lay off. Millicent, by then a wily political operator, did not fall into the potential trap of being used as an intermediary. Instead, she responded that the violence would stop once women had the vote: 'People will begin to laugh at riot and tumult when it is abundantly clear that the reform desired can be obtained by the ordinary constitutional channels.'[31] She, too, was playing something of a double game. While saying little against the militants in public, in private correspondence with other constitutionalists she condemned them in the strongest terms: 'There seems very little probability that the militants will cease from outrage. I think they would rather lose Women's Suffrage than give up their own way of demonstrating,' she wrote to one colleague.[32] By 1914, though, things had gone too far. The National Union was forced to issue a leaflet headed 'Militant Outrages' confronting the issue head-on. 'NUWSS is compelled once more to dissociate itself as publicly and emphatically as possible from all tolerance of such outrages,' it said.[33]

Such public discord between suffragists and suffragettes was to become redundant within months. At the outbreak of war both wings reacted in similar fashion, pledging to do their patriotic duty, suspending their political work and making plans to support the war effort. Millicent, though neither a pacifist nor opposed to the war, admitted later that the thought of it had filled her with dread and depression – and well it might. She would lose no fewer than twenty-nine members of her extended family, including two nephews. Now, though, the National Union's tradition of rejecting Pankhurstian autocracy for a more open, democratic style came back to haunt its leadership. Holding together a constitutional suffrage movement in the face of militancy was one thing; holding together a women's war work movement in the face of pacifism was quite another. The union was to suffer a deep schism during the course of the war, with most of its officers resigning *en masse* in protest after Millicent and a small group refused to support a 1915 women's peace conference in the Hague. The pacifists in the union seem to have been in the majority, but such was the strength of Millicent's position that it was they, not she, who felt they had to leave. 'She stood like a rock in their path, opposing herself with all the great weight of her personal popularity and prestige to their use of the machinery and name of the union,' according to her colleague and early biographer Ray Strachey.

Millicent seems to have been incapable of giving up suffrage work. In early 1916, with a coalition government in place and signs emerging that Asquith might be softening on the issue, she began lobbying and speaking on the subject again. In May that year she wrote to him arguing that if men were to win the vote for their war efforts, women should have it for theirs. In August 1916 the Prime Minister made a clear statement in Parliament that he intended to include women in a general widening of the franchise after the war. No sooner had he spoken than an MP named Carlyon Bellairs rose to say he had been authorised to give Mrs Pankhurst's view on the subject: women 'would not allow themselves to be used to prevent soldiers and sailors from being given the vote'.[34] Millicent did not agree. She spent part of that summer on a suffrage tour of the South-west and North-west, and by the end of the year a Speaker's Conference had been set up to address the issue. Just after Lloyd George became Prime Minister that December a new and surprising recruit to the suffrage cause – Lord Northcliffe, whose newspapers had previously been vehemently against – helped arrange for Millicent to lead a delegation to him. Now all the old suspicion and distrust had disappeared, and it was clear the political wind was set fair for reform. In January 1917 the Speaker's Conference recommended that women already on the local government voting register, the wives of men on that register and graduates should be given the vote – broadly the measure that was passed. The only major point of doubt was whether the cut-off age for women should be thirty or thirty-five. Millicent, who throughout the spring of 1917 was engaged in a series of meetings with cabinet ministers, was able to use the threat of militancy to her advantage. On at least one occasion, she told friends, a grown man turned pale while hearing her talk of the potential terrors ahead if the move should fail. After all, she argued, militancy was fierce enough when the prospects of success were slight and the country divided. Now, with public opinion swinging in favour and hopes raised, all hell could result if things went awry. Emerging from a minister's office she turned to her companion with a mischievous grin: 'I think that settled him. Who's next on the list?'[35]

While the WSPU were now prepared to accept votes for women on any terms the government had to offer – and even to give up altogether if their demand stood in the way of votes for soldiers – the NUWSS continued to press its old case for equality with men. Even the partial deal on offer delighted Millicent, though. It suited her gradualist approach. 'Men in this country have never been enfranchised in this wholesale fashion,' she explained later.[36] Even her characteristic equanimity was shaken on the day the bill passed through the House of Lords, though, and she confessed to feeling the tension. Lord Cromer, an ardent anti-suffrage campaigner, was by then Leader of the House of Lords, and his attitude would be crucial in determining how the vote would go. Millicent chanced upon her old sparring partner Mary Ward in the waiting room and they went into the chamber together, taking adjacent seats in the gallery. Mary was incandescent, according to Millicent, when her erstwhile comrade told the House that to vote against the measure would put it into fruitless conflict with the Commons.[37] The bill was passed by 134 to 71, with Lord Curzon and a dozen others abstaining.

Millicent, then aged seventy-one, was urged to stand for Parliament in 1918 but she did not consider it seriously. Her last suffrage tour in 1917 had left her ill with bronchitis, and she felt it was time to retire. Although she bowed out of the NUWSS leadership she continued to take an active interest, particularly on the international front. She had long been a key member of the International Woman Suffrage Alliance and in 1919 she went to Paris with other NUWSS colleagues to lobby world leaders on women's rights at the postwar peace conference. She continued to live an active life, apparently unaffected by her age, visiting Palestine in 1920 and again in 1921 with her sister Agnes. She also continued to attend executive meetings of the National Union, but her power within the organisation was finally gone. In 1924, unhappy about moves by Eleanor Rathbone to lobby for mothers' pensions and family allowances, she resigned her membership. She was in the House of Commons in 1928 to see the full enfranchisement of women enacted, and in July 1929, in her eighty-third year, she and Agnes returned there to attend a lunch for women MPs. It proved to be Millicent's last public appearance. Soon after she confessed to feeling tired and consented to stay in bed. She died a little more than a fortnight later, on 5 August.

It is appropriate that Millicent Fawcett should have died so soon after the suffrage battle came to an end. Others regarded the struggle as one of highs and lows, setbacks and advances, but Millicent always saw it, as she saw the onward march of humanity, as a steady but sure-footed journey towards enlightenment. She once shocked a journalist who asked her to describe the ups and downs of the movement by replying that she could not do so because there had been none. 'The history of the women's movement for the last fifty years is the gradual removal of intolerable grievances. Sometimes the pace was fairly rapid, sometimes it was very slow; but it was always constant, and always in one direction,' she explained.[38] It was her core philosophy. The final act in the suffrage drama marked the completion of her project. Millicent's friend Frances Balfour, summing up her feelings about her after her death, explained it thus:

> Florence Nightingale used to say and act on, 'The Son of God goes forth to *war*,' and at the darkest hour of our cause, by instinct, Mrs Fawcett went out to war ... How often have I watched her, after some seemingly disastrous defeat, when many of us thought the cause thrown back for years, come into the committee room, her face beaming with smiling defiance.[39]

Constance Markievicz.

XI

Constance Markievicz – Born Rebel

When long ago I saw her ride
Under Ben Bulben to the meet
The beauty of her countryside
With all youth's lonely wildness stirred
She seemed to have grown clean and sweet
Like any rock-bred, sea-borne bird

W. B. Yeats describing Constance Gore-Booth in her youth

On 20 February 1919 a small and now largely forgotten piece of Parliamentary history was made. The first woman elected to Westminster entered the House, not to take her seat but to view the only tangible evidence of her new status – a cloakroom peg with her name on it. The new session had started nine days earlier but the Countess Markievicz had been unable to attend. She had been detained in Holloway for her activities as an Irish Republican rebel and even now, newly released, she had no intention of taking an active part in the business of an institution she loathed. But, never one to miss out on an opportunity for a dramatic gesture, she could not leave London without making her presence felt.

The election of December 1918, in which sixteen other female candidates had stood and been defeated, had been a strange time for Constance Markievicz. Little news of the proceedings had reached her in prison. She had been given permission to write an election address but remained unsure of whether the censor had allowed it to reach its destination. She could not make a speech, visit her constituency or communicate directly with her electorate. And yet, she wrote to her beloved sister Eva, her election as Sinn Fein member for the St Patrick's division of

Dublin was a foregone conclusion. After years of working and agitating in the city's slums, she knew most of the voters personally.

Constance's electoral victory in December 1918 was a galling one for Christabel Pankhurst, who had had high hopes of becoming Britain's first woman MP during her own campaign at Smethwick. For although the suffrage struggle had played a part in Constance's political development she had not chosen to make it her life's work. Her sister Eva, living in England, was a lifelong suffrage campaigner and one of Christabel's own early mentors, but Constance believed British votes could never make Irish women free. If she had grown up in England she would very possibly have become one of the militant suffragettes' greatest assets – fearless, beautiful and daredevil, she brought romance to every one of her life's ventures. By 1919 she had already been imprisoned twice and condemned to death once for her republican activities, in particular for her part in the 1916 Easter Uprising. She had often carried a gun.

With hindsight it would be easy to argue that Constance was born, in 1868, to be a rebel. Certainly hers was never destined to be an ordinary life. The eldest daughter of an Anglo-Irish baronet, she spent much of her childhood roaming or riding across the lush green Sligo countryside that surrounded her family seat, a Grecian Revival mansion named Lissadell, or along the dunes by its shoreline. Her father, Sir Henry Gore-Booth, went away periodically on Arctic expeditions and came back with stirring tales of gales, ice-floes and daring rescues of marooned comrades. Constance learned to stalk deer on her father's estates and from an early age rode with the County Sligo Harriers on her pony, Storeen. Her parents, who had four more children after Constance, allowed her a great deal of freedom and she rode unescorted or sailed her small boat alone in the bay. Only once did she suffer a serious accident, when she tried to jump her pony over a cow and the cow responded by getting to its feet.

Throughout her life Constance would think of Lissadell as her spiritual home – the core of what Ireland meant to her. It provided her with images of beauty to which she could cling during her long years in prison. And, perhaps more importantly, it provided her with qualities and skills for which she would always be grateful. She learned stoicism, resourcefulness and courage. Perhaps even more usefully, she learned to shoot. In the words of one biographer: 'There can be few more effective trainings for a female revolutionary than the nineteenth century childhood of a country tomboy in a troubled land.'[1]

Constance's family never set out to prepare her for the life she eventually chose. But growing up in post-famine Ireland even a relatively unobservant child would have found it hard to ignore the desperate poverty that surrounded her, and Constance, despite her daredevil streak, was a sensitive and warm-hearted girl. Her family were said to be among the better landlords, but the standard against which they were judged was shockingly low. Constance's grandfather, Sir Robert Gore-Booth, was remembered locally for spending thousands of pounds on food relief during the famine – unlike the absentee landlords in England he could see the plight of his tenants. But he was also remembered for an incident in which he extended his lands and evicted large numbers of tenants. Although it seems there was no truth in the local legend that he sent many of them to their deaths in an unseaworthy 'coffin ship', there were complaints that many of those to whom he offered money to emigrate were too old or infirm to make a life in America.[2] In 1879, when Constance was eleven, the potato crop failed, though not as badly as it had done during the great famine of the late 1840s, and the Gore-Booth family were forced again to provide food for their tenants. Families on their estates lived in one-roomed houses which they shared with their animals, and their diet consisted mainly of milk, oatmeal and poor-quality imported Indian meal.

It would be many years before Constance distilled these images into the basis of a political philosophy. As a girl and as a young woman she was able to devote much of her time to enjoyment. She loved to dress up, and was once turned away from the back door of Lissadell after showing up there in a beggar's clothes. She once persuaded a friend to climb the steeple of the local Church of Ireland and hang on it an invitation for local people to attend a Methodist sermon. On another occasion she shocked the assembled company at a formal dinner when she held aloft the hand of the male diner sitting next to her and declared loudly: 'Look what I've just found in my lap!' Yeats, who visited Lissadell as a young man, became a confidant of the more fragile, ethereal Eva and confessed to her his hopeless love for the revolutionary Maud Gonne, later a close compatriot of Constance's. Despite his disapproval of their politics, he would create an immortal image of the young sisters:

The light of evening, Lissadell
Great windows open to the South

Two girls in silk kimonos, both
Beautiful, one a gazelle.

As was usual with girls of her time and class, Constance was a London debutante at eighteen and was presented at the court of Queen Victoria. She brought a certain panache to the role, attending Ascot in a red dress slashed with black satin stripes and a black hat with three ostrich feathers. During a 'season' in Dublin she once walked a drunken soldier back to his barracks in her dressing gown and tiara after finding him clinging to her gatepost when she returned from a ball. Lissadell, much as she loved it, could contain her no longer. After a spell as a student at the Slade School of Fine Art in London she eventually persuaded her parents to let her study painting in Paris. What Constance's fellow students made of her is a mystery – one who dared to tease her about her accent found herself with her head under a tap. A friend from this period described Constance as an eye-catching figure: 'A tall thin slip of a girl with tawny red-gold hair which she wore *a la Mérode* over her ears under a sailor hat [with] a pink cotton blouse, much open at the collar, from which a long throat rose very triumphantly.'[3]

Constance wore a ring on her wedding finger and declared herself 'married to art'. But not for long. In 1899 she was introduced at a student ball to Count Casimir Dunin-Markievicz, a Polish-Russian nobleman whose background and interests seemed strikingly to mirror hers. Casi, as Constance knew him, had grown up in a large country house and, like herself, enjoyed country pursuits such as hunting. Like Constance he had thrown over the life allotted to him – in his case the study of law in Kiev – to travel to Paris and become an artist. Despite these seemingly good portents her announcement in early 1900 that she intended to marry Casi caused a certain amount of consternation. First, her chosen bridegroom was six years her junior – she was then thirty-two – and a widower with a young son who was being looked after by his family. Second, he was a Roman Catholic. There was also the question of his lineage, about which inquiries were instituted through the Tsarist authorities. They brought bad news. Russian intelligence agents reported back that there had never been a Count Markievicz in Poland.[4] A family friend who knew Casi told Constance's brother Josslyn, now head of the family, that she was 'much perturbed' about the marriage. 'I don't think there is the smallest chance of his making her happy … I think marriages between English girls and foreigners a great mistake.'[5] Constance was determined, though, despite all these objections, and she sought to mollify her brother. 'Thank goodness he hates politics and has never meddled in any plots or belonged to any political societies,' she wrote in one of many letters to Josslyn on the subject.[6] After many months of arrangements and negotiations the couple were eventually married in London on 29 September 1900.

Upon their return from a cycling honeymoon in Normandy, Constance and Casi planned a future as artists in a four-roomed apartment off the Boulevard Montparnasse. A little more than a year later, despite Constance's protestation to her brother that with her tiny 'portion' and Casi's £160 per year they would be too poor to have children, their only daughter, Maeve, was born. The birth, at Lissadell, was a difficult one and Constance nearly died. A few months afterwards, when Constance and Casi departed, they left the infant with Constance's mother. Although Maeve later lived with her parents for a time, most of her childhood would be spent with her grandmother. In 1902 and again in 1903 the couple took long trips to stay with Casi's family in the Ukraine, where Constance met his young son, Staskov. After the second of these visits they decided to bring him back to live with them – but in Dublin rather than in Paris. There they took a grand double-fronted Georgian house named St Mary's, in Frankfort Avenue, Rathgar.

Dublin suited both Constance and Casi. Despite Constance's complaints over her marriage settlement they were able to uphold their family traditions with a grand lifestyle, attending functions at the castle and cutting a dash at the annual horse show. Casi loved to drink, though Constance did not, and both enjoyed entertaining. But while they continued to socialise in the circles dictated by their aristocratic backgrounds, there was a more bohemian side to their lives. Their friends included many of Ireland's best-known literary and artistic figures, among them Maud Gonne and Yeats, with whom they helped to found the Dublin Arts Club in 1905. The upper-class 'West Britons' tended to regard the artistic set with suspicion, fearing they had Fenian tendencies. Maud Gonne had long been involved in campaigning to protect people evicted from their homes, and in 1900 had founded a revolutionary women's movement named Inghinidhe na h-Éireann, Daughters of Ireland. With Yeats, Gonne had also helped to found the Abbey Theatre in 1902, and the Markieviczs became involved there too. Casi turned his back on a moderately successful painting career to write plays, and Constance took a number of acting parts at the theatre.

Even during these hedonistic years Constance was not entirely without social conscience. As early as the mid-1890s, while she was a student at the Slade, she joined a suffrage society in London. Her early political education was interlinked with that of her sister Eva, who had contracted tuberculosis and had been sent to Bordighera, in Italy, for a cure. While there she had met Esther Roper, a clergyman's daughter from Cheshire who had been one of the first female students at Manchester's Victoria University and who was secretary of the Manchester National Society for Women's Suffrage. In December 1896, during a break at Lissadell, the sisters organised a suffrage meeting at which Constance made her first public speech. The audience was a sympathetic one, with both Sir Henry and Lady Gore-Booth in attendance, and soon afterwards the local paper reported that Constance had become president of the newly formed Sligo Women's Suffrage Association. Eva probably garnered the facts for Constance's speech, in which she quoted John Stuart Mill and pointed out that the numbers of women signing petitions in favour of the suffrage had risen from 11,000 in 1873 to 257,000 in 1893. 'We are told the principal argument against our having votes is that we don't make noise enough. Of course it is an excellent thing to be able to make a good deal of noise, but not having done so seems hardly a good enough reason for refusing the franchise,' she said to cheers and a great deal of amusement.[7]

Constance's involvement with the women's suffrage movement ended, at least for the time being, when she went to Paris in 1898. Eva, meanwhile, continued to become more deeply involved while also gaining recognition as a poet. Her work with Esther, both in agitating for the vote and in organising the Lancashire textile workers, brought her into contact with the Pankhursts at the beginning of the twentieth century. Sylvia commented later that despite her delicate health Eva was 'a personality of great charm': 'Christabel adored her, and when Eva suffered from neuralgia, as often happened, would sit with her for hours massaging her head. To all of us at home this seemed remarkable indeed, for Christabel had never been willing to act the nurse to any other human being.'[8] Eva and Esther went to the gates of Strangeways to meet Christabel and Annie Kenney on their release from their first imprisonment in 1905, but they were pacifists and never joined the WSPU. Instead they continued their work with the constitutional suffrage organisations. In 1908, though, they came together with the militants to oppose the candidacy of Winston Churchill at the North West Manchester by-election. May Billinghurst was prominent among the suffragettes campaigning at this election, along with the Pankhursts. Constance came over from Dublin to help, and made her presence felt when she rode her horse-drawn carriage into the midst of a hustings crowd. 'Can you cook a dinner?' a man shouted out at her. 'Yes. Can you drive a coach and four?' Constance responded.[9]

The militant suffrage movement in Ireland did not begin until 1908, when Hanna Sheehy-Skeffington and Margaret Cousins founded the Irish Women's Franchise League. From the beginning the organisation, although non-party, had Irish nationalism as one of its main reference points. Just as the militant WSPU in England sprang largely from frustration over male attitudes in the labour movement, the IWFL was born of anger at the failure of many Irish politicians to recognise the women's potential as future citizens of their country. 'We were as keen as men on the freedom of Ireland, but we saw the men clamouring for amendments which suited their own interests and made no recognition of the existence of women as fellow citizens,' Margaret Cousins wrote.[10] The WSPU had also provided inspiration. 'I eagerly followed the doings of the militants with full understanding of their aims, methods and spirit,' wrote Margaret Cousins. 'I felt so much one of them that I longed for some way in which the women of Ireland might be colleagues in such a soul-stirring and needed movement.'[11] During the ensuing six years Constance would be regularly associated with the organisation, but it would become less central to her life as she grew increasingly absorbed by her work for socialist and republican causes.

For her, 1908 marked a watershed. It was the year she ceased to focus on Dublin Castle and its smart social occasions, and turned more firmly towards radical politics. That year, too, Constance was invited by the Inghinidhe na h-Éireann to help them launch a new magazine, *Bean na h-Éireann*, 'The Woman of Ireland'.[12] Constance caused consternation when she arrived in full evening dress with a fur coat and diamonds in her hair – apparently straight from the castle, the centre of all that was loathed by the 'daughters'. She agreed to design a heading for the cover page of the magazine and to contribute regular gardening notes, reflecting one of her lifelong passions. As Hanna Sheehy-Skeffington remarked later, she was 'not a feminist ever and only a mild suffragist', but she was always interested in direct action against any kind of authority.[13] In July 1910 Constance made a speech calling on the young women of Ireland to refrain from joining any suffrage society that did not have 'the freedom of the nation' as part of its programme, as the IWFL did. Her notes for *Bean na h-Éireann* always had a nationalist flavour. 'It is very unpleasant work killing slugs and snails but let us not be daunted. A good nationalist should look upon slugs in the garden in much the same way she looks on the English in Ireland,' she wrote on one occasion.[14]

All this activity began to take its toll on Constance's marriage. One of Casi's main sources of income had been as a portrait painter to the gentry, and as his wife became more publicly militant such work became harder to find. At the same time, Constance seems to have begun a lifelong habit of giving away most of her own income from a shares portfolio set up for her on her marriage. The couple's finances grew increasingly precarious. By 1910 they were receiving final demands for late rent, and Casi was writing in despair to Constance's brother Josslyn: 'It's impossible to know what Constance gets, what does she do with her money, as she generally flies into a temper if I ask her any question about it.'[15] There were more fundamental problems in the marriage. While Constance plunged headlong into each of her life's ventures Casi was more of a *bon viveur*, drifting along cheerfully and sociably but without any great sense of direction. Once at an afternoon gathering at which tea was being served he turned in frustration to his wife and exclaimed: 'Constance – please tell these people I *drink*!' By now he was spending several months each year with his family in the Ukraine, often returning to find the house full of radicals of varying complexions with whom he had little in common.

The WSPU would later set up a Dublin branch in apparent competition with the IWFL in the hope of attracting protestant women to its cause, but for the time the two organisations worked closely together – so much so that the Irish group would be accused of being little more than an adjunct of the London one. Indeed, letters written by Annie Kenney to Hanna Sheehy-Skeffington in 1912 suggest she felt justified in handing out orders: 'I will let you know in the course of a day or two the best time for you to come to London to lobby … Do as we do in England – simply pester the lives out of Cabinet ministers, leaders of the Irish Party, the Labour Party,' she wrote.[16] There were a number of militant incidents in Ireland and some IWFL members were imprisoned, but the suffrage battle never reached the intensity it did in England. The most spectacular incident happened in July 1912 during a visit to Dublin by Herbert Asquith in support of his plans for Irish Home Rule. Both IWFL and WSPU activists were there to greet him, with the Irish campaigners sailing out to meet his boat at Kingstown, now Dun Laoghaire, and raining confetti on him from a window as he walked with the Nationalist leader John Redmond in a torchlight procession. The real trouble was caused by two English suffragettes, Mary Leigh and Gladys Evans, who first threw a hatchet into the Prime Minister's carriage and then tried to set fire to the Theatre Royal with petrol. In response, angry crowds began heckling IWFL women at an outdoor meeting near the theatre and the police were forced to protect them. Constance, some little distance away, was mobbed and took refuge in Liberty Hall, the headquarters of the Irish Transport and General Workers' Union.[17]

By now Constance was a regular visitor to Liberty Hall. In the summer of 1910, during a brief phase in which she attempted to set up a co-operative market garden outside Dublin, she had cycled into the city to hear the union leader James Larkin propound his belief that Irish labour should not be controlled from England. Constance had been an instant convert, and her association with Larkin had also brought her into contact with the republican socialist James Connolly. Soon she was attending the meetings of a variety of organisations: the Gaelic League, Sinn Fein and the labour movement as well as the women's causes with which she had for some time been involved. But while she took on board the philosophies of these groups, Constance's *métier* was always in action rather than in deep thought or in political manoeuvrings. And in Ireland, in stark contrast to the comparatively tame activities of the English suffragettes at the time, that action was beginning to take on the qualities of a real revolution. Constance's co-operative venture, Belcamp Park, became the first headquarters of a new scout movement set up to train and drill the young people of Ireland for the fight ahead. Constance's 'boys' in the Na Fianna Éireann took target practice in the grounds – a receipt from the same year shows she spent £59 in a shop which sold guns. A friend recalled later:

> Although she had only armed the boys with miniature rifles we may claim that Madame had put arms into the hands of the future Irish Volunteers ... Madame had much the character of a boy and the Fianna, although they took up a great deal of her time and energy, also helped to lighten her burden and to give her hope to continue the struggle. She was as agile as a boy, and as full of enterprise, and she had a mischievous sense of fun which the scouts enjoyed.[18]

These boys were soon engaged not just in target practice but also in tearing down Union Jacks and swarming up lampposts to put up posters urging young men to boycott the British Army. Later, during the First World War, Constance learned of a boys' paper which was printing troop movements and she sent her scouts with anti-recruiting literature to every point at which the soldiers were due to arrive. The army's intelligence officials were both horrified and puzzled that such information should have got into enemy hands.

During 1913 the Irish Transport and General Workers' Union, founded by Larkin in 1909, came into direct conflict with the employers. The main protagonist on the employers' side was William Martin Murphy, owner of both the Dublin United Tramways company and the *Irish Independent* newspaper, and a man implacably opposed to Larkin. Murphy sacked 100 tram workers for joining the union. Workers at Eason's, Ireland's largest newspaper distributor, followed suit and the dockers began refusing to handle their goods. On 29 August at the behest of Murphy, 400 employers agreed to lock out the members of the union, including 3,000 from the building trade who had refused to sign a pledge not to join the union. Soon 25,000 men were out of work, and Larkin and four colleagues had been charged with seditious libel and seditious conspiracy.

It was to Constance's home, Surrey House in Rathmines, that Larkin fled when a warrant was issued for his arrest. The following day he emerged, dressed as an elderly man with a beard, and managed to speak from the balcony of the Imperial Hotel in O'Connell Street before being arrested. Throughout the five-month lock-out Constance was fully occupied in providing food for children who were close to starvation. With Larkin's sister Delia, she was put in charge of welfare at Liberty Hall. There she produced huge vats of soup from bacon bones and potatoes cadged from sympathisers, and crowds of people queued up with mugs and old tin cans to receive it. The playwright Sean O'Casey later accused her of doing little real work and of taking up a soup ladle only to pose, in a pristine white apron, for the press.[19] But a trade union leader who was constantly in Liberty Hall during the strike remembered her toiling ceaselessly, her sleeves rolled up, a sack tied around her for an apron and a cigarette usually hanging from her mouth.

Two months into the strike a curious incident occurred which may have sprung from Constance's links, through Eva, with the English suffragists. Dora Montefiore, a prominent suffrage campaigner and friend of

Eva's who had split from the WSPU in 1907, tried to organise the evacuation of a number of starving Irish children to England. Other ex-Pankhurst devotees, including Emmeline Pethick-Lawrence, offered accommodation for them. For whatever reason – maybe because Dora had previously been at the centre of a scandal when a Labour activist had left his wife for her – the Catholic Church did not take kindly to the idea. The well-wishers were accused of trying to kidnap innocent Catholic children, possibly for some sort of white slave trade, and the few who tried to go were dragged off the boat by the priests. Dora was imprisoned in Dublin and had to be bailed out by Constance. Later, a quiet evacuation of some children did take place and a group, along with the mother of one of them, went to stay at the Pethick-Lawrences' country cottage in Surrey. Meanwhile Sylvia had irked Christabel by agreeing to speak at a meeting in support of Larkin, who had been jailed in October. The incident was one of the main catalysts for her expulsion from the WSPU.

The locked-out workers were eventually forced back on their employers' terms, but the conflict had forged new relationships between different rebel groups in Ireland.[20] In November 1913 an Irish Citizen Army had been formed by the transport workers' union in response to the setting up of the Ulster Volunteer Force in the North, which aimed to stop Home Rule. Constance was one of the first recruits to the Irish Citizen Army. At the same time a separate army, the Irish Volunteers, was set up under the auspices of the Irish Republican Brotherhood. On Sunday 26 July 1914 the Volunteers landed 3,000 rifles at Howth, near Dublin, from a yacht named the *Asgard*, owned by the novelist Erskine Childers. Constance was at her country cottage in Balally when she heard the news that as the Volunteers made their escape with the guns British soldiers had opened fire, killing three and wounding thirty-eight. She spent the ensuing days making wreaths for the funerals. The news also brought Sylvia Pankhurst over from England with another suffragette, Maud Joachim, to interview the families of the dead and injured. She was still there when the First World War was declared nine days later.

War did not bring an instant end to suffrage agitation in Ireland as it had done in England. But while the Irish campaign for the vote continued – Sylvia promised to speak in 1915 and caused fury by cancelling at the last minute – Constance had now turned her attentions firmly to the nationalist cause. Her house in Rathmines became a hub of activity. James Connolly, her great friend and mentor, was by then staying there. Others were welcome to turn up at any time and to stay, talking until the early hours. The house was always full, always chaotic. One visitor recalled seeing Michael Collins reciting Emmet's speech from the dock at the top of his voice late one night.[21] When not talking and plotting at home, Constance was often out on night-time route marches with the Citizen Army or her Fianna boys.[22] She struggled to make ends meet, particularly as she was still burdened by debts she had incurred helping the desperate during the lock-out. At least once she wrote to her brother Joss to ask for a loan. Casi, who had been spending a great deal of time in Russia for the past several years, had joined an Imperial Hussar regiment. Constance's stepson, Staskov, stayed with her until the middle of 1915 and then set off on the long and treacherous journey across Europe to rejoin his father's family.

At Christmas 1915 Constance heard news that a shipload of arms from Germany would land in Ireland at Easter. In January Connolly disappeared for three days for a council of war with the Irish Republican Brotherhood group in the Volunteers. Connolly had to be persuaded that the labour cause should be sacrificed for the sake of an armed insurrection; Constance did not. During his absence she apparently met Padraic Pearse in the street and told him the Citizen Army was going to storm Dublin Castle, with or without Connolly's approval. By now both Liberty Hall and Constance's home were being regularly raided by the police, and she and her comrades were being watched intently by British intelligence. A Fianna boy was arrested after mistakenly delivering a consignment of gelignite to Surrey House; the gelignite was never found. Constance was often in her Citizen Army uniform, either on manoeuvres or taking her turn as a sentry at Liberty Hall, where a much-prized printing press was under threat.

The uprising, when it came, began amid confusion. Some of the republican leaders were still set against it, and when news reached them of the capture of the arms ship and the arrest of Sir Roger Casement, a former British consul who had negotiated with Germany for its safe passage, they tried to stop it. Orders to the Volunteers to mobilise were countermanded by a newspaper announcement, causing confusion across the country. In Dublin, the insurgents had an army of little more than 800 – 700 Volunteers and 120 from the Citizen Army. Constance began the day with her friend Dr Kathleen Lynn, driving a batch of medical supplies to the City Hall. Before she even reached her destination she had her first taste of action when Connolly shot dead a policeman who tried to stop them. She was then left in charge of trench digging on St Stephen's Green, from where the holiday crowds had been hurriedly ejected. The rebels seized the Post Office and several other key buildings around Dublin, though they failed in their aim of capturing the castle.

At about noon on Easter Sunday Constance drove up to St Stephen's Green, dressed in a green uniform with a brown belt and feathers in her hat. An army doctor gave evidence at the court martial that followed, claiming she had leant against the Eglinton monument on the green and shot at him from 50 yards' distance as he sat in an open window of the University Club.[23] She was carrying a Mauser pistol with a fitting that allowed it to be fired from the shoulder. She stayed at the green until Tuesday morning, when she and the other rebels seized the College of Surgeons. By the Thursday, the GPO had been isolated by the British and Connolly had been wounded. On the Sunday, the news reached the College of Surgeons that a surrender had been negotiated. Ironically the British officer who arrived to receive it, Captain Henry de Courcy Wheeler, was a distant relative of Constance by marriage. He offered her a car to take her to the castle, but she chose instead to march with her comrades.

Constance was quite prepared to die, and even discussed with another rebel on the march to the castle whether they would be hung or shot. But the next few days must have been some of the most traumatic of her life, as she sat in a cell and listened to the sound of her closest friends and colleagues being executed. Eva, in London, read in *Lloyd's List* that Constance's body had been found on St Stephen's Green. Several days later, when she learned her sister was alive, she almost wished she had been dead – the prospect of an execution was so much worse.[24] When she was finally allowed to see Constance, her mind was full of just one dreadful thought: did Constance know Connolly had been shot that day? Would she have to tell her? But Constance knew everything. It had all been, in her view, 'splendidly worthwhile. For one glorious week Ireland had been free,' Eva recalled.[25] Just one death was causing Constance real grief – that of Francis Sheehy-Skeffington, husband of Hanna and a pacifist who had been trying to stop the looting of city properties when he was shot by the British Army. Hanna would later enlist the help of the Pethick-Lawrences and other British political contacts to highlight the injustice of his killing. 'Why on earth did they shoot Skeffy?' Constance asked her sister in confusion. 'He wasn't in it. He didn't even believe in fighting. What did it mean?'[26] For herself, she said, she would not have minded being summarily shot. But she did object to her 'trial', at which there were few witnesses and no defence solicitor. She pleaded guilty to participating in the uprising but not guilty to 'assisting the enemy' – the enemy were surely the Germans, she said – and not guilty to causing disaffection, for which she blamed the British. Not long afterwards she greeted a fellow female prisoner with a radiant smile and the words: 'Did you hear the news? I have been sentenced to death!'[27] Constance asked Eva for news of Maeve, but her daughter, now fifteen, did not visit her.

Clemency was requested in view of Constance's gender, and she was moved from Dublin to Aylesbury gaol in England, where she served the rest of her imprisonment. 'I shall be quite amiable, and am not going to hunger-strike as I am advised by comrades not to. It would suit the Government very well to let me die quietly!' she wrote to Eva.[28] Meanwhile her family was in turmoil. Casi had been injured, and though messages were sent to him it was not clear for some time that he knew his wife was in prison. Josslyn, saddled with the task of sorting his sister's rather untidy personal affairs, was beset by accusations that she had shot an injured policeman as he lay on the ground. Constance never admitted to this, nor was she ever charged with such an offence. Indeed, she had urged her comrades not to shoot a British squaddie who had wandered into the College of Surgeons just after the news of the surrender, on the grounds that it would be pointless at that stage. She told Eva she had held a gun against a policeman's chest but had been unable to shoot him because she recognised him. She thought she might have hit one officer in the arm, she added. But the press reports did not reflect this, and it was suggested Constance's family connections, not her gender, saved her life. Even Eva's companion Esther Roper believed the Prime Minister had intervened to stop her being executed.[29] Constance told Joss to ignore the rumours. 'My enemies will make a monster of me; my friends a heroine and both will be equally wide of the truth! I really did very little we were not in the thick of it at all,' she wrote to him.[30] Josslyn seems to have spent a great deal of time trying to get to the bottom of these tales, while Constance's youngest brother Mordaunt was convinced she had, indeed, shot a policeman. Old friends, too, were shocked by her behaviour. Yeats's sister Lily wrote to her father in disparaging terms of the uprising:

What a pity Madame Markievicz's madness changed its form when she inherited it. In her father it meant looking for the North Pole in an open boat. Very cooling for him and safe for others. Her followers are said to have been either small boys or drunken dock workers out of work ... I would not have followed her across the road.[31]

Constance spent a year at Aylesbury, isolated from all her political comrades. She was the only Irish woman prisoner there, and her companions were mostly women convicted of killing their children. She worked cheerfully in the kitchens, though, and her friends' concern for her welfare was much greater than her own. 'All my life in a funny sort of way seems to have led up to the last year, and it's been such a hurry skurry sort of a life. Now I feel I have done what I was born to do. The great wave has crashed up against the rock, and now all the bubbles and ripples and little me slip back into a quiet pool of the sea,' she wrote to Eva.[32] Constance was allowed to receive visits from her sister, and she smuggled out messages via an intermediary with instructions to 'make capital' of her grim surroundings. Eva did as she was asked, drawing an angry response from the prison governor that Constance's companions were not, as was claimed, 'the dregs of the population'. Several were 'quite decent well-behaved women', he retorted.[33]

In June 1917 Constance was released as part of a general amnesty and was welcomed back to Dublin as a heroine. Even as the boat train left London, Irish men and women gathered to sing patriotic songs on the platform. At Kingstown harbour the crowds were so dense she could barely get on her train. Traffic had to be diverted in the centre of Dublin as her car made its way to the remains of Liberty Hall, which had been shelled during Easter week. Other prisoners were released on the same day, but Constance was the best known. She was almost the only leader of the uprising to have survived. A week later she took the final step in her personal identification with Ireland and its struggle for freedom, when she was received into the Roman Catholic Church.

It was hard for Constance to adjust to life in post-1916 Dublin. Many of her closest friends were dead, her home was shut up and her belongings looted or in storage. She moved back into Surrey House only briefly, and for most of the following ten years she stayed with friends during the brief times when she was not either in prison or touring the country. Not much more than a month after her release, British intelligence officers tracked Constance as she set off to County Roscommon. They followed her to Cork, Meath, Down, Clare and Kerry during the ensuing months, becoming a familiar sight at her meetings.[34]

Constance was arrested again in the spring of 1918 along with more than seventy Sinn Fein leaders. Field Marshal Lord French, the new Viceroy of Ireland and coincidentally the brother of the suffragette and republican Charlotte Despard, had become worried about the possibility of a 'German plot'. A shipwrecked man rescued off Galway had sparked off the arrests by telling police he was a member of Casement's Irish Brigade. This next spell in prison was much more sociable than Constance's last. She was held in Holloway with Kathleen Clarke, whose husband Tom had been executed in 1916, with Maud Gonne and later with Hanna Sheehy-Skeffington. The women were kept apart from other prisoners on a special landing with its own bathroom, and they exercised separately. It was difficult to get news of the outside world, though, and Constance asked Eva to send the *Daily Herald, The Socialist* and Sylvia's *Workers' Dreadnought*. 'I am radiantly happy! Don't be alarmed. "Stone walls do not a prison make" etc,' she wrote to Eva.[35]

The war over, the political world began preparing for a general election. While the former suffragettes groomed their candidates – Emmeline Pethick-Lawrence and Christabel Pankhurst among them – Sinn Fein began picking its own. There was talk that its candidates might be released from prison for the duration, but this came to nothing. When Constance first learned that she was to stand for election, she did not even know for which constituency. She was one of two women candidates fielded by Sinn Fein, the other being Winifred Carney in Belfast. Although she could not be there herself, those of her female friends and supporters who were at liberty were prominent in working for her election.

The *Dublin Evening Mail* reported on polling day that by early afternoon 6,000 votes had been cast in the St Patrick's division: 'A vast number of women voters supported Countess Markievicz and the consensus of opinion favours her return by a sweeping majority. The district was liberally decorated with republican flags.' 'Vote for the Countess. Victory means release,' read some of the banners.[36] Constance polled more than twice as many votes as her Irish Party rival. Early predictions that Sinn Fein might take twenty-six seats proved wildly pessimistic. The party took seventy-three of the 105 seats, and the unionists took twenty-six.[37] The nationalists were almost wiped out.

Constance again arrived back in Dublin to a public reception and adoring crowds in the streets. Bands played by the Liffey, 'The Red Flag' and Constance's own 'Hymn of Battle' were sung and the *Irish Citizen* commented that a queen or a president might have been envious. By then Constance's republican colleagues had announced the advent of the first Dail

Éireann, which had begun meeting at the city's Mansion House. The censor at Dublin Castle had forbidden the press to publish its programme or its declaration of Irish independence. In February 1919 Michael Collins had helped to spring Eamon de Valera and two other Sinn Fein prisoners from Lincoln gaol in England, and when de Valera returned to lead the Dail in March he appointed Constance as Minister of Labour. In reality, her life was little different from before, except that she now had the Mansion House as her headquarters. Much of her time was spent travelling the country, speaking at meetings where her words were taken down assiduously by British intelligence officers. In April she addressed an audience of 10,000 in Glasgow, urging them to form demobilised soldiers into a Citizen Army. In May she was arrested again and sentenced to four months in Cork female prison for using seditious language in a speech in which she urged a boycott of the police. Cork was quite the nicest prison she had been in, she wrote to Eva. The governor even allowed her to work outside, making a garden in the yard which continued to bloom for many years. While she was there, the Lord Lieutenant of Ireland explored the possibility that as a foreign national by marriage she might be deported to Russia.[38] It was decided that since the authorities had no reason to believe she had ever been to Russia and the whereabouts of her husband were unknown, this course of action would not be advisable.

Constance was released in the autumn to find herself a minister in a banned parliament. She was, to all intents and purposes, a fugitive. She would never contemplate giving up her political activities, and by undertaking them she made herself liable to arrest. The Dail continued to meet as often as it could, though, and Constance continued to attend without fail. She also carried on speaking at public meetings – though only ever for a few moments, and always with an escape route carefully planned so that she would not be arrested while leaving. She moved around Dublin dressed in various disguises, often as an old lady in a bonnet and cape. She was recognised by tram conductors and news boys, but never given away.

> The first day I went down town on my bike I had great fun watching the police as I whizzed by. The first I met turned his back most deliberately and stared at the sky, I next met two who burst out laughing in my face then two who looked as if they would have liked to knock me down but I was past them in a flash. I returned to the Abbey Theatre one night to see Desmond FitzGerald's beautiful little miracle play 'The Saint',

she wrote her comrade Joe McGarrity in America.[39] This life continued for nearly a year while guerrilla war was waged against the British, until in September 1920 the inevitable happened and Constance was arrested again. This time she was court-martialled on charges of conspiracy to promote the Fianna Éireann, which was said to be conspiring to kill members of the police and military. According to press reports, she refused to recognise the court and ate chocolates during the hearing. She was sentenced to two years' imprisonment.

While in Mountjoy Prison Constance had news of Staskov, who had been imprisoned in Russia for reasons that remained obscure. She worried about his fate and that of Casi, from whom she had not heard for some years. 'Poor Russia!' she wrote to Eva. ' I often think about my Polish relations. Poor Casi hated wars, revolutions and politics: and there he is – or was – in Kiev, or in the Ukraine.'[40] Finally, after her release in the summer of 1921, she received a letter from Casi. He had been living in Warsaw and working as a legal adviser to the American consul. His letter has not survived but her reply was friendly, though rather formal: 'You ask me what are my plans? Well I have none, it's quite impossible to make any at a time like this! I am so glad that you have been successful with plays, and only hope that you are fairly comfortable, I've often been very unhappy thinking of all you and your people must have suffered.'[41] It was perhaps fortunate that Constance and Casi were now separated by such great physical as well as emotional distance. They had drifted so far apart that their earlier equanimity in the face of their growing differences must surely have deserted them by then if they had been in the same country. 'Casi's letter very cheerful,' Constance had written to Joss after receiving his previous letter in 1917. 'He says he wrote a book about Ireland when he heard I was released and that it made a "great row". All the nobility's privileges have been taken from them – time too!'[42]

While her husband, in Warsaw, bemoaned the loss of his aristocratic privilege, Constance, in Ireland, continued to agitate for a workers' republic. In 1922 she wrote to Staskov, who shared his father's views: 'You rail against the Bolsheviks, I know little about them but one thing I do know is that our people suffered far worse from the English. What I begin to believe is that all Governments are the same and that men in power just use that power to get more power for themselves.'[43] The sentiments seem odd from someone in the midst of a struggle for democratic government but Constance, even with her boundless optimism and appetite for life, was

tired. She had split, along with de Valera, from Michael Collins after rejecting the October 1921 treaty designed to give Ireland Dominion status. She
had ceased to be Minister of Labour when the 'Free State' forces formally
took over Dublin Castle under Collins's leadership, and spent much of the
later part of 1922 on a tour of the US. The upheavals of her life had left her
estranged from almost her entire family, with the exception of Eva. Even
Maeve had become a virtual stranger, to the extent that on Constance's return to London from America her daughter had to ask to be introduced to
her when she saw her in the hotel – she was not even sure whether the
changed woman she saw was her mother. Her biographer describes her as
a mere imprint of her earlier self:

> The young intellectual republicans who met her during these last years of
> her life found it hard to penetrate the mask of tense exhaustion, the gum-
> chewing, the chain-smoking, the shabby clothes, in order to perceive the
> exceptional being that still lay behind the ruins of her beauty and her phys-
> ical elan.[44]

Back in Dublin, she was also depressed by the parlous state in which ordinary people were being forced to live as civil war raged around them.
'Conditions here are awful and seem to get worse and worse every day.
There is starvation on every side, not only among the very poor but among
people who were quite well off,' she wrote to Staskov.[45] Still, Constance's
life was not all sadness, nor had she abandoned her political work. She
continued to agitate against the government – now the Free State government – and when violence broke out she was often in the thick of it, engaging snipers from the roof of Dublin's Hamman Hotel in June 1922 after
British-backed Free State troops drove the Irregulars from their Four
Courts headquarters. There was straightforward political work, too. In
May 1923 Constance regained her constituency, which she had lost in June
1922. She could not take up her seat in the Free State Parliament, though,
any more than she could previously take up a seat in the British Parliament. In November 1923 she began a final period of imprisonment, for
urging action on behalf of republican prisoners including de Valera, who
was in solitary confinement. She joined a number of other republican
women who had been hunger-striking in the North Dublin Union, and
now decided to join them. Constance described the experience in a letter
to Eva as being far less unpleasant than she had expected, though she may

have been trying to calm her sister's fears for her. 'I did not suffer at all but just stayed in bed and dozed and tried to prepare myself to leave the world. I was perfectly happy and had no regrets,' she wrote.[46]

When Eva died in 1926, Constance lost her last real link to the Gore-Booth family and to her past. She did not attend the funeral, which took place in London, saying she 'simply could not face it all'. To attend would have meant seeing her brothers and remaining sister, and in such circumstances she could not bring herself to do so. The loss of Eva was a terrible blow, and it is not surprising that, brought low by grief and depression, she became ill herself the following year. In early July 1927 Joss received a telegram to say that his elder sister had been operated on for appendicitis and was in a critical condition. A few days later she seemed to be better, though still very weak. Casi travelled to Dublin with Staskov to see her. On 15 July she relapsed and died with her husband and Eamon de Valera at her bedside.

The funeral was a public one, with both Casi and Joss in attendance as well as all the major Irish republican figures who remained alive and at liberty to attend. The address was given by Jim Larkin and the Citizen Army marched to Glasnevin cemetery under a red banner inscribed in Russian. But Constance's funeral, appropriately perhaps, had its moments of conflict too. The military attended to prevent a volley from being fired over her grave, and it was decided she should not be buried under armed surveillance. Her coffin was placed in a vault and interred the following day.

Constance's friend Sydney Czira, who wrote under the alias 'John Brennan', said that anyone who tried to describe her to a stranger would seem to be talking not of one woman but of a whole company of women. 'The wide scope of her genius, and the energy and enthusiasm of her character made her not only an outstanding figure but an almost indispensable part of all national work in the years before 1916,' she wrote.[47] Certainly, although her life's work was mainly concerned with the Irish cause, she managed to make her mark on the history of women's political liberation too. Everything she did on the public stage seemed to be writ large. Yet much of what she did behind the scenes, of the work which won her the love and affection of Dublin's poor, was on a scale that was barely perceptible on the political radar. Every time she served a bowl of soup, or drove into Dublin with her car filled with peat for the unemployed, she won a vote. Her actions may have been varied in pattern but her character was not. Constance Markievicz was a doer. Her deeds were the deeds of a woman who lived in strange times, but whatever her time or her surroundings, they were always bound to be extraordinary.

Margaret Grace Bondfield.

XII

Margaret Bondfield – In Power

Since I have been able to vote at all I have never felt the same enthusiasm because the vote was the consequence of possessing property rather than the consequence of being a human being … At last we are established on that equitable footing because we are human beings and part of society as a whole. To me the enfranchisement of women is not so much a question of rights as of opportunity – not a privilege but an obligation to add their share to the common stock in the building of ever-nobler forms of social life … It is an entire mistake, and I always said it was a mistake on the part of some of the ultra-feminist suffragists, to argue the specific woman point of view in connection with political questions.

Margaret Bondfield speaking in the debate on the second reading of the Representation of the People (Equal Franchise) Bill, 29 March 1928

On the face of it the Labour Party should be proud of Margaret Bondfield: one of its first women MPs; first woman minister; first woman cabinet minister. A staunch trade unionist throughout her life, she gave up her chance of promotion in the business world in order to expose the sweat-shop conditions which were prevalent in London's major stores. If that were not enough, she was also a long-term campaigner for the right of women to have a vote.

A week may be a long time in Westminster, but in the Labour Party old enmities die hard. In 1995 Barbara Castle – Britain's fourth female cabinet minister – was asked if she would write a preface for a Fabian pamphlet celebrating Margaret Bondfield's life. She refused. Her predecessor had 'sailed very near the wind of political betrayal', she said, when she served in Ramsay MacDonald's cabinet between the years of 1929 and 1931. In the end Stephen Byers, by then the incumbent of Margaret's former seat, wrote a half-hearted appraisal of her service for Wallsend: 'She failed to develop close links with Tyneside ... the position was well expressed by the Soviet spy Kim Philby when he said "to betray you must first belong".' 'In 2001, when Tony Blair made his centenary speech to the Labour faithful, Margaret Bondfield's name was nowhere to be found on the party's historical roll of honour. Keir Hardie was praised for his devotion to the women's cause, Aneurin Bevan for founding the health service, even Michael Foot for being 'a wonderful human being'. Just one woman featured among the dozens singled out for praise: Barbara Castle.

The suffragettes were no less forthright in their dislike of this inoffensive woman. Sylvia Pankhurst sniped that Margaret 'had proved useless, if not hostile, to the Women's Suffrage cause',[2] while Keir Hardie, a close Labour colleague, was just as outspoken. Her attitude towards the franchise – that it should be available to everyone – was 'that of the dog in the manger', he said.[3] What could have caused such condemnation by people who were essentially working for the same end? Then, as now, political spats can be at their most vehement when they involve personalities whose views are similar. Margaret Bondfield's crime, in the eyes of the Pankhursts and their followers, was to campaign not as a feminist but as a socialist. She believed that at a time when two-thirds of males still did not have the vote, it would be iniquitous to fight for votes for women on the same terms as men. What the suffragettes wanted was not just the vote, or even just the empowerment the vote could bring. What they wanted was legal recognition of their equal status with men. What Margaret Bondfield and her friends in the adult suffrage movement fought for was the sweeping away not of the gender divide but of the class divide. They wanted not votes for women but votes for workers. The fact that the workers, in their eyes, would always include women was not enough for the suffragettes. It was a distraction. In their turn, adult suffrage campaigners saw the militants as fanatics who would happily destroy much that was precious in society by promoting a sex war.

Margaret Bondfield never won the hearts of these radical women, nor even of many of her constituents on Tyneside, but the Labour Party could not deny she was one of its own. Not only did she occupy during her long career some of the most coveted positions within the movement; she also carried impeccably proletarian credentials. Her family hailed from the West Country and her paternal grandmother could trace her ancestors back to the Monmouth rebellion. Her father, a foreman lacemaker, had in his youth been secretary of the Chard Political Union, whose activities were regarded with such suspicion that a division of militia was diverted to the area while *en route* to the Crimea in order to suppress it. There were riots as a result. Later William Bondfield joined the Anti-Corn Law League.[4]

William married Ann Taylor in 1852, and by the time Margaret was born in 1873 her father was sixty years old and the couple already had nine children. Margaret and another girl, Katie, completed their family. A change of ownership brought an end to William's lifetime in the lace factory and, unable any longer to earn a good living, he became a sad figure, haunted by the fear of the workhouse. Margaret felt he was remote from her, 'a stranger who punished with quotations and a slipper'. But he retained a lively mind. Margaret later recalled how he once came home with a new geological hammer when his children all needed boots. She wished she had known him in his more carefree youth, when he helped a friend to invent a flying machine which was exhibited at the Crystal Palace in London.

The family had very little money, but William and Ann worked to ensure their children got an education – one of Margaret's brothers went on to work for the *Financial Times*, while another edited a local newspaper. The Bondfield children never went hungry, not least because they lived in a pair of rural cottages where they could grow their own fruit and vegetables. But the family resources did not stretch to keeping Margaret in secondary education, and from the age of thirteen she had to earn her living – as a class monitor at the school where she had previously been a pupil. She had always had a facility with words, and had a stock of recitations as well as piano pieces for which she was often in demand at Sunday School gatherings and parties. Throughout her life she would have the ability to hold the attention of a crowd, no matter how large and how hostile. The course of Margaret's life was set, though, when she was sent to Brighton at the age of fourteen. A short apprenticeship with an embroideress came to an end when her employer retired, and the young girl was then taken on as a junior in the outfitting department of Hetherington's store in Western Road. It was a salutary experience. Although Margaret's employer was by no means one of the worst, she was employed, like most shop assistants at the time, under the 'living in' system. Under this system workers had to live in accommodation provided by their employers, for which rent and board was deducted from their pay. The food was often execrable, they had no personal freedom or privacy and they were often expected to work very long hours – Margaret recalled one shop owner who would put up his shutters at 11.55 p.m. on a Saturday so as to observe the sanctity of the Sabbath.

It was in Brighton that Margaret's political education began under the tutelage of a Mrs Martindale who was a keen member of the local Liberal Party. Although Margaret never had any intention of joining she happily accepted invitations to visit Mrs Martindale to talk and to borrow political books and literature. Mrs Martindale's daughter Hilda later recalled Margaret at sixteen as 'an eager, attractive and vividly alive girl' whose descriptions of her dingy dormitory and consumptive room-mate opened the older woman's eyes to the unsavoury reality behind the respectable facades of her local shops.[5] Pictures of Margaret in her teens show a neat, small and bright-eyed teenager whose lace collar seems incongruously grown-up in contrast to her rounded, childish features. Even at this early age, though, Margaret was showing signs of being a leader among her friends. There were no washing facilities at Hetherington's so on a Friday evening when the store closed she would lead her workmates in a half-mile dash to the public baths, where they then had fifteen minutes to wash and dress before that, too, closed for the evening.

At the age of twenty-one, with a hard-earned £5 savings in her pocket and a testimonial praising her as 'a thoroughly smart business young person', she left Brighton for London.[6] The following three months were some of the hardest of her life, spent in a near-hopeless search for work. One day she walked all the way up Oxford Street and down the other side without success. She survived only because her sympathetic landlady believed in her and was prepared to wait for the rent until Margaret found a job. Eventually she succeeded but the conditions were even worse than those she had encountered in Brighton. She was forced to work sixty-five hours a week for around £40 a year, half of which was deducted for bed and board. One day while eating fish and chips from a newspaper she noticed an article about the National Union of Shop Assistants, Warehousemen and Clerks, and immediately decided to join up.

Soon Margaret was writing reports for the union newspaper, *The Shop Assistant*, under the pseudonym Grace Dare. So little time and personal freedom did she have that she was forced to work on these pieces when her fellow workers were asleep – she would have been sacked if she had been discovered. Margaret's articles tended towards the personal, bringing injustice to life through the stories of young women she met in her daily life. On one occasion she told the story of a very young assistant who was being taken advantage of by her manager. 'Grace' described, with a flourish of Victorian melodrama, how the manager explained the eventual disappearance of the girl by saying she had found a better job. Later she had encountered her, drunk and miserable, on a railway platform in the East End, and had reproached herself for not discovering sooner what was happening to her. On another occasion she wrote about a young assistant who became undernourished and sick while trying to live on the meagre rations her employer provided, and who eventually died after being repeatedly told she did not need a doctor.[7] Margaret was an engaging figure, often described by those who met her as having the pert energy of a small bird. 'Small in stature with dark hair, wide brows, and bright dark eyes, she reminded her hearers of a courageous robin as, in her clear, resonant, musical voice she told them that the unions must get together for political action if they were to achieve their larger aims,' ran one description.[8] By 1898 her work for the shop assistants' union was taking up all the little free time she had. When she finished work on a Saturday night she would often take an overnight train to some far-flung town where a meeting was taking place, retracing her steps overnight on Sunday in order to be at her post on Monday morning. Margaret's employers were pleased with her and had she not become involved in politics she would have slowly climbed the management ladder. Instead she gave up full-time shop work for the trade union, visiting and leafleting workplaces to seek out potential new members.

In 1906 Margaret was asked to undertake what would prove to be one of her most remarkable pieces of work – a full-scale investigation into conditions of service among shop workers, which would lead eventually to changes in the law to curb the 'living in' system. Margaret went back to her old career, moving from shop to shop and taking jobs, first in well-appointed stores then, as her references grew shorter, in less salubrious areas. In addition to the poor conditions she had already encountered herself, she was able to expose how workers' wages could be further eroded through a series of fines for minor misdemeanours. One such list of fines included the following items:

Addressing customer as 'Miss' instead of 'Madam,' 3d; wearing flowers in business hours, 2d; standing on counters, chairs and fixtures, 2d; private writing or reading, talking to each other while serving, talking to another customer unless strictly business, standing in groups or lounging about in an unbusinesslike manner, 6d; not using paper or string with economy, 3d.[9]

At one store in the Commercial Road she found workers living in rooms with no windows; in some districts grocers' and drapers' assistants were expected to work ninety hours a week. In the East End she discovered a world she had not known before, and though a church-going teetotaller herself she developed sympathies for behaviour in which she would never have indulged. In one article for *The Shop Assistant* she protested against moves to stop women drinking in pubs. 'These are women who have lost hope, whose hearts are dead, whose lives are a dark blot on the Victorian era. Will these be benefited by being turned from the public house to the street? I think not,' she wrote.[10]

As for her own social life, it was mostly taken up with politics. In the early 1900s a series of personal losses had beset Margaret. First her younger sister Katie died of tuberculosis and then her older brother Ernest died of pneumonia while on active service in the Boer War. In the same year Margaret's father died and her brother Frank, with whom she had been sharing lodgings in London, moved back to Chard to be near their mother and to start a small printing business. From then on, Margaret wrote later, she lived mostly for her work. She did not believe she was cut out for marriage or motherhood, and felt sure she could make a more valuable contribution through the union movement.

> I concentrated on my job. This concentration was undisturbed by love affairs. I had seen too much – too early – to have the least desire to join in the pitiful scramble of my workmates. The very surroundings of shop life accentuated the desire of most shop girls to get married. Long hours of work and the living-in system deprived them of the normal companionship of men in their leisure hours, and the wonder is that so many of the women continued to be good and kind, and self-respecting, without the incentive of a great cause, or of any interest outside their job … I had no vocation for wifehood or motherhood, but an urge to serve the Union – an urge which developed into 'a sense of oneness with our kind'. I had 'the dear love of comrades.[11]

Coincidentally Margaret was quoting a Walt Whitman poem which several years later Emily Wilding Davison would send to her friend Mary Leigh.

However, Margaret's political activities did gradually begin to broaden. Soon after moving to London she had joined the Ideal Club, an intellectual group which held poetry and social evenings as well as hosting discussions on political or moral issues. Among its other *habitués* were social reformers such as George Bernard Shaw and the Webbs. In 1900 Margaret had supported the setting up of the Labour Representation Council, the forerunner of the modern Labour Party, and in 1902 she began a long and fruitful friendship which shaped much of her life for the two decades that followed. Margaret was immediately taken with Mary Macarthur, the daughter of a wealthy Scottish store-owner, who had been converted – to her father's dismay – to trade unionism, when she met her at a conference in 1902:

> I saw a thin white face and glowing eyes, and then I was enveloped by her ardent, young hero-worshipping personality. She was gloriously young and self-confident. It was a dazzling experience for a humdrum official to find herself treated with the reverence due to an oracle by one whose brilliant gifts and vital energy were even then manifest. So might a pigeon feel if suddenly worshipped by a young eaglet.[12]

The two soon became close friends and colleagues, and within a year Margaret had found a job for Mary as secretary of the Women's Trade Union League. They went on to work together at the National Federation of Women Workers, which Mary founded and continued to run until her death in 1921.

It could only be a matter of time before Margaret became involved in the debate over women's suffrage. Already her union work had brought her into contact with Charlotte Despard, later to become president of the Women's Freedom League, and in 1904 she travelled to the International Congress of Women in Berlin with Dora Montefiore, the Women's Social and Political Union representative at the event. But Margaret never accepted the militants' line on the suffrage, let alone their tactics. She was first and foremost a socialist – indeed she had briefly flirted with the Marxist Social Democratic Federation, of which Charlotte Despard was a member, and had spoken on its platforms in London. In 1904 Margaret 'came out' as an adult suffrage campaigner, in opposition to the more explicitly feminist WSPU. Sylvia Pankhurst was asked by the Fulham Independent Labour Party to debate the issue on a public platform with Margaret Bondfield as her opponent. Sylvia, then a student and inexperienced as a speaker, asked Isabella Ford to stand in for her. The young Margaret tore to shreds the argument that a limited women's franchise was the way forward. Industrial organisation would improve women's lot much more efficiently than votes, she said. If women were to have the vote at all, they should have it as part of a much more radical move towards universal suffrage for both men and women. Her attack was also surprisingly personal, according to Sylvia:

> Miss Bondfield appeared in pink, dark and dark-eyed with a deep, throaty voice which many found beautiful. She was very charming and vivacious and eager to score all the points that her youth and prettiness would win for her against the plain middle-aged woman with red face and turban hat ... Miss Bondfield deprecated votes for women as the hobby of disappointed old maids whom no-one had wanted to marry.[13]

Sylvia admitted that in her heart she, too, was a believer in adult suffrage. But the incident led to a lifelong personal dislike of Margaret, fuelled by indignation that she should have subjected Isabella Ford to such humiliation. Sylvia's reaction also reflected the more widespread animosity of the WSPU to anyone who opposed its precise stance on the suffrage. So committed was the suffragette movement to its aims, and *only* to its own precise aims, that through the years it split several times with those who failed to toe its line. Charlotte Despard would break away in 1907 in protest at the despotism imposed on the union by Emmeline and Christabel Pankhurst. In addition to the Pethick-Lawrences Sylvia herself would be expelled later. It would have been hard for any of the WSPU's leaders to claim any convincing political or moral argument for opposing the universal franchise, but they opposed the adult suffragists almost with the passion that they opposed the Liberal government.

By 1906 Margaret became involved with the newly formed Adult Suffrage Society, and she later became its president. Although the society regularly debated the issue in public with its opponents and also held its own major rallies, it never ceased to be regarded with suspicion by the militants. Believing that to broaden the agenda in this way would be to delay the granting of votes for women, they suspected the adult suffragists of foul play. Keir Hardie had already opposed the setting up of a Women's Labour League which he saw as a potential rival to the WSPU. Now, writing in the *Labour Leader*, he came close to accusing the ASS of being little more than a front for those who opposed votes for women: 'It holds no meetings, issues no literature, carries on no agitation on behalf of Adult Suffrage. It is never heard of, save when it emerges to oppose the Women's Enfranchisement Bill.'[14]

This was unfair. In 1906 the Adult Suffrage Society was particularly active in support of a bill brought by Sir Charles Dilke, which reached a second reading in the House of Commons before being talked out by an anti-suffragist MP. The bill, which proposed nothing less than full adult suffrage, was vehemently opposed by all the main women's suffrage societies, who saw it as a deliberate attempt to frustrate their efforts to break down the gender barrier. Sir Charles's bill even included a clause which would have allowed women to stand for election to Parliament – something which had barely been thought about at that time. Margaret, in an interview given to *Tribune*, confessed herself delighted.[15] She heartily approved of the idea of women becoming MPs, she said. For the past twelve months she had spoken frequently at meetings in favour of adult suffrage, and she was sure the public were ready for such a radical move. In 1907 she was challenged to a major debate on the subject by Teresa Billington-Greig, who had just broken away from the WSPU with Charlotte Despard to form the Women's Freedom League. Although the former WSPU organiser came off best, winning the vote by 171 to 139, Margaret was pleased with the result. She told her audience:

> I work for Adult Suffrage because I believe it is the quickest way to establish a real sex-equality … I have always said in my speeches and in conversation that these women who believe in the 'same terms as men' Bill have a perfect right to go on working for that Bill, and I say good luck to them and may they get it! But don't let them come and tell me that they are working for my class.[16]

Margaret was prepared to argue long and loud for adult suffrage, but she was not prepared to damage her relationship with the Labour Party for it. In 1909, at the party conference, she moved an amendment which would have committed the party to complete opposition to any government franchise bill that excluded women. Arthur Henderson, a long-term party colleague, persuaded her to water down the wording. The militants of the WSPU were furious, and accused Margaret and her colleagues of treachery. Soon afterwards the ASS reformed itself into a new People's Suffrage Federation and more than 100 MPs signed up to its adult suffragist aims. The WSPU was less than impressed. 'Those who are anxious to obtain Votes for Women at the earliest possible date will have nothing to do with the new Suffrage Federation,' its newspaper warned. 'Their campaign has all along been directed towards blocking and injuring the agitation for the simple removal of the sex disqualification; and at the same time they have carried out no genuinely constructive agitation for the vote.'[17] The paper accused the organisation of being a 'decoy duck' for the government. The *Manchester Guardian*, far more sympathetic to the adult suffragists than the WSPU, admitted it was easier for the government to ignore such an unwieldy demand than to ignore the more modest proposal pursued by the militants. Even the ability of the adult suffragists to attract 6,000 people to a meeting at the Royal Albert Hall, as they did on one occasion in 1913, could not make much impact in a political atmosphere dominated by the more spectacular activities of the militants.[18]

Sylvia sniped that none of the women who later secured political office had been prominent in the fight for the vote. Margaret had 'remained during the greater part of her public life uninterested in the question', she remarked.[19] This was partially true. Although Margaret did take an active part in campaigning for the vote, and in 1910 spent five months in America lecturing on the suffrage with another People's Suffrage Federation stalwart, Maud Ward, it was not the main focus of her life. The suffragettes were prepared to give up their entire lives, their incomes, their homes, even their health, for the cause. Margaret Bondfield and her colleagues lacked the suffragettes' fanatical zeal, their almost cult-like attachment to their leaders. Margaret rarely even commented on the WSPU's militant tactics, but she thought them misguided. In December 1912, in an article for the *Labour Leader* urging members to work hard for a doomed government franchise reform bill, she warned: 'The "anti" press is glorying in the tactical mistakes of our friends, and asserting that "the suffrage cause is dead – killed by the Peths and the Panks".'

The strain of union politics could take its toll as much as that of suffrage agitation. In 1908 Margaret left her job with the shop assistants' union, exhausted after ten solid years as its assistant secretary. She described the decision as 'alike a grief and a deliverance'.[20] It was the first of several times when her health would give way under the strains of the life she had chosen. After a holiday in Switzerland with her friend Maud Ward, with whom she shared a house in Hampstead for a time, she began working as a freelance lecturer on trade unionism and on the suffrage. By then an acknowledged expert on conditions in the retail trade, she was often in demand to talk about her experiences. She also threw herself unreservedly into the politics of the Independent Labour Party, and easily carried the day at a debate in the Caxton Hall in which she proposed the motion that 'the full development of women is possible only under Socialism'. Women had everything to gain from the transformation of society, she argued, having seen the decline of the birth rate and a sustained attack on the family under capitalism. Although Margaret Bondfield was emphatically not a feminist, she shared with the militants the view that motherhood was a noble calling. In one speech she decried the modern notion that the only worthy career for a woman was one in which she worked outside the home. Women who chose to stay at home and look after their husbands and children should be supported in their desire to do so, she believed.

This attitude was perhaps reinforced by Margaret's intimate knowledge of the hardships suffered by those married women who were forced to work both outside and inside the home. In 1910 she was asked by the Women's Industrial Council, with which she had had a long association, to investigate the conditions of married women in textile industries. This took her to the woollen mills in the North of England, where she found women forced to abort their children because they could not afford to raise them. Many mill women also worked as prostitutes, she reported, and Bradford had the highest illegitimate birth rate in the British Isles. What she saw inspired her to join a 'War against Poverty' campaign being waged by Ramsay MacDonald, George Bernard Shaw, the Webbs and Keir Hardie. Women had gained the right to sit on county and borough councils in 1907. In 1910 she stood for election for the first time, as a Labour candidate in the London County Council election for Woolwich. The seat was a double-member one and Margaret came third.

In 1911 personal loss again caused Margaret to suffer collapse. This time it was the deaths of two close colleagues, Mary Middleton and Margaret MacDonald, who had worked together as joint secretaries of the Women's Labour League. Margaret had visited Ramsay MacDonald's wife just before she died of a poisoned hand, then returned to Lancashire to complete a tour of lectures. In the middle of a speech in Manchester she found herself suddenly unable to continue, her mind a complete blank. The chairman of the meeting took over and Margaret was ordered to rest. She retired to Cornwall but found herself haunted by anxiety about her abandoned work. Even when she returned to London in April 1912 she was still not well. 'Attended meeting at Woolwich. Tired and excited before. Tired and depressed after,' her diary recorded one evening.[21] She rested for several more months, taking a fortnight abroad with a colleague from the Co-operative Women's Guild and visiting the West of Ireland, before she was finally well enough to return to work. Now she stepped into her departed friends' shoes, as organising secretary of the Women's Labour League. In 1913 she took on a new role within the ILP, as a member of the party's National Administrative Council. She added further to her burdens by becoming a special campaigner on maternity issues for the Women's Co-operative Guild, gathering information on the 300,000 women who found themselves excluded from newly introduced maternity benefits because their husbands had not paid for sufficient 'stamps'.

All this work was interrupted by the war, which Margaret opposed along with many of her ILP colleagues including Keir Hardie and Ramsay MacDonald. Sylvia Pankhurst was also working to oppose the war, but this unity of purpose did not soften her attitude to Margaret. Nor did the fact that both were directing their efforts to help those left destitute by the outbreak of hostilities. All over the country, and particularly in the poorest areas, women who had relied on their husbands' wages were suddenly plunged into poverty. The Queen Mary's Needlework Guild had planned to collect clothing for these families but the Women's Trade Union League, with Margaret at its fore, protested. Women in the textile trades were being put out of work by a sudden economic collapse caused by the war, they said – it would be better to provide them with work making garments for others. Margaret was delighted with the result, which was the setting up of workshops. Sylvia was less impressed, dubbing the centres 'Queen Mary's Sweatshops' and claiming they paid young girls as little as five shillings a week. Margaret and her union colleagues 'had proved useless, if not hostile, to the Women's Suffrage cause; but it was believed they were staunch on the industrial side ... alas the committee speedily covered itself with ignominy', she claimed later.[22] The truth of the matter is now hard to untangle but other, less partisan commentators have since praised Margaret's wartime efforts to promote equal pay for women hard hit by the war.[23]

While former suffrage campaigners of all hues were fully engaged in their war efforts – Emmeline's supporters working to back the government; others including Margaret and Sylvia working equally hard to oppose it – the suffrage debate moved on. In October 1916 a new National Council for Adult Suffrage was set up, featuring a number of senior Labour figures on its committee including Mary Macarthur and the Labour MP George Lansbury, a former WSPU supporter. Emmeline Pethick-Lawrence spoke on one of its platforms in 1917. The main work of this committee was to press the government to reconsider its plans for a limited extension of the franchise. In this, it failed. The measure which became law in 1918 gave the vote only to women over thirty, and then only to those who were property owners or graduates. Margaret later described it as ' a mean and inadequate little Bill, creating fresh anomalies which had to be overcome'.[24] It would be a further ten years before Britain would have universal adult suffrage.

The end of the war saw Margaret renewing her efforts on behalf of the labour movement. In 1918 she was elected to the Parliamentary Committee of the Trades Union Congress, and in the months that followed she travelled as its delegate to conferences in Berne and in Washington. In America she made speeches denouncing the peace imposed on Germany as unjust. One newspaper recorded that her remarks had been greeted 'with moderate applause'. Another expressed surprise at her small stature and apparently mild manner: 'Miss Bondfield does not look like the representative of 4,500,000 workers. She is a typical English "gentlewoman", small, well poised and with a low, modulated voice far from the popular conception of the English Labour agitator.'[25] But her political efforts were now to be focused much closer to home. She had been selected as parliamentary candidate for Northampton. Although her first two efforts in the constituency, in 1919 and in 1922, were unsuccessful she acquitted herself well and impressed the media. The *Manchester Guardian* noted that she was one of the best female speakers in the country: 'She is a little woman but her pleasantly toned, deep voice has great carrying power. I have often seen her sway an audience and lift it for the moment to the height of some great idea by the force of her own feeling and deep sincerity,' its correspondent commented.[26] The National Union of Women's Suffrage Societies even sent a helper to join her campaign – after she had correctly answered a list of questions on franchise reform.

Following Mary Macarthur's death in 1921, which came as a major blow to Margaret, her National Federation of Women Workers merged with the

National Union of General and Municipal Workers. Margaret became its chief women's officer, a post she held until 1938. In 1923 she became the first woman chairman of the TUC. But her main aim at this time was to get elected to Parliament, though there were suggestions Labour could have found her a better seat. In 1922, during her second election campaign, she wrote to ask her old friend George Bernard Shaw to come and help. 'Why Northampton?' he replied. 'You are the best man of the lot and they shove you off on a place where the water is too cold for their dainty feet ... and keep the safe seats for their now quite numerous imbeciles.'[27] Despite his reservations Shaw did come and speak for her, but she still lost by 5,000 votes. The following year, on her third attempt, she finally became an MP. Three women – Nancy Astor, Mabel Philipson and Margaret Wintringham – had previously taken their seats in Parliament, none of them Labour. Margaret Bondfield was one of a trio of Labour women MPs now elected, with Susan Lawrence and Dorothy Jewson. Her supporters, 'nearly crazy with joy', placed her on the high seat of a charabanc and hauled her by hand for two hours around the town.[28] There was even more celebrating to come. The Tories had lost eighty-eight seats while Labour had gained forty-seven, and though the Tories remained the largest party with 258 seats to Labour's 191, they could no longer form a government. After some weeks of deliberating the Liberals, who had 158 seats, decided not to form a coalition government and the first, minority, Labour administration was formed with Ramsay MacDonald as Prime Minister. The next day Margaret was chairing a meeting of the TUC council when a note was passed in to say the new Minister of Labour, Tom Shaw, was downstairs and would like to see her. He offered her a job as his parliamentary secretary.

Thus Margaret, along with several of her colleagues, was placed in a position that would be rare today. She had become a minister less than a week after making her maiden speech in Parliament. Inexperienced both in the workings of Westminster and in the workings of government, she was also part of a minority administration that would have struggled even if it had had dozens of experienced ministers. Later Margaret would describe the experience as 'a strange adventure'.[29] Her office in Montague House had an elaborately painted ceiling but no women's toilet. After a joyous reunion with old friends at an International Labour Organisation meeting in Geneva, where she represented the British government, she returned to an atmosphere of deepening gloom. The fledgling Labour government was beset by financial problems, industrial unrest, rising unemployment and general economic gloom. The financial world, of course, was not sympathetic. But at fifty-one Margaret still possessed a certain youthful energy and was able to tackle her task with gusto – so much so that sometimes she would upset people by forcing an issue when it would perhaps have been better to retreat. It was this quality which would so upset some of her colleagues in the Labour movement. One historian would later accuse her of 'monumental tactlessness'.[30] Even Mary Agnes Hamilton, who wrote a gushing biography of Margaret at around this time, admitted she had faults but claimed they were always tempered by an attractive personality: 'Any deficiencies … are offset by her personal charm: that winsomeness which won the hearts of the staid trade unionists at her first appearance at Congress.'[31]

Beset by difficulties in defending the government's record on unemployment, Margaret was relieved to escape to Canada in 1924 for a series of meetings about the problems of British immigrants. At home, though, the crisis was deepening. She returned to find the government embroiled in the controversy surrounding the infamous Zinoviev Letter, which suggested Russia was plotting with British communists to overthrow the government. Margaret's own personal troubles in the ensuing election were further exacerbated by the accusation that she had been gallivanting abroad while the government plunged into chaos. She lost her seat.

Re-elected to the TUC general council, which she had quit on becoming a minister, she now turned her attentions to finding a new constituency. There was other work to do, though, and it would prove controversial. Margaret was given a place on the Blanesborough Committee, set up to consider the issues of unemployment insurance and the problem of escalating benefits bills. Although she said later that she did not personally agree with all the recommendations of the committee's report, which called for cuts in benefits, she signed it and defended it in the interests of unity. The result was that many unemployed people were excluded from receiving benefits because they had paid insufficient contributions in the preceding two years. When the Tory government brought in a bill to implement the committee's findings, Margaret was accused by many in the Labour Party of treachery. The issue would leave a blot on her character for the rest of her career. She argued later that on such a pressing issue it was imperative to bring in a unanimous report. The labour movement would never forgive her.

While the committee was sitting Margaret's Labour friends were still working on her behalf, seeking a new seat for her. In the North-east Arthur Henderson, always a close ally, achieved what Stephen Byers would one day describe as 'a classic trade union fix' in which Margaret was adopted as prospective parliamentary candidate for Wallsend. Later she would face allegations that she neglected the town and that she acted against the interests of its poorest citizens when she signed the Blanesborough report. At first, though, she was welcomed by Labour supporters there, particularly the women supporters, who were delighted by the prospect of having a female MP.

On by-election day in 1926, more than 20,000 people could be seen milling around outside Wallsend Town Hall, waiting for the result. It was a sunny June day and when the returning officer pronounced Margaret the winner her supporters threw their summer bonnets in the air.[32] Women danced in the street, men burst into song and the crowd began to chant: 'Maggie, MP! Maggie, MP!' To the modern eye, the election address for which the town had voted would look unavowedly socialist.[33] It accused the Tories of deliberately failing to maintain the industrial peace, of supporting the coal-owners against the workers, and of discriminating in favour of the wealthy by removing £42 million from the shoulders of higher-income taxpayers at the expense of the poor. The fact was, though, that Margaret had been slowly drifting to the right for some time. The Blanesborough débâcle, which led to her being unsuccessfully challenged in the 1929 election by an unemployed workers' leader, was symptomatic of a deeper change in her political outlook.

Before being plunged afresh into controversy, Margaret was able to speak in Parliament on the second reading of the bill which finally gave the vote to women over the age of twenty-one. Although even then there were some 'fancy franchises', such as university or business franchises, which gave some people a second vote, all adults could now vote if they or their husbands had lived at their current address for six months. The bill increased the total number of voters from 21.5 million to 26 million, and most of those who benefited were women. In fact, according to Sir William Joynson-Hicks, who introduced the Bill, there were now 14 million women voters and only 12 million men. In her speech Margaret welcomed the move, 'peculiarly so because I have never been able to be enthusiastic about reforms of the franchise hitherto proposed'.[34] Although she supported the measure she pointed out that Britain would not reach the end of this particular road until all adult men and women had a single vote, regardless of property or status.

The following year, having been re-elected despite growing unhappiness in Wallsend about her performance and about her infrequent appearances there, Margaret entered the cabinet as Minister of Labour. The official cabinet photograph shows her dwarfed by her taller male colleagues but her sober suit echoing theirs, the uniform lacking only collar and tie. Although the Blanesborough controversy had dragged on for years she felt it had left her stronger, for she had fought with her usual energy. Characteristically she was looking forward with relish to the task ahead. Perhaps less characteristically, she was also touched with a sense that she had just been handed a place in history: 'It was part of the great revolution in the position of women which had taken place in my lifetime and which I had done something to help forward,' she explained later.[35] She also became the first woman Privy Counsellor, which involved a certain amount of delicate negotiation about whether or not she should remove her hat before being presented to the King. The prevailing view was that she should not but Margaret disagreed and eventually won the day.

In the country at large unemployment was continuing to rise, and it was Margaret's job to find a route through this increasingly impenetrable swamp. The job was never going to make any minister popular, and as a Labour minister she was particularly vulnerable to accusations of betrayal. The low murmur of complaint that genuine claimants were being refused benefit because they could not prove they were 'genuinely seeking work' soon became a rising clamour. Margaret protested, impotently, that such decisions had been delegated to local boards of referees and were therefore not her responsibility. This would not stand up under scrutiny. Even if she had been personally responsible she did not have the money to fund benefits for all claimants. She had discovered, on taking office, that the Unemployment Insurance Fund was £40 million in debt. The main focus of her activity during her first months in the post was the passing of a bill to ensure that employment exchanges proved work was available before refusing benefit, and to authorise the Exchequer to contribute £3.5 million to balance the books. The bill, although passed, found favour neither with the Tories nor with the Labour left. Nor did the issue then disappear. In 1931 it was central to the collapse of Ramsay MacDonald's second government and the ending of Margaret's parliamentary career.

By June 1931 the Unemployment Insurance Fund was in debt to the tune of £115,000. But a far bigger problem was also facing the government – a £2 billion War Loan which fell due for repayment that year. Drastic cuts in spending were proposed. When Ramsay MacDonald crossed the floor of the House of Commons to form his National Government, Margaret did not support him. It was inevitable that she would lose her seat. Attacked by the Tories for allowing the Unemployment Insurance Fund to run out of control, and by the left for failing properly to provide for those out of work, it would have been a miracle if she had been re-elected. Even if she had been popular with her constituents, which she was not, she would have struggled. As it was the entire Labour government, with the exception of George Lansbury, lost their seats.

Her seat lost and her parliamentary career at an end, Margaret suffered a complete breakdown. She was ordered to bed with fibrositis – generalised muscle pain – for which she underwent painful treatment, but it was clear she was in poor emotional as well as physical shape. After a long rest she spent several months touring the US before returning to fight Wallsend again in 1935 without success. She was then adopted as Labour candidate for Reading, but she gave up her candidature when it became clear the election would be long delayed by the Second World War. During the war, reversing the role she had played in the First World War, she supported the government and toured America again lobbying for US support for the Allies.

Margaret still had energy for one last fling before retiring. At the beginning of the war she was selected to sit on the Women's Group on Public Welfare, which conducted a study into problems arising from wartime evacuation. Its report was called 'Our Towns: A Close-Up', which highlighted how the extreme poverty of the inner cities had been exposed by this sudden contact between their residents and those in the countryside. In September 1939 more than a million people had been evacuated from the major cities and billeted on families in the country, often against their will. A torrent of 'extraordinarily intense and bitter' complaint arose almost instantly, according to the committee.[36] The evacuee children were accused of being dirty, disease-ridden, disobedient, foul-mouthed and dishonest. Their mothers, who in many cases accompanied them, were said to be abusive, lazy and verminous, 'insanitary in their habits and loose in their morals'. The children rejected good food and clamoured for chips and sweets, while their mothers liked nothing better than to spend time in the local pub. The committee accepted most of these complaints, but pointed out that they had arisen as a result of the appalling conditions which existed in Britain's cities.

When Margaret Bondfield died in June 1953, the Labour Party buried her with full honours. Clement Attlee gave the address, and the congregation at the Golders Green Crematorium sang her favourite hymns, which included 'To Be a Pilgrim'. Her obituary in *The Times* praised her as 'a woman of lovable temperament and unusually wide human sympathies … Her generous nature and real sense of humour looked out from a pleasant, alert, bright-eyed countenance surmounted by a broad and thoughtful brow.' But in later years, both the Labour Party and the suffrage movement were to judge her more harshly. It is sad, then, that she chose to assess her own life solely in relation to the political achievements which would be so largely forgotten. 'If, occasionally, it is difficult to separate my personal adventure from the history of the Labour Party that is perfectly in harmony with the facts. I have been so identified with the movement that it is not always possible to say where one ends and the other begins,' she wrote.[37]

What did Margaret Bondfield, Labour politician and trade unionist, do for women? Despite claims to the contrary, she did a great deal. She fought for and won better conditions for some of Britain's worst-treated women workers and she highlighted the parlous conditions women faced in many inner-city areas. More than that, she flew the flag for working women's votes when the mainstream suffrage organisations had turned their backs. All of this pales, though, in the face of her key achievement: her quiet, steady rise through the male-dominated ranks of the labour movement to positions both at the head of the Trades Union Congress and in a Labour cabinet. For that alone, Margaret Bondfield's figure should stand tall in the rich and nostalgic landscape of Labour mythology.

*Emmeline Pankhurst and Elizabeth Garrett Anderson on the steps of
the House of Commons, November 1910*

Conclusion

The window smashing has roused great hostility against the women. No greater blunder could be conceived ... It seems as if devised purposely to show that women are incapable of political restraint. My conviction is now and always has been that the Pankhursts have been the bane of the women's movement.

Bruce Glasier's diary, April 1912

The morning of 21 June 1910 must have found Herbert Asquith feeling irritable. King Edward VII was dead, George V as yet uncrowned, yet instead of enjoying a sombre respite from the political battlefield the Liberal government was embroiled in fraught negotiations over the future of the House of Lords. Some way would have to be found of dealing with the troublesome Peers, who had precipitated a political and financial crisis by rejecting the 1909 Budget. The cabinet had finally extricated itself from that particular mess, but only with the help of the Irish Nationalists. That meant further trouble ahead, for the Irish had given their support only after extracting a firm promise that Home Rule would follow. This, of course, would be resisted with extreme vehemence by the Ulster Unionists. To the Prime Minister, who had recently returned from a holiday on Skye, the joys of office must have seemed obscure.

And now he was expected to receive not one, not two but *three* deputations on the issue of women's suffrage. There was but one small ray of light – at least the dreadful Pankhursts were not among them. First came the constitutional suffragists, led by Millicent Fawcett, with a tedious plea for the Conciliation Bill for women's votes which had recently been drawn up by a cross-party committee. All the suffrage societies had been agitating vigorously for this bill, but the government had given no indication of its views.

Herbert Asquith was no advocate for the women's cause; indeed he feared the narrow measure they proposed would enfranchise more Conservatives than Liberals. However, the Conciliation Bill had proved useful in some respects, for the militants had called off their dogs in order to give it a calm passage. At least he could travel the country without mayhem breaking out around him. Now here was Mrs Fawcett, of all people, offering a veiled threat that the maenads would arise again if women did not get the vote this session. Asquith had no time for this. He would announce his intentions in the Commons, he responded tersely.

Then, after a second group of constitutionalists came the anti-suffragists, claiming the established social order would break down if women *were* given the vote. Asquith had some sympathy with this. His own wife, Margot, had a tendency to meddle in politics and always, he felt, with disastrous effect. He had had to stop telling her things, for she was deeply indiscreet.[1] The Prime Minister's often sphinx-like visage softened now. Of course, he told his interlocutors, the cabinet must decide. But they should know they were preaching to the converted. If he had his way, there would be no votes for women.

Asquith held no brief for women's suffrage. For the vote to be won, something fundamental must change. Either the political climate must alter in order to make the women's case a more pressing one, or the Prime Minister must change. Neither of these things would happen in time for women to get the vote before the First World War.

Historians tend to take the view that Herbert Asquith was an honourable man. There is little or no evidence of this in his relations with the women's suffrage campaign. The story of the Prime Minister's dealings with the suffragists between the years of 1910 and 1914 is a shameful one, peppered with political chicanery and pock-marked with the scars of dishonesty. When the Conciliation Bill had its second reading in July 1910, Asquith voted against it. Surprisingly, for a Prime Minister's lead is usually followed by the ambitious within his party, the bill was still carried by a majority of 110, with the bulk of Liberal and Labour members supporting it. Asquith then announced that the bill would receive no more government time that session, and the campaigners resigned themselves to starting afresh when the House reassembled in November after its summer recess. Before that could happen, though, there was more Liberal fancy footwork. With a general election looming, rumours began to circulate that the government wanted to bring in its own bill – not to enfranchise women but to increase the numbers of *male* voters. Militancy broke out anew with the 'Black Friday' demonstration in November 1910, at which large numbers of women were injured. In a partially successful bid to restore peace, the government promised a smooth ride for the Conciliation Bill on condition that it should be drafted to allow amendments to widen the franchise for men.

Asquith's duplicity on the question knew no bounds, though, and once the Liberals were returned to power the prospect of votes for women began once more to recede. In May 1911 the Conciliation Bill again passed its second reading, this time with a majority of 167. For a while, hopes were high. So high, in fact, that the WSPU held a celebration dinner and even invited both Millicent Fawcett and Charlotte Despard, a leader of the breakaway Women's Freedom League. With the House of Lords problem coming to a head in July, though, there was again no more time for the bill. The women, understandably, agreed to wait. Then, while the MPs enjoyed a summer holiday, rumours of a male suffrage bill began to circulate, only to be denied categorically by Asquith. His promise of facilities for the women's bill in 1912 would be 'strictly adhered to, both in the letter and in the spirit', he wrote to the Conciliation Committee chairman, Lord Lytton.[2]

Asquith was lying. In November 1911 he announced that the government was, after all, to introduce its own male suffrage bill. This would be drafted to allow a women's amendment, but he made it clear he would oppose such a move. His words were met with furious protests, a huge demonstration at the opening of Parliament and several more suffragist demonstrations. It was even rumoured that Asquith would resign if women got the vote through his proposed bill. There would be no need for such a step, for he had done his work well. The Conciliation Bill, undermined by the prospect of a separate government measure coming up behind it, was defeated when it came up yet again for a second reading. Then Asquith announced, at the second reading of his own Reform Bill, that as MPs had voted against women's enfranchisement there was clearly no desire among them to bring it in at all!

There was worse to come. A further debate on the Reform Bill was set for January 1913. By that time the militants had completely given up hope of any help from this government and were devoting their efforts to secret arson, pillar-box firing and general insubordination. Meanwhile the constitutionalists, led by Millicent Fawcett, were still clinging to the shreds of their belief in Liberalism. They spent the remaining months of 1912 in discussing, negotiating over and drafting a range of possible amendments which could enfranchise women. The militants were proved right. The government, it transpired, had drafted its bill in such a manner that it could not be amended to include women. A ruling to this effect was made by the Speaker of the House of Commons, and the women's hopes finally died. Asquith affected to be shocked by the development but as suffragists of all hues pointed out, he had been proven to be either criminally incompetent or downright wicked. Whatever else he may have been, Asquith was not a stupid man. He was implacably against a women's measure and the parliamentary draftsmen had made the way clear for him. To cap it all, he then proceeded to compound the mischief by refusing to receive any more deputations from the women.

Asquith did later begin to soften, receiving a deputation of East End suffragists in 1914 and admitting during the war that the time had finally come for a change. 'When the war comes to an end … have not the women a special claim to be heard on the many questions which will arise directly affecting their interests? I say quite frankly that I cannot deny that claim.'[3] There had been threats that militancy might be renewed after the war, and it is possible these mollifying words were simply another trick designed to stave off such an eventuality. Asquith did allow the setting up of a Speaker's Conference on the franchise, but we will never know whether he would have followed through. In December 1916 he resigned and Lloyd George became Prime Minister.

All this is pertinent because it has a tremendous bearing on what, if anything, the militant suffragettes actually achieved. Did the Pankhursts and their allies win votes for women? They did not. Indeed they could not, for they were operating in a political climate so inclement that it is hard to see how the vote could possibly have been won before 1916. Major constitutional measures do not usually get enacted through Private Member's bills. They especially do not get enacted through Private Member's bills when the Prime Minister of the day, not to mention a large portion of his cabinet, is either against them or indifferent to them.

So what difference did the militants make, if any? In truth, they made a huge difference. They raised the issue of the vote from the level of drawing-room chit-chat and chattering class indignation to the very top of the political agenda. This was no mean achievement. Where would the franchise question have been, by 1918, if the militants had not come along when they did? Just one of a number of worthy but dull campaigns, deserving of serious consideration but easily ignored. Its protagonists would have been – indeed, were – a group of well-meaning pensioners whose day had long since passed.

By the time the WSPU entered the scene, the intellectual argument over votes for women had already been won. More than thirty-five years of agitation by the more polite constitutional suffragists had, by the end of the nineteenth century, turned the tide of influential opinion. Parliament had demonstrated its intent to enfranchise women in 1897 when it gave a second reading to Mr Faithfull Begg's doomed Private Member's Bill. From then on, all that remained for the suffrage campaign was to create the political will to see the deed actually done. They had to push their issue to the fore so that it could not be ignored. This was easier said than done, for they lacked the traditional tools of politics. The women needed a lever, and they had struggled to find one.

Other causes were more pressing than theirs; other agitators better equipped for the fight. The workers, for example, were fast discovering the economic lever of the withdrawal of their labour. During the years before the First World War they used this to great effect, and in doing so they won results. Wages had been falling in real terms for several years, and now the country was nearly paralysed by a wave of strikes. London was brought to a halt by a transport stoppage. In 1912 the miners' demand for a national minimum wage brought a million men out. In 1908 there had been 400 recorded labour disputes; in 1912 there were almost 900. There was only one way forward for the government – capitulation. A minimum wage bill, imperfect but good enough to quell the worst of the revolt, was rushed through Parliament.

The Irish Nationalists, meanwhile, had discovered a political lever – their parliamentary muscle. The second election of 1910 left the Liberals clinging to power with 272 seats, just one more than the Conservatives. The only way they could continue to function as a government, and in particular the only way they could quell the House of Lords, was with the votes of John Redmond's eighty-five Nationalists. The price extracted for that was a Home Rule Bill. The constitutional suffragists had no such weapons. But the militants had loud voices, they had hammers, they had matches and they had kindling, and they used them to great effect. The fact that ministers troubled themselves at all with votes for women during the turbulent pre-war years was entirely due to their shock tactics. Millicent Fawcett, herself all too easily brushed off with vague promises, admitted as much in more than one way. In the early stages of militancy, she praised the WSPU's efforts warmly, remarking that the militants seemed to have learned the valuable lesson from the Irish that 'it was useless to try to get any concessions … from a minister of either party unless you approached him with a cow's tail in one hand and the head of a landlord in the other'.[4] Later she gently wielded militancy as a weapon of her own, quietly whispering into ministers' ears that it would be bound to revive – horror of horrors! – if the vote were not won before the war was ended.

Before that had happened the WSPU had already played its part and left the stage. When the vote was won, the Pankhurst loyalists were too busy supporting the war effort even to give it much thought. They never won the unequivocal statement of equal women's rights they had sought, the narrow measure over which they could have planted their flag and proclaimed victory. They had played their part, of course, and a great part it had been. For that, they staked their rightful claim to a place in history. But the real achievement of the WSPU was much more than that. Its true victory was in raising for the first time a truly female, feminist consciousness in Britain.

The most vicious criticism of the militant suffragettes often tended to centre on their femininity, or lack of it. The *Daily Chronicle*, for example, described in these terms the arrests of ten WSPU members in Parliament in October 1906: 'The bodyguard was quickly dispersed, leaving a trail of hatpins and hairpins behind them, and even bonnets. The leaders proved the most refractory, and they had to be bodily carried off the bench. With shrieks and screams they were carried from the central hall down the steps into St Stephen's Hall.' Time and again, the hostile press would describe the women in such terms, emphasising the inappropriateness of their behaviour. Conversely, those who wished to praise a militant would underline how demure, how ladylike she was. 'Mrs Pankhurst, a small, gentle-looking woman in a gray checked travelling wrap … looks younger than the pictures which have reached America before her – more like a nice, home-keeping mother than a political leader,' said the *New York Times* in 1909.[5] George Dangerfield, in his 1935 work *The Strange Death of Liberal England*, posits the odd notion that what the suffragette in fact sought was not so much the vote but her own inner masculinity:

With a vital energy, the manifestations of which were abandoned and eccentric, she pursued her masculinity first into politics – which seemed the

most likely thicket in which to bring it to bay – then into the secret recesses
of her own being; and though her quarry was always agile enough to remain one jump ahead of her, her pursuit was to be of incalculable service
to the women who came after … Beneath the political and economic mo-
tives in the disintegration of Liberal England, there lies the psychological
motive – the abandonment of security. In the case of the women it was the
abandonment of what was, in the worst sense of the word, a *feminine* security.[6]

In one sense, Dangerfield was right. What the suffragettes did, or tried
to do, for the women of England was to shake off the stultifying cultural
corsets and stays of the Victorian age. They brought a new, younger, more
vibrant thread into the nation's political life. In their early years they
breathed fun and laughter into the process. It was a tricky business, of
course. On the one hand, they had to convince the government they were
serious in their intent. On the other, they wanted to carry the public with
them through humour. They were having fun, and their irrepressible,
youthful energy was one of their more charming features. More often
than not, they could exploit the funny side of a situation. Take this description of what happened when Emily Wilding Davison and friends invaded a minister's meeting at the White City pleasure park in
Manchester:

> The Suffragettes entered the American Cake-Walk and the American
> Dragon Slide, situated on either side of the hall, and from these places of
> entertainment flung small stones through the windows into the meeting,
> and made their voices heard. A policeman dashed on to the cake-walk to
> arrest them, but mounted the wrong platform. To the screaming amuse-
> ment of the onlookers the machine compelled him to cake-walk backward,
> whilst the offending women were equally obliged to cake-walk forward, a
> ludicrous spectacle indeed!'[7]

The policeman, clinging to his dignity, was made ridiculous while the
suffragettes, who had cheerfully dispensed with theirs, were able to laugh
with the crowds.

What the suffragettes discovered was not their own masculinity, but a
new form of feminine consciousness. This was not the first time women
had gathered together in such numbers, for they had been thrown together

in the workplaces of the nineteenth century and had worked together alongside men in many radical movements. But the Women's Social and Political Union was one of the world's first exclusively female political movements. It had male supporters, but not male members. Even Fred Pethick-Lawrence was not a member. Sylvia Pankhurst said he was, in fact, one of the four key figures in the union but for most of his time in the movement he held no formal position. Later, a separate Men's League for Women's Suffrage was set up by Emmeline Pethick-Lawrence's brother-in-law, Mortimer Budget.

The suffragette movement borrowed its tactics and much of its style from the politics it saw around it, but it adapted them and made them its own. From the start, there was a closeness, a sense of camaraderie in the movement's work. Many of those who joined it described how their lives changed instantly, almost overnight. Paradoxically, by going out on to the streets the women separated themselves from conventional society, for the very act of speaking in public was regarded as radical. Millicent Fawcett had faced criticism in the 1860s for her decision to speak at a public meeting; the suffragettes went much further. With every new militant step they took, they set themselves more clearly apart from the world they had left behind. 'Had I found on my return that I had taken on a new body, I should not have been in the least surprised. I felt absolutely changed. The past seemed blotted out,' Annie Kenney wrote of her feelings on emerging from her first term of imprisonment. The women withdrew into a world of their own, in which the old social mores did not apply. Annie Kenney, describing her new life in London, said it was 'a revolution in itself':

> No home life, no one to say what we should do or what we should not do, no family ties, we were free and alone in a great brilliant city, scores of young women scarcely out of their teens met together in a revolutionary movement, outlaws or breakers of laws, independent of everything and everybody, fearless and self-confident.[8]

The suffragettes revelled in the notion of their exclusivity, even devising a language in which they could communicate without being understood. At the trial of Emmeline Pankhurst and the Pethick-Lawrences in 1912, the suffragettes' 'code book' was read out in court amid gales of laughter. Archibald Bodkin, the prosecutor, produced a telegram which read: 'Silk, thistle, pansy, duck, wool, EQ.' This, he said, translated as 'Will you aid protest Asquith's public meeting tomorrow evening but don't get arrested unless success depends upon it. Christabel Pankhurst, Clement's Inn.'[9]

These young women regarded themselves as different from their mothers, and their personal relationships, as well as their political ones, were coloured by this feeling. Teresa Billington-Greig, for example, was described by Sylvia as 'one of the "new" young women who refused to make any pretence of subordinating herself to others in thought or deed'. When 'an honest fellow' made unwelcome advances to her, he blamed the suffragette movement for her rejection. 'Doubtless the movement had caused her to be more exacting in her demands on life, and had roused her to insistence that marriage should provide a satisfying intellectual companionship.'[10] Those who were most deeply involved in the movement often had their most intense relationships with each other. When Emily Wilding Davison died, among her papers was found a tiny volume of Walt Whitman's poetry, dated December 1912, with an inscription: 'From Comrade Davison to Comrade Leigh'. Various passages had been underlined: 'I hear it is charged against me that I seek to destroy institutions', 'I dreamed a city of friends', and on the title page, 'The institution of the dear love of comrades'.

Some of these relationships may have been physical, others were not. But they often contained the same essential qualities of intensity and a sense of separateness from the accepted norms of society. Increasingly, as time went by, the women regarded men with suspicion. While Fred Pethick-Lawrence was involved, he worked doggedly to keep the WSPU sailing on a steady course, enabling it to use the power and influence of its male political friends. After the split with the Pethick-Lawrences, a much more overt exclusivity began to creep in. Ethel Smyth wrote disparagingly to Emmeline: 'Sylvia will never be an Amazon. If it weren't Hardie on a pedestal it will be someone else.'[11] Emmeline wrote to Ethel that she was going 'off men'. Annie Kenney said: 'If all the world were on one side and Christabel Pankhurst on the other, I would walk straight over to Christabel.'

In 1913 this anti-male sentiment burst forth in one of the most extraordinary pieces of suffragette propaganda. In a series of articles for *The Suffragette*, followed up by a pamphlet, Christabel expounded her theories on venereal disease. More than three-quarters of all men were infected with gonorrhoea and a further quarter with syphilis, she said. She painted a picture of men as creatures at the mercy of their sexual urges; tainted and violent in their habits. Women, on the other hand, were vessels of purity and

rectitude. Already, she argued, increasing numbers of women were rejecting the notion of marriage. It was the only way for them to preserve their
delicate cleanliness. They now realised that many of the evils of the world,
including childlessness and infant mortality, were due to the diseases
spread by men. Her campaign culminated in a glorious slogan: 'Votes for
Women and Chastity for Men!' Her ravings were not taken entirely seriously, even within suffragette ranks, yet there was a grain of truth in them.
In 1915 a Royal Commission on Venereal Diseases reported that 10 per cent
of the population in large cities was infected with syphilis, and that half the
women who failed to conceive did so because of gonorrhoea. What 'The
Great Scourge' really did, though, was to expose fully the extent of the sexual hatred now running through the psyche of the militant movement. As
Sylvia put it:

> The deduction was clear: women were purer, nobler and more courageous,
> men were an inferior body, greatly in need of purification … masses of
> women, especially of the middle class, were affected by this attitude, even
> though they remained outside the ranks of the union. The pendulum had
> swung far, indeed, from the womanly humility of Victorian times.[12]

Even in their most radical phase, the suffragettes continued to acknowledge that they borrowed much of their *modus operandi* from the
male world around them. Indeed, when criticised for their methods they
would point this out in justification. When the *Manchester Guardian* attacked the women for stone-throwing, Emmeline responded haughtily:

> Why, bomb-throwing, shooting and stone-throwing are time honoured
> masculine political arguments … women … have exercised the greatest
> self-restraint and done the very minimum of violence because they have
> been forced against their will to the belief that the Government would yield
> to nothing else … It is apathy and indifference on the part of men who pro-
> fess to believe in our cause that is responsible for all that has happened and
> that may happen in the future.[13]

Yet the suffragettes always adapted these male tactics to fit their own peculiarly feminine style. They emphasised, after their window-smashing raids,
that the women who took part had their own little silver hammers, easily
hidden in their muffs.

Even the thread of militarism that wound its way throughout the history of the militant suffrage movement had its feminist twist. Almost from the beginning, in its own rhetoric the WSPU was not a union – messy, untidy concept! – but an army of noble women marching out for their just cause. 'The spirit of the WSPU now became more and more that of a volunteer army at war,' Sylvia wrote of the period after 1907. 'It was made a point of honour to give unquestioning assent to the decisions of the leaders, and to obey the command of the officials, paid or unpaid, whom they had seen fit to place over one.'[14] Obedience was always a key strand in the autocratic WSPU, and resentment of the demand for it led to all the major splits that occurred along the way. The militaristic rhetoric grew more overt as the years went by. 'When you put an army in the field,' Emmeline said in 1913, 'you want to do as much damage to the enemy as you can and sustain as little yourself … I congratulate our soldiers.'[15]

Yet the suffragettes' military uniform was never a masculine one. Unlike the women of the Irish rebellion, who discussed the appropriate colour for puttees and wondered whether feathers were a suitable adornment for a rebel soldier's hat, the WSPU always emphasised its feminine qualities, even when it was marching four abreast. Such matters were carefully planned. The funeral of Emily Wilding Davison was typical: suffragettes in white bearing laurel wreaths followed by women in purple with crimson peonies, and a battalion in black with purple irises. Such spectacles had been a feature of the movement throughout its history. Sylvia, whose own artistic talents were often employed by the union for the making of huge decorative banners and set-pieces for exhibitions, attributed the origins of its colour and symbolism to the aesthetic senses of Emmeline Pethick-Lawrence: 'Processions and pageantry were a prominent feature of the work, and these, in their precision, their regalia, their marshals and captains, had a decided military flavour. Flora Drummond was called the General and rode at the head of processions with an officer's cap and epaulettes.'[16] Military women were exalted on these occasions: Joan of Arc and Boudicca were often writ large on the carefully choreographed scenes. Gentler female occupations were emphasised too. One such procession included a 'pageant of empire and history', with women dressed as abbesses and peeresses summoned to Parliament by Edward III, as well as models of motherhood, science, art, nursing, education, poverty, youth and age.

It may seem odd to hail these fripperies as achievements of this early

feminist movement. But if not this, then what? We cannot say unequivo-
cally that the suffragettes, or even the constitutional suffragists, won the
vote for women. They certainly played a major, even a heroic part. In the
end, though, British women would have had the vote. There was too great
an accumulation of social change during the nineteenth century, both here
and across the world, for the freedom of women to have been held back for
ever. Before 1910 women had the vote in New Zealand, Australia and Fin-
land. Before 1940, in Russia, Austria, Canada, Germany, Holland, America,
Thailand, Brazil, Cuba, Turkey and the Philippines.

The militant suffragette movement did much more than this. What it
did, for the first time and with lasting effect, was to inject a new, modern
notion of femininity into women's consciousness. The notions of sisterhood, of female bravery and nobility, even of women's purity, were taken
up again by later feminists and developed into new and different threads.
Were the anti-pornography campaigns of the 1970s and 1980s really so different from Christabel's 'Great Scourge'? Was the spirit of sisterhood at
Greenham Common so far removed from the 'dear love of comrades' ap-
propriated by Emily Wilding Davison from Walt Whitman? Was the sense
of sheer freedom gained from casting off the stays of the Victorian age
really different in essence from the feeling of liberation that swept through
the late 1960s? The suffragettes gave women a sense of self that has never
left them.

Sylvia Pankhurst, writing in 1931, foresaw much of this future development:

> The militant movement had effected far more than the winning of the po-
> litical franchise for this country: it had stimulated the women's emancipa-
> tion movement in all countries … It had acted as a leaven from which
> public spirit, self-confidence and initiative had spread amongst the women
> of its time and had accelerated the building of a new, a higher and freer sta-
> tus for the womanhood of all races.'

Sylvia's last words summed up the future of the movement: 'Great is the
work which remains to be accomplished!'[17]

Notes

Introduction

1. Quoted in Joyce Marlow, *Votes for Women: The Virago Book of Suffragettes*, p. 1
2. Brian Harrison, *Separate Spheres*
3. For a full account of these early beginnings, see Ray Strachey, *The Cause*

Chapter I. Elizabeth Wolstenholme Elmy –
A Long Struggle

Abbreviations:

Crawford: Elizabeth Crawford, *The Women's Suffrage Movement*
TSM: Sylvia Pankhurst, *The Suffragette Movement*

1. *Votes for Women*, 5 November 1908
2. Early biographical details from Ben Elmy, 'A Woman Emancipator', *Westminster Review*, Vol. CXLV, pp. 424–83
3. Crawford, pp. 188–9
4. 'Campaign Against the Contagious Diseases Acts', undated, in British Library
5. Crawford, p. 189
6. 'The Criminal Code in its Relation to Women', 3 March 1880
7. All correspondence with Harriet McIlquham is in the British Library, Mrs Elizabeth Wolstenholme Elmy Letters, Add 47,449
8. Elmy, 'A Woman Emancipator'
9. TSM, pp. 31–2
10. Ibid., p. 34
11. Ellis Ethelmer, 'Life to Woman', 1896
12. Correspondence with Harriet McIlquham in Elizabeth Wolstenholme Elmy Papers, Manuscript Department, British Museum

13. TSM pp. 183–4
14. *Manchester Guardian*, 31 October 1906
15. Ibid., 18 February 1907
16. *Votes for Women*, 25 June 1908
17. Ibid., 23 July 1908
18. *Manchester Guardian*, 18 July 1912
19. Reported in *Votes for Women*, 27 June 1913
20. *Manchester Guardian*, 13 March 1918
21. Dora Montefiore, *From a Victorian to a Modern*, p. 43
22. *Workers' Dreadnought*, 23 March 1918

Chapter II. Emmeline Pankhurst – Matriarch

Abbreviations:
LEP: Sylvia Pankhurst, *Life of Emmeline Pankhurst*
MOS: Emmeline Pankhurst, *My Own Story*
TSM: Sylvia Pankhurst, *The Suffragette Movement*
 1. TSM, pp. 54–5
 2. MOS, pp. 5–6
 3. LEP, p. 15
 4. Ibid., p. 71
 5. Ibid., p. 19
 6. MOS, p. 19
 7. TSM, p. 90
 8. Ibid., p. 164
 9. MOS
10. LEP, p. 46
11. MOS, p. 56
12. Ibid., p. 62
13. Incident described in TSM, p. 181
14. MOS, p. 93
15. LEP, p. 76
16. MOS, p. 129
17. LEP, p. 94
18. Autograph Letter Collection, The Women's Library, London
    Metropolitan University
19. Recollections of Emmeline Pankhurst from Ethel Smyth, *Female
    Pipings in Eden*
20. MOS, p. 153

21. Smyth, *Female Pipings*
22. MOS, p. 316
23. Smyth, *Female Pipings*
24. Ibid.
25. David Mitchell, *The Fighting Pankhursts*, p. 142
26. Ibid. p.145
27. Quoted in Jane Purvis, *Emmeline Pankhurst*, p. 251

Chapter III. Annie Kenney – Mill to Militancy

Abbreviations

MM: Annie Kenney, *Memoirs of a Militant*

TSM: Sylvia Pankhurst, *The Suffragette Movement*

1. Details of Annie Kenney's life from her autobiography, *Memoirs of a Militant*
2. MM, p. 192
3. Emmeline Pethick-Lawrence, *My Part in a Changing World*
4. Martin Pugh, *The Pankhursts*, pp. 210–13
5. TSM, p. 164
6. Descriptions of Annie Kenney from TSM, p. 185
7. MM, p. 35
8. Ibid., p. 42
9. Ibid.
10. TSM, p. 195
11. MM, p. 62
12. Emmeline Pethick-Lawrence, *My Part in a Changing World*, p. 151
13. Autograph Letter Collection, The Women's Library, Vol. XXD, folio 193
14. MM, p. 72
15. Ibid.
16. Ibid., p. 110
17. Ibid.
18. Ibid., p. 96
19. B. M. Willmott Dobbie, *A Nest of Suffragettes in Somerset*
20. *So Rich a Life*, quoted in Elizabeth Crawford, *The Women's Suffrage Movement*, p. 134
21. MM, p. 108
22. Ibid.
23. TSM, p. 413
24. MM, p. 227

25. Ibid., p. 231
26. Ibid., p. 239
27. Ibid, p. 266
28. Pugh, *The Pankhursts*, p. 326
29. MM, p. 289
30. MM, p. 298

Chapter IV. Fred Pethick-Lawrence – Godfather

Abbreviations:

FHBK: Frederick Pethick-Lawrence, *Fate Has Been Kind*

PL: Pethick-Lawrence Papers, The Wren Library, Trinity College, Cambridge

TSM: Sylvia Pankhurst, *The Suffragette Movement*

1. Public Record Office, quoted in Angela John and Clare Eustance, *The Men's Share*, p. 143
2. FHBK, p. 15
3. PL, Box 5
4. FHBK, p. 22
5. Ibid., p. 34
6. James Marchant, *If I Had My Time Again*, p. 142
7. Brian Harrison, *Prudent Revolutionaries*, p. 244
8. PL, Box 7
9. Ibid.
10. Ibid.
11. Emmeline Pethick-Lawrence, *My Part in a Changing World*, p. 124
12. PL, Box 3
13. Vera Brittain, *Pethick-Lawrence: A Portrait*, p. 40
14. FHBK, p. 69
15. Pethick-Lawrence, *Changing World*, p. 170
16. TSM, p. 283
17. Brittain, *Pethick-Lawrence*, p. 32
18. TSM, p. 297
19. Museum of London, Ada Flatman Letters
20. PL, Box 6
21. Pethick-Lawrence, *Changing World*, p. 266
22. FHBK, p. 96
23. Emmeline Pankhurst, *My Own Story*, p. 255
24. PL, Box 9
25. Ibid.

26. Ibid.
27. Pethick-Lawrence, *Changing World*, p. 278
28. FHBK, p. 100
29. Autograph Letter Collection, The Women's Library, letter from Emmeline Pethick-Lawrence to Mrs Cavendish Bentinck, 6 November 1912
30. Elizabeth Crawford, *The Women's Suffrage Movement*, p. 539
31. Quoted in Brian Harrison, *Prudent Revolutionaries*, p. 250
32. FHBK, p. 119
33. Brittain, *Pethick-Lawrence*, p. 96
34. Ibid., p. 135
35. Fred's letters from India in PL, Box 6
36. PL Box 6
37. Ibid.
38. Autograph Letter Collection, The Women's Library, London Metropolitan University
39. Ibid.
40. PL, Box 1

Chapter V. Adela Pankhurst – Forgotten Sister

Abbreviations:
TSM: Sylvia Pankhurst, *The Suffragette Movement*
VC: Verna Coleman, *Adela Pankhurst: The Wayward Suffragette*
1. Emmeline Pethick-Lawrence, *My Part in a Changing World*, p. 162
2. TSM, p. 88
3. VC, p. 15; quoted from an article in *Empire Gazette*, 1938
4. VC, p. 17; quoted from A. Pankhurst Walsh, 'Looking Backwards', *Stead's Review*, October 1928
5. Museum of London, letter to Helen Fraser Moyes, 1961
6. TSM, p. 67
7. VC, p. 28; quoted from Pankhurst Walsh, 'Looking Backwards'
8. Museum of London, letter to Helen Fraser Moyes, 1961
9. Dora Montefiore, *From a Victorian to a Modern*, p. 117
10. Molly Murphy (*née* Morris), *Suffragette and Socialist*, p. 10
11. Museum of London, Suffragette Fellowship Collection, Hannah Mitchell statement
12. Ibid.
13. *Labour Record*, November 1906
14. West Yorkshire Archive Service, Kirklees, Edith Key Papers, KC 1060

15. Ibid.
16. *Votes for Women*, November 1907
17. Ibid., December 1907
18. Ibid., May 1908
19. John Copley, *The Women's Suffrage Movement in South Yorkshire*
20. West Yorkshire Archive Service, Kirklees, Archie Key Memoirs, KC 1060
21. Diary, 16 August; quoted in B. M. Wilmott Dobbie, *A Nest of Suffragettes in Somerset*
22. Helen Fraser Moyes, *Woman in a Man's World*, p. 30
23. Scottish Office Prison Commission files, Scottish Record Office
24. Museum of London picture collection
25. Ibid., David Mitchell Papers
26. *Votes for Women*, 10 November 1910
27. Molly Murphy, *Suffragette and Socialist*
28. TSM, p. 184
29. Museum of London, Helen Fraser Moyes Papers
30. Ibid.
31. TSM, p. 406
32. Craigie Collection; quoted in June Purvis, *Emmeline Pankhurst*, p. 233
33. Ibid., p. 257
34. Sylvia Pankhurst, *The Home Front*, p. 65
35. Ibid.
36. Quoted VC, p. 80
37. Museum of London, David Mitchell Papers
38. Ibid.
39. Ibid.
40. Museum of London, Helen Fraser Moyes Papers
41. Ibid.
42. Ibid.
43. Museum of London, David Mitchell Papers

Chapter VI. Keir Hardie – Westminster Friend

Abbreviations:

CB: Caroline Benn, *Keir Hardie*
PP: Pankhurst Papers, International Institute of Social History, Amsterdam
TSM: Sylvia Pankhurst, *The Suffragette Movement*
  1. Sylvia Pankhurst, *The Home Front*, p. 227

2. CB, p. 4
3. TSM, p. 131
4. Ibid.
5. Quoted CB p. 198
6. Ibid., p. 169
7. Hansard, 29 March 1928
8. CB, p. 185
9. TSM, p. 177
10. Ibid., p. 185
11. Ibid., p. 210
12. Biographical notes on Hardie, PP, File 55
13. Hardie in *Labour Leader*, 15 August 1906.
14. Recorded in Bruce Glasier's diary; quoted Kenneth D. Morgan, *Keir Hardie, Radical and Socialist*, p. 160
15. National Library of Scotland, MSS 20670
16. Quoted CB, p. 239
17. *Votes for Women*, 1 October 1909
18. *Votes for Women*, 1 October 1909
19. Quoted in CB, p. 268
20. PP, File 9, Folder 9c
21. CB, p. 275
22. *Daily Sketch*, 22 November 1911
23. *The Suffragette*, October 1912
24. Ibid., December 1912
25. TSM, p. 450
26. Ibid., p. 491
27. Ibid.
28. Ibid.
29. PP, File 9, Folder 9c
30. Pankhurst, *The Home Front*, p. 227
31. *Labour Leader*, 30 September 1915

Chapter VII. Mary Ward – True Victorian

Abbreviations:
PH: Pusey House, Oxford: Mary Ward Papers
WR: Mrs Humphry Ward, *A Writer's Recollections*
1. G. P. Wells, *Wells in Love*
2. Janet Penrose Trevelyan, *Life of Mrs Humphry Ward*, pp. 2–3

3. Ibid., pp. 5–6
4. WR, p. 39
5. Ibid., p. 23
6. WR, p. 96
7. J. A. Sutherland, *Mrs Humphry Ward: Eminent Victorian, Pre-eminent Edwardian*, p. 49
8. WR, p. 143
9. Ibid., p. 152
10. Sutherland, *Mrs Humphry Ward*, p. 64
11. WR, p. 152
12. Ibid.
13. PH, 1/4, statements on book sales
14. Ibid., 3/3, letter to Louise Creighton
15. Sutherland, *Mrs Humphry Ward*, p. 200
16. Gertrude Bell Archive, University of Newcastle
17. WR, p. 290
18. *The Times*, 2 February 1906
19. Sutherland, *Mrs Humphry Ward*
20. *Votes for Women*, 19 August 1910
21. *Evening Standard*, 17 October 1911
22. Sutherland, *Mrs Humphry Ward*, p. 199
23. PH, 2/9, items 353–98, 5 July 1907, letter to Arnold Ward
24. Brian Harrison, *Separate Spheres*, p. 134, from Curzon and Cromer Papers
25. PH, 2/10, letter to Dorothy Ward, 21 February 1909
26. Ibid., 3/3, letter to Louise Creighton, 11 November 1909
27. Harrison, *Separate Spheres*, p. 134
28. Sutherland, *Mrs Humphry Ward*, p. 201
29. Quoted in Harrison, *Separate Spheres*, p. 193
30. *The Times*, 12 April 1912
31. PH, 2/9, items 353–98, letter to Arnold Ward
32. Sutherland, *Mrs Humphry Ward*, p. 353
33. Quoted in Harrison, *Separate Spheres*, p. 204
34. WR, p. 370
35. Sutherland, *Mrs Humphry Ward*, p. 375
36. Harrison, *Separate Spheres*, p. 22

Chapter VIII. May Billinghurst – Fighting Spirit

Abbreviation:

TSM: Sylvia Pankhurst, *The Suffragette Movement*

1. Ethel Smyth's 'March of the Women'
2. May Billinghurst Papers, The Women's Library
3. Autograph Letter Collection, Vol. 29, The Women's Library
4. May Billinghurst Papers, The Women's Library, item 81
5. Public Record Office, 1901 census
6. May's speech to the jury, Old Bailey 10 January 1913, May Billinghurst Papers, The Women's Library
7. Ibid.
8. Ibid.
9. Iris Dove, 'Yours in the Cause'
10. *Manchester Guardian*, 21 April 1908
11. TSM, p. 280
12. Cutting in May Billinghurst Papers, The The Women's Library, item 83
13. *Votes for Women*, 26 April 1908
14. May Billinghurst Papers, The Women's Library, item 83
15. Lilian Lenton, *Women's Bulletin*, 11 September 1953
16. *Votes for Women*, 3 September 1908
17. *Daily News*, 14 October 1908
18. Report in *Lewisham Journal*, May Billinghurst Papers, The Women's Library
19. Dove, p. 8
20. Autograph Letter Collection, The Women's Library, letter from Mrs Pittman to Miss Burton
21. *Daily Mail*, 22 November 1911
22. *Votes for Women*, 8 March 1912
23. Lenton, *Women's Bulletin*, 11 September 1953
24. TSM, p. 376
25. Alice Ker, Autograph Letter Collection, The Women's Library, 7 April 1912
26. TSM, p. 415; Sylvia Pankhurst says the WSPU's own figures were much higher
27. Lenton, *Women's Bulletin*, 11 September 1953
28. Ibid.
29. Notes on arrest and trial, May Billinghurst Papers, The Women's Library

30. May Billinghurst Papers, The Women's Library, item A13/a, 27 December 1912
31. Autograph Letter Collection, The Women's Library, 31 December 1912
32. May Billinghurst Papers, The Women's Library, item A21–b
33. Ibid.
34. Ibid., item B3/5
35. Autograph Letter Collection, The Women's Library, 8 January 1913
36. Ibid., 17 January 1913
37. Ibid.
38. Ibid., 18 January 1913
39. Reprinted in *Votes for Women*, 24 January 1913
40. Autograph Letter Collection, The Women's Library, 30 January 1913
41. May Billinghurst Papers, The Women's Library, item B3/28
42. Newspaper cutting, May Billinghurst Papers, The Women's Library, item B3/30
43. Lenton, *Women's Bulletin*, 11 September 1953
44. For a full account see TSM, pp. 551–3
45. Ibid., p. 552
46. *The Suffragette*, 21 May 1914
47. Autograph Letter Collection, The Women's Library, Miss Pittman, 15 November 1970
48. Lenton, *Women's Bulletin*, 11 September 1953

Chapter IX. Emily Wilding Davison – First Martyr

Abbreviations:

Colmore: Gertrude Colmore, *The Life of Emily Davison*

TSM: Sylvia Pankhurst, *The Suffragette Movement*

1. Most of the information on Emily's early life comes from Colmore.
2. Colmore, p. 9
3. Emily Wilding Davison Papers, The Women's Library, item A2/1
4. Colmore, p. 14
5. Sleight, *One Way Ticket*
6. Emily Wilding Davison Papers, The Women's Library, London Metropolitan University, item A2/1
7. Sleight, p. 16
8. TSM, p. 328
9. Emily Wilding Davison Papers, The Women's Library, item 7A 2/1
10. Public Record Office, 1901 census

11. Register of County and Parochial Electors, Westminster Archives

12. Emily Wilding Davison Papers, The Women's Library, item L3: letter from Isabella Bell, mother of Winifred Stobbart

13. Ibid., item L4, letter from Winifred Stobbart of Longhorsley, 14 September 1989

14. Brian Harrison tapes, The Women's Library, tape number 55

15. Emily Wilding Davison papers, The Women's Library, item L3

16. Ibid., item L4

17. Sleight, p. 112

18. Colmore, p. 22

19. *Votes for Women*, 11 June 1909

20. Letter in Suffragette Fellowship Collection, Museum of London, 14 October 1909

21. Colmore, p. 30

22. Ibid., p. 32

23. Emily Wilding Davison Papers, The Women's Library, item A3-1-1, letter from Emily to Mary Leigh, 3 November 1909

24. *Sunday Chronicle*, 22 October 1911

25. TSM, p. 468

26. Public Record Office, 8/174 43451 – 9 – 16 February 1912

27. Ibid.

28. Ibid., 8/174 43451 – 19

29. Colmore, p. 44

30. Ibid.

31. TSM, p. 435

32. Quoted in Elizabeth Crawford, *The Women's Suffrage Movement*, p. 161

33. Quoted in Liz Stanley and Ann Morley, *The Life and Death of Emily Wilding Davison*, p. 160

34. Fionnula McHugh, quoted in Stanley and Morley, *Life and Death*, p. 160

35. Emily Wilding Davison Papers, The Women's Library, item A3 7-5

36. Letter to the press, 9 December 1912

37. Colmore, p. 51

38. Emily Wilding Davison Papers, National Library of Women, item A2-2; letter from Harriet R. Kerr, Secretary *pro tem* for the WSPU

39. Ibid., item A6-2, letter from Ella M. Elliot, 20 February 1913

40. Ibid., undated item, A3-5 to A3-6

41. Ibid., item A5-4-1

42. Metro Radio, 5 June 1986, copy in Emily Wilding Davison Papers, National Library of Women, item L/5
43. Colmore, p. 56
44. Emily Wilding Davison Papers, The Women's Library, item A7-4
45. Sleight, *One Way Ticket to Epsom*, p. 18
46. *The Suffragette*, 13 June 1913

Chapter X. Millicent Fawcett – Pacifist Warrior

Abbreviations:
MGF: Millicent Garrett Fawcett Papers, The Women's Library
MGFP: Millicent Garrett Fawcett Papers, Manchester Central Library
Strachey: Ray Strachey, *The Cause*
TSM: Sylvia Pankhurst, *The Suffragette Movement*
What I Remember: Millicent Garrett Fawcett, *What I Remember*
1. Early life taken from *What I Remember*, pp. 1–17
2. Strachey, p. 36
3. Ibid., p. 46
4. Ibid., p. 53
5. *What I Remember*, p. 113
6. Strachey, p. 101
7. Ibid., p. 106
8. Autograph Letter Collection, The Women's Library, 21 February 1885
9. MGFP, M50 2/26/40, December 1886
10. Ibid., M50/2/26/17, March 1891
11. *Votes for Women*, 11 August 1911
12. *The Star*, 5 May 1898, MGFP, M50 4/22/1-51
13. MGFP, M50 4/22/1-51
14. Elizabeth Crawford, *The Women's Suffrage Movement*; David Rubinstein, *A Different World for Women: the Life of Millicent Garrett Fawcett*
15. Strachey, p. 228
16. Autograph Letter Collection, The Women's Library, January 1906, letter from Helen B. Taylor to Mrs Sterling
17. Ibid., Frances Balfour to Millicent Fawcett
18. *What I Remember*, p. 181
19. Ibid., p. 185
20. MGFP, M50 2/1/246; M50 2/1/247
21. Ibid., M50 2/1/247

22. Ibid., M50 2/1/270
23. MGF, 55, Millicent to Elizabeth Garrett Anderson
24. Strachey, p. 221
25. MGF, 63, Elizabeth to Millicent, 12 March 1912
26. Strachey, p. 234
27. MGF, 39, 1909
28. Strachey, p. 250
29. Ibid.
30. *What I Remember*, p. 193
31. MGF, 57, letter from Sir Edward Grey; MGF, 53 and 54, exchange of letters with Lloyd George
32. Ibid., 50, June 1914
33. Quoted Strachey, p. 268
34. TSM, p. 601
35. Strachey, p. 314
36. *What I Remember*, p. 243
37. Strachey, p. 319
38. *English Review*, quoted Strachey, p. 321
39. *Contemporary Review*, September 1929

Chapter XI. Constance Markievicz – Born Rebel

Abbreviations:
Marreco: Anne Marreco, *The Rebel Countess*
NLI: National Library of Ireland
PRONI: Public Record Office of Northern Ireland, Lissadell Papers
TSM: Sylvia Pankhurst, *The Suffragette Movement*

1. Marreco, p. 2
2. See notes on family history in PRONI
3. Marreco, p. 65
4. *Irish Times*, 4 April 1994
5. PRONI, D/4131/K/1/356
6. Ibid., D/4131/K/1
7. Marreco, p. 63
8. TSM, p. 164
9. Marreco, p. 111
10. Quoted in Mary Cullen and Maria Luddy, *Female Activists – Irish Women and Change, 1900–1960*, p. 42
11. Ibid., p. 118

12. Marreco, p. 102
13. NLI, Sheehy-Skeffington Papers, ms 24, 189
14. Quoted in Marreco, p. 111
15. PRONI, K3; K6A
16. NLI, Sheehy-Skeffington Papers, ms 22,663
17. Rosemary Cullen Owens, *Smashing Times*, p. 60
18. NLI, Sydney Czira Papers
19. Marreco, p. 161
20. Liz Curtis, *The Cause of Ireland*, p. 234
21. Frank Kelly, quoted in Marreco, p. 192
22. PRO, British intelligence reports, HO144
23. PRONI, K/6A
24. Ibid., K/7/1
25. Ibid.
26. Ibid.
27. NLI, Sheehy-Skeffington Papers, Hanna Sheehy-Skeffington memoirs
28. PRONI, K/7/4
29. Marreco, p. 210
30. PRONI, D/4131/K/5, 17 October 1916
31. Anne Haverty, *Constance Markievicz: Irish Revolutionary*, p. 161
32. Marreco, p. 227
33. PRO, HO144, 21 December 1916
34. Ibid., HO144
35. PRONI, K/7/2
36. *Dublin Evening Mail*, 14 December 1918
37. Curtis, *The Cause of Ireland*, pp. 306–7
38. PRO, HO144
39. NLI, Joe McGarrity Papers
40. PRONI, K7/12
41. NLI, Markievicz Papers, ms 13,778, autumn 1921
42. PRONI, K/6A, 28 December 1917
43. NLI, Markievicz Papers, ms 13,778, May 1922
44. Marreco, p. 284
45. NLI, Markievicz Papers, ms 13,778, summer 1924
46. PRONI, K/7/12
47. NLI, Sydney Czira Papers

Chapter XII. Margaret Bondfield – In Power

Abbreviations:

LSE: London School of Economics and Political Science, Independent Labour Party and Fabian collections

TSM: Sylvia Pankhurst, *The Suffragette Movement*

1. Annie Lockwood, 'A Celebration of Pioneering Labour Women'
2. Sylvia Pankhurst, *The Home Front*, p. 53
3. Quoted TSM, p. 245
4. Family and childhood details all from Margaret Bondfield, *A Life's Work*, unless otherwise stated
5. Mary Agnes Hamilton, *Margaret Bondfield*, p. 34
6. Bondfield, *A Life's Work*, p. 26
7. *The Shop Assistant*, August 1897; February 1898 (TUC library, London Metropolitan University)
8. *Dictionary of National Biography*
9. Bondfield, *A Life's Work*, pp. 64–9
10. *The Shop Assistant*, July 1897
11. Bondfield, *A Life's Work*, p. 36
12. Obituary in *The Woman Worker*, quoted in Hamilton, *Bondfield*, pp. 98–9
13. TSM, p. 177
14. Quoted in TSM, p. 245
15. Quoted in Bondfield, *A Life's Work*, p. 82
16. Bondfield, *A Life's Work*, p. 83
17. *Votes for Women*, 22 October 1909
18. LSE, ILP collection, file 3/56
19. TSM, p. 334
20. Bondfield, *A Life's Work*, p. 80
21. Ibid., p. 126
22. Sylvia Pankhurst, *The Home Front*, p. 53
23. See, for example, Lockwood, 'A Celebration', p. 31
24. Bondfield, *A Life's Work*, p. 126
25. *The Evening Public*, 26 June 1919, *The Telegram*, New York, 23 June 1919 (TUC library)
26. Undated cutting in TUC library
27. Quoted in Bondfield, *A Life's Work*, p. 245
28. Bondfield, *A Life's Work*, p. 251
29. Ibid., p. 255

30. Robert Skidelsky, *The Labour Government of 1929–1931*
31. Hamilton, *Bondfield*, p. 18
32. Lockwood, 'A Celebration', p. 34
33. Bondfield, *A Life's Work*, p. 269
34. Hansard, 29 March 1928
35. Bondfield, *A Life's Work*, p. 276
36. LSE, Fabian Society, file K17/2
37. Bondfield, *A Life's Work*, p. 9

Conclusion

Abbreviation:

TSM: Sylvia Pankhurst, *The Suffragette Movement*

1. Martin Pugh, *The Pankhursts*, p. 175
2. TSM, p. 356
3. Ray Strachey, *The Cause*, p. 354
4. Millicent Garrett Fawcett, *What I Remember*, p. 176
5. Quoted in Pugh, *The Pankhursts*, p. 202
6. George Dangerfield, *The Strange Death of Liberal England*, p. 125
7. TSM, p. 314
8. Kenney, *Memories of a Militant*, p. 110
9. George Dangerfield, *The Strange Death of Liberal England*, p. 146
10. TSM, p. 188
11. Quoted in Caroline Benn, *Keir Hardie*, pp. 298–9
12. TSM, p. 523
13. Pugh, *The Pankhursts*, p. 193
14. TSM, p. 265
15. Quoted in Pugh, *The Pankhursts*, p. 258
16. TSM, p. 266
17. Ibid., p. 609

Bibliography

Books

Benn, Caroline, *Keir Hardie*, Hutchinson, 1992

Billington-Greig, Teresa, *The Non-Violent Militant*, Routledge & Kegan Paul, 1987

Bondfield, Margaret, *A Life's Work*, Hutchinson, 1948

Brittain, Vera, *Pethick-Lawrence: A Portrait*, George Allen & Unwin, 1963

Coleman, Verna, *Adela Pankhurst: The Wayward Suffragette*, Melbourne University Press, 1996

Codd, Clara M., *So Rich a Life*, Institute for Theosophical Publicity, 1951

Colmore, Gertrude, *The Life of Emily Davison*, The Woman's Press, 1913

Crawford, Elizabeth, *The Women's Suffrage Movement: A Reference Guide*, Routledge, 2001

Cullen, Mary and Luddy, Maria (eds.), *Female Activists – Irish Women and Change, 1900–1960*, The Woodfield Press, 2001

Cullen Owens, Rosemary, *Smashing Times: A History of the Irish Women's Suffrage Movement, 1889–1922*, Attic Press, 1984

Curtis, Liz, *The Cause of Ireland: From the United Irishmen to Partition*, Beyond the Pale Publications, 1994

Dangerfield, George, *The Strange Death of Liberal England*, Paladin, 1966 (first pub 1935)

Dictionary of Labour Biography, Volume II, Macmillan, 1974

Fawcett, Millicent Garrett, *What I Remember*, Fisher Unwin, 1924

Ford, Linda G., *Alice Paul and the Triumph of Militancy, One Woman One Vote, Rediscovering the Woman Suffrage Movement*, ed. Marjorie Spruill Wheeler, NewSage Press, 1995

Fraser Moyes, Helen, *Woman in a Man's World*, Alpha Books, 1971

Fry, Amelia R, *Conversations with Alice Paul*, University of California, 1976

Fulford, Roger, *Votes for Women*, Faber, 1957

Hamilton (Iconoclast), Mary Agnes, *Margaret Bondfield*, Leonard
    Parsons, 1924
Harrison, Brian, *Separate Spheres: The Opposition to Women's Suffrage in
    Britain*, Croom Helm, 1978
—, *Prudent Revolutionaries*, Clarendon Press, 1987
Haverty, Anne, *Constance Markievicz: Irish Revolutionary*, Pandora, 1988
Huws Jones, Enid, *Mrs Humphry Ward*, Heinemann, 1973
John, Angela, and Eustance, Clare, *The Men's Share*, Routledge, 1997
Kenney, Annie, Memories of a Militant, Edward Arnold, 1924
Kent, Susan Kingsley, *Sex and Suffrage in Britain, 1860–1914*, Routledge,
    1990
Leaming, Barbara, *Katharine Hepburn*, Crown Publishers, 1995
Leneman, Leah, *A Guid Cause, The Women's Suffrage Movement in
    Scotland*, Aberdeen University Press, 1991
Lunardini, Christine A., *From Equal Suffrage to Equal Rights*, New York
    University Press, 1986
Macardle, Dorothy, *The Irish Republic*, Corgi, 1968
Marchant, James, *If I Had My Time Again*, Odham's Press, 1950
Marlow, Joyce, *Votes for Women: The Virago Book of Suffragettes*, Virago,
    2000
Marreco, Anne, *The Rebel Countess*, Wiedenfield and Nicolson, 1967
Mitchell, David, *The Fighting Pankhursts*, Cape, 1967
—, *Queen Christabel*, MacDonald and Jane's, 1977
Montefiore, Dora, *From a Victorian to a Modern*, Archer, 1927
Morgan, Kenneth O., *Keir Hardie, Radical and Socialist*, Weidenfield and
    Nicolson, 1975
Murphy, Molly, *Suffragette and Socialist*, University of Salford, 1998
Pankhurst, Emmeline, *My Own Story*, Eveleigh Nash, 1914
Pankhurst, Sylvia, *The Home Front*, Hutchinson, 1932
—, *Life of Emmeline Pankhurst*, T. Werner Laurie, 1935
—, *The Suffragette Movement*, Virago 1977 (first published 1931)
Pethick-Lawrence, Emmeline, *My Part in a Changing World*, Gollancz,
    1938
Pethick-Lawrence, Frederick, *Fate Has Been Kind*, Hutchinson, 1942
Pugh, Martin, *The Pankhursts*, Allen Lane, 2001
Purvis, June, *Emmeline Pankhurst*, Routledge, 2002
Rubinstein, David, *A Different World for Women: The Life of Millicent
    Garrett Fawcett*, Harvester Wheatsheaf, 1991

Skidelsky, Robert, *The Labour Government of 1929–1931*, Pelican, 1970

Sleight, John, *One Way Ticket to Epsom, a Journalist's Enquiry into the Heroic Story of Emily Wilding Davison*, Bridge Studios, 1988

Smyth, Ethel, *Female Pipings in Eden*, P. Davies, 1933

Stanley, Liz, and Morley, Ann, *The Life and Death of Emily Wilding Davison, a Biographical Detective Story*, Women's Press, 1988

Strachey, Ray, *The Cause: A Short History of the Women's Movement in Great Britain*, G. Bell, 1928

—, *Millicent Garrett Fawcett*, John Murray, 1931

Sutherland, J. A., *Mrs Humphry Ward: Eminent Victorian, Pre-eminent Edwardian*, OUP, 1990

Trevelyan, Janet Penrose, *Life of Mrs Humphry Ward*, Constable, 1923

Ward, Mrs Humphry, *A Writer's Recollections*, Collins, 1919

Wells, G. P., *Wells in Love*, Faber and Faber, 1984

Willmott Dobbie, B. M., *A Nest of Suffragettes in Somerset*, Batheaston Society, 1979

Wollstonecraft, M., *Vindication of the Rights of Women*, J. Johnson, 1792

Yeo, Eileen, *Mary Wollstonecraft and 200 Years of Feminisms*, Rivers Oram Press, 1997

Pamphlets

Dove, Iris, 'Yours in the Cause – Suffragettes in Lewisham, Greenwich and Woolwich', Lewisham Library Service and Greenwich Libraries, 1988

Hardie, Keir, 'From Serfdom to Socialism', George Allen, 1907

Lockwood, Annie, 'A Celebration of Pioneering Labour Women', North Tyneside Fabians, 1995

Pethick-Lawrence, Frederick, 'Women's Votes and Wages', 1911

Wolstenholme Elmy, Elizabeth, 'The Criminal Code in its Relation to Women', 3 March 1880, British Library

—, 'Woman's Franchise, the Need of the Hour', ILP, 1907

—, 'The Campaign Against the Contagious Diseases Acts', undated, British Library

Archives and personal papers

British Library: Hansard records; Mrs E. C. W. Elmy Letters; Ellis Ethelmer, *Life to Woman*, 1896

British Library of Political and Economic Science, LSE: ILP Papers; Fabian Society Papers

International Institute of Social History, Amsterdam: Pankhurst Papers

London Metropolitan University: Trades Union Congress Library Collections

Manchester Archive Service, Manchester Central Library: Millicent Garrett Fawcett Papers

Museum of London: Suffragette Fellowship Collection; Ada Flatman Letters; Helen Fraser Moyes Papers; David Mitchell Papers

National Library of Ireland: Markievicz Papers; Sheehy Skeffington Papers; Sydney Czira Papers; Joe McGarrity Papers

National Library of Scotland: Keir Hardie Papers

Public Record Office, Kew: Home Office Files; Prison Office Records; Foreign and Colonial Office Records; 1901 Census

Public Record Office of Northern Ireland: Lissadell Papers

Pusey House, Oxford: Mary Ward Papers

Scottish Record Office: Scottish Office Prison Commission files

Sheffield Local Studies Library: John Copley, 'The Women's Suffrage Movement in South Yorkshire', (Ph.D. thesis), Sheffield City College of Education, 1965–8

University College London: Ward Family Papers

University of Newcastle: Gertrude Bell Archive

Westminster Archives: Register of County and Parochial Electors

West Yorkshire Archive Service, Kirklees: Edith Key Papers

The Women's Library, London Metropolitan University: Personal Papers: Jessie Kenney, Teresa Billington-Greig, Rosa May Billinghurst, Emily Wilding Davison, Millicent Garrett Fawcett; Autograph Letter Collection; Oral Evidence on the Suffragette and Suffragist Movements, Brian Harrison, Tape 55, Norah Balls

Wren Library, Trinity College, Cambridge: Pethick-Lawrence Papers

Newspapers and periodicals

National Library of Women, London

The Suffragette

Time and Tide

Votes for Women

Woman's Bulletin (journal of the Women's Freedom League)

Workers' Dreadnought

British Library
Nineteenth Century
Westminster Review

British Library Newspaper Library, Colindale, London
Daily Mail
Daily News
Daily Sketch
Irish Times
Labour Record
Manchester Guardian
The Times
Tribune

London Metropolitan University: Trades Union Congress Library Collections
The Shop Assistant

Index